The Theory and Practice of Writing Music for Games

The nature of game music charges the modern-day composer with understanding a whole host of aesthetic and technical principles unique to the medium. Based on years of working in the field, as well as teaching the subject at colleges and universities, *The Theory and Practice of Writing Music for Games* is an invaluable resource for those looking for a classroom tested, directed course of study.

As players and composers, themselves, authors Steve Horowitz and Scott R. Looney share the inspiration and joy of game music with an emphasis on critical thinking and the creative process, exploring the parallels and distinctions to concert music, film, TV, cartoons, and other popular forms.

Each chapter builds on the next and guides the reader step by step through the essentials. Along with all the theory, a multitude of clearly defined hands-on projects and exercises are included, designed to prepare the reader to go out into the field with a complete understanding of the art and craft of music composition for games and visual media.

Key Features:

- Discusses a variety of topics in a simple and easy-to-understand format.
- Provides a valuable resource for teachers and students, anyone who is looking to build a career in music for games.
- Breaks down the fundamentals needed to build your career.
- Includes fun and practical exercises that strengthen your composer chops.

The Theory and Practice of Writing Music for Games

Steve Horowitz and Scott R. Looney

CRC Press
Taylor & Francis Group
Boca Raton London New York

CRC Press is an imprint of the
Taylor & Francis Group, an **informa** business

First edition published 2024
by CRC Press
2385 NW Executive Center Drive, Suite 320, Boca Raton FL 33431

and by CRC Press
4 Park Square, Milton Park, Abingdon, Oxon, OX14 4RN

CRC Press is an imprint of Taylor & Francis Group, LLC

© 2024 Steve Horowitz and Scott R. Looney

Library of Congress Cataloging-in-Publication Data
Names: Horowitz, Steve, 1964- author. | Looney, Scott, author.
Title: The theory and practice of writing music for games / Steve Horowitz, Scott Looney.
Description: First edition. | Boca Raton FL : CRC Press, 2024. | Includes
bibliographical references and index.
Identifiers: LCCN 2023029252 (print) | LCCN 2023029253 (ebook) |
ISBN 9781032540085 (hardback) | ISBN 9781032538631 (paperback) | ISBN 9781003414728 (ebook)
Subjects: LCSH: Video game music—Instruction and study.
Classification: LCC MT64.V53 H67 2024 (print) | LCC MT64.V53 (ebook) | DDC 781.5/4—dc23/eng/20230918
LC record available at https://lccn.loc.gov/2023029252
LC ebook record available at https://lccn.loc.gov/2023029253

ISBN: 978-1-032-54008-5 (hbk)
ISBN: 978-1-032-53863-1 (pbk)
ISBN: 978-1-003-41472-8 (ebk)

DOI: 10.1201/9781003414728

Typeset in Minion
by codeMantra

Access the Support Material: http://gameaudioinstitute.com/crc

Table of Contents and Chapter Synopsis

Here we take the first steps in defining exactly why music for games is special. We begin with an overview of the unique nature of game music and how it differs from all other forms of visual media, exploring the nature of game time, and the intersection between interactive and adaptive composition. We also take a historical tour of indeterminacy from the music of John Cage to a beloved classic game and its musical influence on composers worldwide.

CHAPTER 2 ■ Building Blocks

All of life can be defined by gameplay, and music is no exception. In this chapter, we take a look at the fundamentals of game design, game designers, and some of the tools they use to practice their craft. Then we break down the building blocks of music, specifically in regard to how they can be tied to game design and in game events. Lastly, we break down practical and fundamental compositional concepts and hands-on techniques.

CHAPTER 3 ▪ The Composer's Toolbox   48

It's time to make some noise – musical noise that is. To get ready for production, we start by defining the most important tools of the trade. From orchestration to digital audio workstations and middleware, this chapter covers the most asked questions having to do with what tools a composer really needs to be productive and competitive in the industry, and at the same time, always keeping in mind that creativity is king!

CHAPTER 4 ▪ Music as Information   64

Now that we have built a strong theoretical and practical foundation, we move on to examining the relationship between music composition and the still image. For this chapter, we break down the key components of writing for the screen, and explore the concept of music as information. Then we analyze some iconic game scores, looking at the written page, examining orchestrational techniques, and deciphering their form and function.

CHAPTER 5 ■ Cinematic Transitions

Storytelling is an integral part of games and music. Linear media is part of games and has a rich history. In this chapter, we explore those traditions while breaking down everything composers need to know about scoring cinematics and cutscenes. We then take a critical look at these practices in several well-known game titles, exploring the very heart and soul of creative scoring.

CHAPTER 6 ■ Living in Limbo

This section centers around the idea of form and style. Composers must be aware of the many ways music relates to gameplay. Here we dive headfirst into the thorny topic of transitions and what makes them so challenging. This is vital information that composers need as they level up their skills. We then take a deep dive with a structured analysis of the music for the critically acclaimed title, *Ori and the Blind Forest*.

CHAPTER 7 ▪ Get in the Game: Applied Musical Concepts 120

We continue our discussion by looking at the game engine itself and various game music systems. Everything we do when composing for a game must relate to the structure and function of the project. As we start to focus more intently on the interactive aspect of gaming and how that affects music, many questions of implementation and design start to arise. We answer those questions by breaking down two very important and popular games, highlighting their composers and music systems.

CHAPTER 8 ▪ Middleware Music Concepts and the Technical Composer 134

The usage of audio middleware tools is ubiquitous in the game industry, and games both small and large are using them. In this chapter, we take a brief look at the history of middleware programs and codify some common paradigms. This is followed by a complete system breakdown of the game *Peggle 2*, which helps to illuminate the importance of being a technical evangelist in a tech-crazy world.

CHAPTER 9 ■ Advanced Approaches 148

Since games are driven by code, it is only natural that advanced music systems can be created for a variety of game types. In this chapter, we take a look at some extremely creative, fascinating, and advanced game scoring techniques and present them in plain English, so you can add some of these ideas into your own compositions. From Mini Metro to *No Man's Sky*, the universe of creative ideas has no limit!

CHAPTER 10 ▪ Lessons Earned   161

Here, we take the reader on a journey into the real world, breaking down the who, what, when, where, and how of building a career. Making games is a team sport, and understanding your colleagues is a must. Networking, game jams, and much more are all presented as an essential reference guide that will arm the reader with the fundamental knowledge needed to be successful in the field.

The Theory And Practice of Writing Music For Games *(First Edition)*
By Steve Horowitz & Scott R. Looney

This book is important. It is the first of its kind, based on years of research, and teaching the subject at colleges and universities. It is an invaluable resource for those looking for a classroom tested, directed course of study. Each chapter builds on the next in syllabus fashion, and guides the reader step by step through the subject matter, breaking down the essential information. Along with the theoretical chapters, you will find a multitude of clearly defined hands-on projects and exercises. By the time the full course is completed, students will be ready to go out into the field with a complete understanding of the art and craft of music composition for games and visual media.

Note: Please check out our companion website. This site includes a plethora of videos and extra materials that can be used by both teachers and students to reinforce the subject matter. Simply navigate over to : http://gameaudioinstitute.com/crc

Authors

Steve Horowitz is a creator of odd but highly accessible sounds and a diverse and prolific musician. Perhaps best known as a composer and producer for his original soundtrack to the Academy Award-nominated film *Super Size Me*, Steve is also a noted expert in the field of sound for games. As audio director at Nickelodeon Digital, he has literally worked on hundreds of well-known titles, projects that have garnered multiple Kid Screen, Webby, and Broadcast Design awards. Horowitz also received a Grammy Award in recognition of his engineering work on the multi-artist release, *True Life Blues: The Songs of Bill Monroe [Sugar Hill]*, Best Bluegrass Album (1996). The artist behind 31 albums of mind-bending original music, Steve currently resides in San Francisco.

Scott R. Looney is a passionate artist, sound-smith, educator, and curriculum developer who has been helping students understand the basic concepts and practices behind the creation of content for interactive media and games for over 15 years. He pioneered inter-active online audio courses for the Academy of Art University, and has also taught at Ex'pression College, Cogswell College, Pyramind Training, UC SantaCruz, City College SF, SF State University, and Oregon State University. He has created compelling sounds for audiences, game developers, and ad agencies alike across a broad spectrum of genres and styles, from contemporary music to experimental noise. In addition to his work in game audio and education, he is currently researching procedural and generative sound applications in games, and mastering the art of code.

Introductions

INTRODUCTION BY STEVE HOROWITZ

I think I've discovered why I was meant to be a composer. I can sit down with a blank piece of paper in front of a piano or in front of a computer and just start writing. Suddenly, I look up and five hours have gone by like nothing – music flows so naturally. On the other hand, writing words is really hard, and it takes forever. Music is so ephemeral and hard to pin down, but words are solid as stone. Writing this book has shown me how much of a musician I really am. I can only hope that I've been able to put down on these pages the sum of what I'm hoping to translate to you, the reader. The intention is simply to help you be creative, write your music, and with luck and perseverance, have a chance at a career in this crazy thing called the game industry. It's my sincere hope that I've been at least somewhat successful at this endeavor.

I have been a musician my entire life, or at least as long as I can remember. My first and strongest memories from childhood are musical ones. I clearly remember sitting on the floor of our home in Miami Florida when I was around five years old, my mother operating the record player (I was not allowed to touch it of course), and listening to "The Fox" by Harry Belafonte. I asked her to play it over and over again – she was very patient with me. I still do that with music I love, I play it on repeat, again and again, and I imprint it on my memory. My kindergarten teacher (Mrs. Ormsby) played the autoharp for us, I was entranced, and I can still see her sitting in front of the class strumming, pressing buttons, and singing. Another strong memory from several years later is listening to Jimi Hendrix with headphones on and being completely fascinated with the production and the way the guitar danced in stereo from left to right and back again. I wrote my first piece of music at age ten and it was off to a life of mostly singular focus from there.

Much to my mother's chagrin, I did not go to college out of high school. Instead I chose to be a gigging musician and bandleader. At the age of 24, I hit a technical wall. I was hearing all sorts of things in my head that I could not notate or translate. So, I decided to follow the music to the California Institute of the Arts where I had the tremendous privilege of studying compositions with Michael Jon Fink, Stephen "Lucky" Mosko, Mel Powell, and Morton Subotnick. My teachers told me that I was supposed to write weird music and die poor. I was all in, but a funny thing happened on the road to impecuniousness. I met a very

DOI: 10.1201/9781003414728-1

nice fellow who ran a company that specialized in sound for video games and he asked me this question "Have you ever thought about making your living writing music for games?"

And there you have it – that was the start of my journey into the world of game music. Surprisingly, I found myself completely obsessed with the application of my compositional thought process into this expanding medium. I was intrigued by the non-linear nature and how it fits in with my postmodern conception of music and culture. I was fascinated by the arcane technology that ran the systems and the way they interfaced with my understanding of music production. I fell in love with this shiny new toy.

I have spent the better part of 50 years awash in music of all kinds. I will not bore you with all the details here, but suffice it to say that I still feel like I have only scratched the surface of percipience. Music and the art of composition are such an integral part of who and what I am and meant to do on planet earth. It is an honor to be able to share some of what I have gleaned from experience over the years. I must give sincere thanks and a huge shout out to my co-conspirator and partner in crime Scott Looney. We really do make a good team and this book would not be nearly as strong without his brilliant ideas, friendship, and elbow grease. I would also like to acknowledge Austin Smith who has been super helpful with formatting, image creation, editing, and keeping us both on track. And of course where would we be without our fearless leader and publisher Sean Connelly from Routledge – thank you so much for helping to bring this book out into the light of day.

INTRODUCTION BY SCOTT LOONEY

For most of my life, I've tended toward investigating why and how things happen, rather than taking things for granted. As an improvising musician and experimental artist, I find that since this type of work is less than lucrative, one tends to piece together work in various ways to fit their material needs at the time, and this has led me down a number of different but roughly parallel paths that are associated with music and sound creation in different ways. Some paths end up in a dead end, while others branch off, but the calling to be a teacher or educator started over two decades ago, at the point where computers could start playing audio without expensive sound cards. I became interested in educating music and sound production students in the brave new world of DAWs and MIDI sequencing. Shortly afterward, this path branched off and I ended up teaching web designers with little or no music and audio experience how to produce simple assets for websites which was also when I started writing online curriculum, as well as engineering in my home studio and handling some occasional freelance sound design and composing work. This arrangement continued for a while until the next major shift into a dedicated audio/music department which required me to build an online class covering game audio. While I had friends in the game industry and had some limited experience making assets, and a reasonably sophisticated concept of interactive media, I did not really know much about the game industry itself.

A chance phone conversation with Steve Horowitz, who I had met earlier, as I was involved in a musical project he was producing, changed all of that for me. Steve had been involved in the industry for two decades at that point, and also had worked on a curriculum for game audio through the Interactive Audio Special Interest Group (IASIG). At that point it seemed to me that I had found someone better qualified to teach the course than myself, so I connected him with my dept director at a meeting where I fully expected to have to go find another option to piece together work to fill the quilt covering material needs. Instead it ended up creating one of the major paths that my love of investigation, research, and exploratory curiosity could thrive in, and I'm immensely grateful to him for opening up that path for me as a collaborator, business partner, and close friend.

At the time we started teaching, game audio education online consisted mainly of watching videos of DAWs or if you were lucky, middleware where the instructor would literally say, "let's imagine what this would be like in a game." I was dissatisfied with this interpretation of an interactive medium and after some more research I discovered the Unity game engine that could run on Macs (important for music schools at the time), and I realized if you put a sound in a game engine, you **could** hear exactly what the sound was like in a game – you didn't have to imagine it! There was a bit of a hitch though, in that you had to know a bit about coding to get anything interactively to happen in the game – and although Steve had been in the industry and was familiar with the tech, he had never really been on the technical side. So it fell to me to take up that mantle since I was already leaning in that direction as an ex-IT manager. So I taught myself coding, and figured out ways of adapting existing game demo projects to serve as bases for what became game lessons, while at the same time watching and analyzing hundreds of hours of gameplay, and going to meetups with game developers at the peak of the casual gaming boom, and occasionally getting to work on games as well. As time progressed, I became much more interested in **how** sounds and music were triggered rather than the design or composing process in creating "epic" sound effects and music. Along the way, our partnership led to courses on MacProVideo/AskVideo, the previous book on game audio, and most importantly the establishment of the Game Audio Institute, which I have poured a significant amount of my life and energy into. I believe strongly that any knowledge needs to be taught in as non-denominational a way as possible. There can be multiple tools to accomplish the same task – what's important here is that you know at a base level **how** and **why** sounds and music happen in a game, and especially how much the game's structure and internal operation dictates what can happen in a game. Over my years of teaching the subject I have been in a process of refining out the most important principles and concepts, and I think this book represents our best efforts to date to make this a reality. I hope you find it an enjoyable, challenging, and rewarding experience.

LEVEL UP: MUSIC AND THE BRAIN

The origins of our individual musicality may be easy to understand, but the origins of music itself are a bit more difficult to trace, as it is likely that music has been a part of human culture for as long as people have roamed the earth and it morphs and changes over time. Archaeologists have found bone flutes and other musical instruments that date back 50,000 years. Over time, music has taken on many different forms and has been influenced by a wide range of cultural and technological factors, including religious ceremonies, social gatherings, and entertainment, like video games.

Philosophers wax poetic about the nature and meaning of music. Music and philosophy do intersect in the concept of aesthetics. When used as a part of other art forms, music has the ability to tap into human consciousness and manipulate our emotions. Research shows that music has a wide range of psychological and physiological effects, including the ability to alter mood, reduce stress and anxiety, and improve cognitive function. Neuroscientists use a variety of techniques, including imaging, to study the effects of music on the brain and scientific research has helped to shed light on many aspects of this music and mind connection. Music is closely related to how we perceive time, and we typically digest it in a linear fashion. This sense of progression through time is important, and it helps to give a piece of music a sense of direction and momentum. But, how does that change when we place music into a non-linear medium such as video games?

Game music works on the principle of form follows function. When left alone with nothing to look at and no deadlines to meet, a composer will, in most cases, write very different music from the music that same composer would write for a game. The question is why and how does one gain the theoretical and practical knowledge needed to master the art of interactive and adaptive composition? Furthermore, how do we teach something that is experiential, happens in real time and can only really be taught by doing? Well, if we examine the way we teach and learn the art of composition we might derive some answers. You write a piece of music, hear it, then honestly assess if the result is what was expected, and then move on to the next piece and with luck, the learned knowledge is brought forth. But how do we write that first piece to begin with?

It begins with a creative instinct or passion. We study and apply all of the things that go into this thing we call music. We learn all about melody, rhythm, harmony, and orchestration and then apply all of these concepts to the art of composition. If we do this for live players, we use scores and parts. If we do this in our DAW using MIDI and virtual instruments, we use computers. In the end, the answer is the same; in music composition, we learn by doing. Writing music for games is no different. We have to take all the things that we know about music composition and apply them to an interactive environment. Then we have to test that system in real time and see if what we did garnered the expected results. If it did, great! We take what we learn and we move on. If not, we must go through the process again until we do. This is called iteration.

The technical nature of game music charges the composer with understanding the aesthetic and technical principles of the medium. One of the main defining features of game music is the open-ended nature of the gameplay experience. This indeterminacy poses a unique set of musical challenges. Game composers face a host of issues that just don't exist in linear mediums. The complexities and requirements of the game environment raise many questions. It provides a different aesthetic approach and a fascinating compositional challenge.

We share the joy of game composition with you and others who love games; we are players and composers ourselves. Together we founded the Game Audio Institute in order to help others chart a course through the maze of concepts and techniques that make up this ever changing art form. We deeply appreciate the community of artists who spend their days working on games. Whether you are already working in games, wanting to get into the industry, or working in parallel fields, we believe you will find this book filled with valuable and practical information. From the opening strains of revered classic's like Koji Kondo's *Super Mario* theme to the extended orchestral techniques of BioShock by Gary Schyman, music tells the tale, and helps the player move confidently in the game's world. Whether it is the interactive score to *Naughty Bear* by Phillip Charron or the higher level adaptivity of *Peggle 2* by Guy Whitmore, game composers must be exceedingly creative, technically inclined, and prepared to use vast ingenuity to get the job done.

So if you're up for a challenge unlike any you've had before, then read on! Game composition is interesting and dynamic, and this course can help to guide you through the necessary concepts and techniques commonly used in the industry. We will concentrate on the creativity inherent in the art form of music composition for games, never separating it out from the greater sphere of composers and the world of composition in general. Music composition should never be siloed into "camps." Music for the concert hall, club, home speakers, screen, or wherever it is found should all be taught together – we learn from varying traditions. Game music is no different, it's just approached and applied in a different way. We all use the same skills, knowledge of theory, harmony, melody, and rhythm combined to give the listener goosebumps and send a chill down the spine, using the power of music to create a compelling and unforgettable experience.

Note: Please check out the companion website. This site includes a plethora of videos and extra materials that can be used in the classroom to reinforce the subject matter.

Simply navigate over to: http://gameaudioinstitute.com/crc

INTRODUCTION TO ASSIGNMENTS: TEACHERS' NOTE

What is a game composer? What is game music? Am I a game composer if I only write music for games and don't write music for anything else or is it okay for me to write some chamber music or a song or music for a film? Is it 8-bit chiptunes or is it a much wider range of styles, forms, and concepts? Our contention in this book is that composers who apply their craft and creativity to games are simply composers. Composers write music for all different kinds of reasons. Sometimes constraints are put upon them and sometimes they put the constraints upon themselves. Ultimately, this question will be one for each individual to decide. Our goal is simply to bring our art, craft, and techniques to life.

To that end, the goal of this book is to provide a classroom tested, methodical approach to the art and craft of writing music for video games. In order to demystify the creative and technical challenges involved, we focus on the unique nature of music scoring for game environments, with an emphasis on critical thinking and the creative process. Parallels and distinctions with regard to concert music, film, television, animation, and other linear media are referenced and explored. Technical considerations in game design workflow are addressed for a variety of gameplay styles and forms.

This course is a culmination of many years in the field as well as the classroom. We have found that game composition is both creatively and technically mind bending for composers. There must be pedagogically speaking, a mixture of creative exploration and technical understanding that go hand in hand. This course of study has been developed organically and is currently being successfully used by schools around the country. We feel confident that this book will be a faithful guide into the fascinating and rewarding world of music composition for games and adaptive media.

We also believe this course is unique in its approach. Why? Well, from the get go, we stress the creative, and not the technical. In the early chapters we explore the syntax of writing music for games and how it's different from film or any other form of linear media. Only after that foundation is set, do we ask the student to apply that gained knowledge through targeted hands-on assignments. This is done through a variety of practical classroom exercises that build on those same fundamental principles.

Books having an exclusive focus on music for games (an already rare enough topic, compared to books covering game audio in general) are often anecdotal. This can be useful, but oftentimes these books profess to give composers the secret key to building a profitable career in the world of game scoring. Many claim to be helpful in learning the craft of music scoring from the point of view of folks who have scored some wonderful games; however, where they miss is the rigid underpinning that's necessary to guide students to understanding and success. Charting the growth and positive results from my students has provided a deep sense of satisfaction over the years. Many that have finished this course of study have gone on to fruitful careers and work on great games for companies big and small alike.

The Concepts in This Book Are Based on the Following Pedagogy

- THEORY: Take the most basic concepts at the heart of game music and expose the student to the historical canon and context in a variety of ways—via text, image, videos, and practical exercises.

- COMPREHENSION: The logical application of theory is benefitted by different assessment methods that aid the learning process and help to reinforce the terminology and concepts being taught.

- INTERACTION: In order to learn about a nonlinear medium, students need to encounter the concept firsthand within the gaming environment and then through practical exercises create their own compositions.

The advantage to this approach is the ability to define a concept and then directly apply it. Much like architecture, writing music for games is based on the idea that form follows function. This is not, as many would have you believe, a creative straightjacket. On the contrary, it is a set of parameters that open up a whole world of creative possibilities. Composers deal with limitations all the time, be they self-imposed or provided. Composers are problem solvers.

The student entering a class on composition for games is, in general, insufficiently prepared with respect to the basic principles governing the subject matter. Students from many different walks of life will bring varying experiences in music with them. The very idea of what makes someone a "composer" these days has shifted. The definition has morphed from a human who sits alone with pencil and paper weighed down by history, to include singer songwriters, DJs, electronic musicians, composer performers, sound artists, and others who work with computers, phones, tablets, control surfaces, game engines, and more. These humans may or may not sit alone, they often work in group settings collaborating with others. It is important that as educators, we meet these creative artists where they are. Music and music composition as applied to games meets at the intersection of old and new. Over time, we have come to understand that there is no such thing as "game music" and there is no such thing as a "game composer." There are only composers and musicians who apply their love of music to the art of video games.

Accordingly, the progression of the subject matter in the book should be adapted to match the purposes of each individual teacher and their individual students' needs and learning styles. We encourage teachers to find their own way through the material that best benefits their class structure. It is also easily possible to break this course up into multiple semesters, leaving more time to take a deep dive into each topic area.

ASSIGNMENTS AND PRACTICUM

The assignments in this section are the same ones we use in our classrooms with our students. We have annotated them at the top of each one with a recommendation as to which chapter each assignment best applies. Keep in mind that this is only a suggestion, and teachers should feel free to use them in any order that seems right. There is also no requirement to use them all either – feel free to pick, choose, and adapt to taste.

This course provides not only the theoretical context governing music and games, but also practical hands-on exercises. It is the application of theory through targeted activity that brings complete context. Theory and practice, when put together, solidify a fundamental understanding of how music fits into the art of game design. We can't stress enough how important it is for students and teachers alike to do the exercises provided. Games are not made by talking about making them, and game music must be experienced in real time. Hands-on exercises provide the opportunity to apply concepts and principles and further develop musical skills to improve overall musicianship. They also provide the chance for experimentation, which helps to better understand the fundamental concepts and principles. Overall, this style of game based learning can be a lot of fun, and serves to make the learning process more engaging and enjoyable.

The assignments and exercises provided in this section of the book have all been extensively classroom tested. However, we have found through experience that it is not possible (or at least very unlikely) for students to complete all of them over the course of one semester and as we mentioned before, not all classes are taught in the same manner or have the same student skill level. So, we encourage the teacher to pick and choose, and mix and match the ones that best fit with your course flow and pedagogy. You can also consider varying them from semester to semester to keep things varied and fresh, as well as to pick different assignments to match the skill level of advanced students or students needing more support.

For each assignment we have provided the necessary creative context in addition to technical information. We have also included rubrics when necessary with which you can judge student success.

Additionally, there is a companion website available to use as a resource for course materials, as some assignments require external resources. Over the years, we have found as educators that there has been a shift away from text based curriculum to more visual and practical learning. As a result, the companion site includes a plethora of videos and extra materials in the form of game lessons, which come with their own directions for technical implementation as well, and these can be used in the classroom to reinforce the subject matter in a practical, hands-on and immersive way. All the materials on the site are clearly delineated, and cross referenced to suggested chapters they support. The idea is to provide all the materials you need, easily accessible, and at your fingertips.

Simply navigate over to: http://gameaudioinstitute.com/crc

THE USEFULNESS OF GROUP ASSIGNMENTS

Many of the assignments in this course have students working on and presenting the same game with their own original compositions. Over the years we have found that this is a powerful classroom technique and that much can be learned by looking and listening to multiple versions of a project composed by different people and exploring the discussion questions provided in each assignment. Having used this process in the classroom over many years, we can attest to the fact that it is kind of magical.

This process helps to once again teach the fundamental lesson – there is no one way to score a game! After analyzing several examples in class, over time you may find that interesting patterns of perception emerge within the group as a whole. We must be open to these different ways that music reaches people and the way they express it. Remember, there is no right or wrong. Some may feel that the music for a given project is too repetitive or dull while others may love the repetition and lack of development. Our experience has been that this kind of team exploration leads to dynamic and illuminating conversations that highlight important concepts in an organic way. This kind of learning happens through collective experience in real time. It brings with it sudden awareness, much like a good game does.

In this way, together, we play the game of learning.

Please check out our companion website. This site includes a plethora of videos and extra materials that can be used by both teachers and students to reinforce the subject matter. Simply navigate over to : http://gameaudioinstitute.com/crc

Section-01

CHAPTER 1

The Adaptive Composer

Topic: Introduction to the History and Composition of Nonlinear Music

- Learning Outcomes
- Dynamic Music, Interactive and Adaptive
- Indeterminacy
- Game Pieces
- The Inspiration of Limitation, Musical and Physical
- Koji Kondo and the NES
- Game Engines, Platforms, and Storage
- The Big Takeaway
- Discussion Questions
- Terms

Learning Outcomes

- Explain why game music is unique as compared to film, TV, and video
- Understand the meaning of Dynamic Music
- Differentiate between interactive and adaptive music
- Explore indeterminacy, and how it relates to game music
- General awareness of limitations in music composition and games
- Understanding game engines and platforms, and how they relate to music
- Develop practical solutions for dealing with limitations

DOI: 10.1201/9781003414728-3

DYNAMIC MUSIC, INTERACTIVE AND ADAPTIVE

How Music in Games is Different

Those of us familiar with game music know that game composers create satisfying and compelling music for players to experience. But how does this happen? How can the music just simply know what action you're going to take in a game and respond with the right emotional cue at the right point in time?

The basic answer is that games are largely an **interactive** medium. Loosely translated, an interactive medium is one where the user has to trigger an action of some kind in order to get a result from the game. Put in the simplest terms it's "push a button, music plays." If you don't push the button (or trigger an action), no music will play.

What's missing from this description, though?

The answer you're looking for is *time*. To be more precise, very accurate and predictable time. We don't know *when* something happens, but we only know *how* it happens (in this case, we push a button). Thus games and interactive media are *non-linear* in nature, whereas film and video are *linear* (Figure 1.1).

Let's compare this to a typical suspenseful movie scene:

The keyword in this situation is *predictability*. In a film, if a character goes into the dark spooky castle and opens the door at 13 minutes and 22 seconds, you can easily make an eerie music cue and place it on the timeline in your favorite DAW (Digital Audio Workstation) at that exact point. Once you synchronize it correctly with the film itself, it will always play at the same time. In other words, it's predictable – you know exactly when it will happen. You can then mix the music with sound effects and dialog for the complete audio experience.

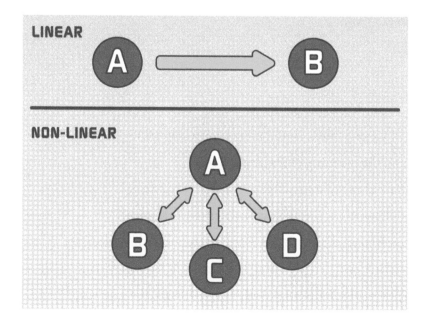

FIGURE 1.1   Linear and nonlinear media. (Image: Austin Smith.)

Now, imagine watching this same scary film, but each time you watch it, the character goes into the house at different times. This is a prime example of the unpredictability and indeterminacy inherent in games. How could you successfully create music for a medium in which you don't know when in time a particular action is going to happen? How can you create a way to trigger the music reliably? The answer, in this case, is that largely, you need to throw away using a specific time as a basis for organizing your music and concentrate on the actions in the movie itself. What we need to do is focus on **how** and not **when**.

Let's think of our spooky house situation from the angle of the action involved. So at some point, the character is going to come up to the house and open the door. It doesn't matter when. So let's list it as an action like this:

Action #001 Spooky Door Opening → Play 'spookymusic.wav'

Now we've defined our action, but how do we trigger it? In a game there's already something that's going to cause the door to move. Most likely this will be some kind of animation code. If we hook up the code that triggers the animation of the door with the spooky music, voila! Instant sync—whenever the character opens the door, the music will play.

However, this seemingly insignificant shift in thinking now requires that each piece of music in the game exists as a separate item. Everything has to be independently mixed and mastered separately. Furthermore, we have to be really organized with all of these audio files so that the programmer knows what to do with these assets in the game. It also means that how the music is triggered in a game is intimately tied up with how the game is designed, and each game is a complete universe unto itself. It's got its own sets of rules and regulations, and any change in the game design can significantly affect how the music is constructed and triggered.

ADAPTIVITY

We have entered the adaptive age. In all parts of our lives, we have come to expect a certain amount of customization from the technology we use in our daily lives. Whether it's clocks that reset themselves for daylight savings time, social media, or the gamification of our health care, algorithms track us. In this regard, games are no exception, because they are built on code. As we play through our favorite game titles, we expect the music to move with us. At the start of a game when we are absorbing information, or later on when we are solving puzzles, the music matches our mood and emotion, and when the action ticks up, we expect the music to follow our interaction and adapt in turn, perhaps getting more exciting and suspenseful. Music composition is adaptive by nature – composition is often said to be improvisation slowed down.

The 20th-century composer Edgard Varese famously opined "Music is organized sound." If this is true, then music for games certainly has a lot of organizing to do. Suddenly composers are free to employ lots of different approaches and techniques. Some composers may start with a specific idea or theme in mind, while others may begin by improvising or experimenting with different sounds and structures. Some composers may work with traditional musical notation, while others may use graphic scores or other experimental methods of representation. Composers may also work in a variety of settings, as solo artists, or part of a band, ensemble, or as part of a larger creative team. Composition often involves a combination of creative and technical skills, and can be a challenging and rewarding process for those who are interested in creating something new.

INTERACTIVE VERSUS ADAPTIVE MUSIC

You most likely have come across these two terms. But what do they mean when applied to a music score for games? Let's take a look at what characteristics are emphasized in one versus the other. First, both of these characteristics fall under the category of **dynamic audio** – audio that is designed to change, either in response to the user or in response to changes in the gameplay environment (Figure 1.2).

INTERACTIVE IS ALL ABOUT CONTROL

Interactive music occurs in response to the player directly. In other words, if a player presses a button, or enters a trigger area, the music will play. As an example, consider a 2D platform game, where different music tension levels are triggered by the player interacting with objects in various locations in the level. In this scenario, the player has control of each of the triggers by encountering them. However, if they don't get to a specific trigger object, the corresponding level of tension won't be triggered. As a result, the player can directly control the varying levels of tension, even though they might not be aware that they are, in fact, doing this.

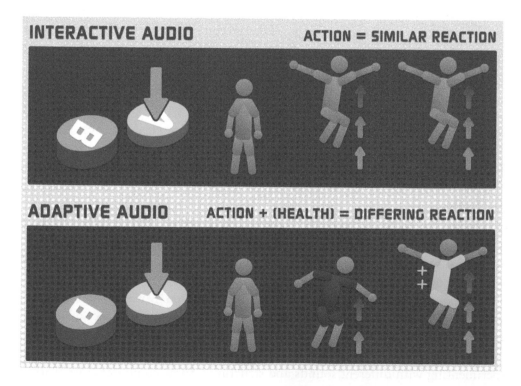

FIGURE 1.2   Interactive versus adaptive audio. (Image: Austin Smith.)

ADAPTIVE IS GIVING UP CONTROL TO THE GAME

In the case of adaptive music, some element of the game itself controls the music, rather than the player directly. A fully adaptive music score is something that is controlled more by the game than the player themselves. One example would be a game where the music is controlled by the player's health. So the more health you have, the lighter the music, but the more health you lose, then the music gains more intensity or changes to match the character state. Another example is music that keeps track of your players' experience level and uses that to determine what music to play. Any type of data that can be tracked in a game can be tied to musical development in this way.

Keep in mind that in practice, interactive and adaptive music are two poles along a continuum, and depending on the game, the developer can set what level of control the player can have over the music soundtrack versus what is controlled by the game itself.

INDETERMINACY

During gameplay, when things happen, the timing of events may be open ended. One player might run through a level or puzzle in one minute, while another takes five. This kind of indeterminacy brings up many questions and causes composers to lose sleep as they ponder exactly what might be going on and how much music needs to be written. The issue of form and time must be addressed in some fashion, and the music of the past helps give us clues to solve today's conundrums. To some extent, indeterminacy has been a long-standing part of our musical heritage. Ancient cultures in Africa, India, and Asia have utilized a musician's choice to play music and rhythms within certain parameters based on that culture's rules about what is acceptable musically or rhythmically. Latin music bases their melodic and rhythmic emphasis on the clave, but allows freedom for musicians to improvise. Indian classical music has a huge array of ragas and talas for melody and rhythm, within which musicians can more or less freely improvise.

For a long time in musical history, this type of "predictable indeterminacy" or improvisation was considered a normal skill that a musician was expected to have, but the emergence of consistent written music from western composers created more of a demand to simply play the score exactly as written. Yet even as written music solidified, chance did still figure into composing as far back as the Baroque Era. J.S. Bach and his Art of The Fugue composition, which is not specified as to instrumentation, means every performance could sound different depending on the instruments involved.

Mozart (Figure 1.3) also was definitely no stranger to using chance techniques in his *Musicalisches Würfelspiel* (Musical Dice Game) which is a composition realized by rolling dice to choose randomized measures from 177 choices. After rolling the dice enough times, you have a short musical composition. Performance of this piece by rolling the dice means that some bars will be heard and others will not, and more importantly that choice is not up to the musician, but an outside (randomized) choice. This is an early example of indeterminacy at work, as well as an adaptive game mechanic. In this case, there are literally billions of combinations of this piece and no two realizations will likely ever be the same.

FIGURE 1.3 Wolfgang Mozart by Barbara Krafft. (Public Domain.)

As we move into the 19th century and the Romantic era of western music, the oppor-tunities for self-expression from performers seem to get more limited, and surprise is largely relegated to cadenzas in concertos and sonatas, and even those are often written out. However, as the 20th century comes into view, more freedom begins to appear for performers to interpret work. Composers such as Charles Ives and Henry Cowell espe-cially begin to utilize unusual and unexpected techniques to create a larger variety of tones and textures unknown to previous composers. Blocks of wood applied to piano keys, arm smashes, and using implements and hand techniques on the strings all become valid modes of expression in a revival of a broadened allowance of player interpretation.

In the Concerto for Piano and Orchestra, he provides 63 pages to be played, in whole or in part, in any sequence. The piece can be performed, in whole or in part, in any duration, with any number of performers. The resulting collaboration is an astound-ing piece of "music," and a fine introduction to the ideas of form, chance, and choice in music.

John Cage by Rob Croes. (CC0 1.0.)

Things get even more interesting as we focus our attention on the so-called "New York school" of composers in the 1950s, who were greatly influenced by newer modes of thinking about art, music, and sound in general. Let's take a look at the most well known of these, the composer John Cage. Arguably the most influential figure of the latter half of the 20th century. Cage was heavily influenced by eastern philosophy and applied his interpretations of the ideas of Zen Buddhism to music. If you have not done so already, please read his book *Silence*, which has been a huge and pervasive influence on the thinking of many composers since its publication in 1961.

CAGE USING CHESS AS A MUSIC/SOUND INSPIRATION

An avid though amateur chess player, Cage utilized other methods of organization for his works. One of his earliest is Chess Pieces written in 1943 for solo piano. It was originally conceived as an ink-and-gouache on masonite painting, created specifically for "The Imagery of Chess" exhibition at the Julien Levy Gallery in New York City (1944–1945), an exhibition that was comprised of works that were in some manner related to the artist Marcel Duchamp's interest in chess (in his earlier life, Duchamp was a master chess player who won several competitions).

Cage's artwork, entitled Chess Pieces, is a painting depicting 64 light and dark squares (in the pattern of a chessboard), with a series of light and dark lines superimposed on top. On closer inspection, the lines turn out to be musical notation.

Decades later, when the "Imagery of Chess" exhibit was revisited, it was discovered that the musical notation in the painting was actually a real composition for piano, and in 2005, Margaret Leng Tan performed the musical piece contained in the painting. For her interpretation, she constructed a form that consists of 22 systems read conventionally from left to right. Each system is a self-contained musical unit of 12 bars, translating collectively into 22 modular segments.

Other composers of the New York school like Morton Feldman employed the use of graphic notation to guide the performers. Interestingly, Feldman in later years abandoned the use of graphic notation and returned to conventional writing. Game music, which emerged as a visual medium in the later part of the 20th century, must also deal with the concept of indeterminacy, although the results are rarely as chaotic as early Cage pieces can be.

For example, it is interesting to note the visual similarities between the game Sound Shapes (Published by Sony) and the score for December 1952 by composer Earle Brown,

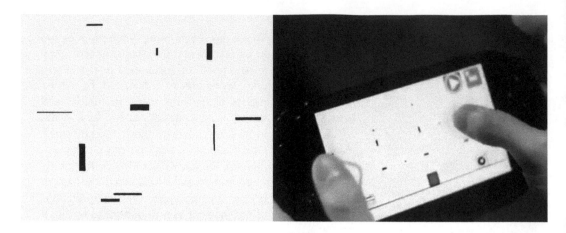

FIGURE 1.4   Sound shapes and December 1952 comparison. (Image: Austin Smith.)

another member of the New York school, and the one most open to the player's musical freedom, due to his earlier background as a jazz musician (Figure 1.4).

If you listen to both of these pieces, you'll notice significant differences. The original is a flexible art piece that can be attempted by any number of performers creating any sounds at a determined duration, whereas the game music for Sound Shapes creates unexpected choices of notes from predetermined scales and modes.

This ebb and flow of control and freedom is also represented in the compositions and improvisations of jazz musicians. These artists have always been masters of the art of spontaneous creation. From Charlie Parker and Thelonious Monk, Duke Ellington, and Charles Mingus, to Eric Dolphy and Anthony Braxton, form and improvisation are baked into the language of jazz.

In jazz charts sometimes called lead sheets, players are given a structure on which to express their own musical ideas and creativity in real time, just like in games. However, in a game, a player's actions may not always result in the music following suit.

GAME PIECES

In music, the game concept first explored in Mozart's musical puzzle can be expanded into systems to allow freedom and structure. These "game pieces" can refer to a variety of different things, depending on the context. Here are a few examples:

1. In a board game that is based on music, the game pieces might be miniature instruments or notes that players move around the board. In a musical performance, game pieces might refer to the various instruments or parts that the musicians play.

2. In a compositional game, game pieces might refer to specific musical elements (such as melody, harmony, or rhythm) that the composer manipulates to create a piece of music. This is similar to what we already saw in Mozart's work mentioned earlier – in that case, it was fully composed musical segments.

3. In some improvisation games, game pieces can refer to certain forms, structures, or guidelines that the improvisers must follow while creating music in real time (Figure 1.7).

Composer and saxophonist Anthony Braxton's music crosses over all lines of genre and form, employing modernist classical as well as jazz and improvisatory techniques. He uses graphic notation frequently in his compositions.

Image sourced from Wikimedia Commons. (CC BY-SA-2.0.)

Butch Morris was an American jazz cornetist, composer, and conductor known for his unique "conduction" method of leading improvisational music performances. Morris developed the concept of "conduction" as a way to lead improvisational ensembles. He defined it as a "system of hand and facial gestures that enable the conductor to sculpt the sound and shape of an ensemble in real time." This method is based on a set of gestures that indicate the structure and form of the improvisation, such as the number of repetitions of a phrase, changes in dynamics, the introduction of new elements, and the overall direction of the music. Morris's system of conduction is not fixed but rather a flexible system that allows for improvisation and spontaneity on the part of the musicians; it also allows the conductor to compose in real time with the ensemble. Over the years, Morris's conduction method has been used in many types of music, including jazz, classical, and experimental music. Morris passed away on January 29, 2013.

Butch Morris by Jack Vartoogian. (Via Getty Images.)

FIGURE 1.5   John Zorn by digboston. (CC BY 2.0.)

John Zorn's (Figure 1.5) Cobra takes the idea of a musical game even more literally. Based on a simulation board game published in the 1970s, Cobra, like the board game, is filled with permissible moves and strategies that the players adhere to. The ensemble generates spontaneous compositions in real time using these rules and strategies. Cobra has a leader who conducts the game, and the musicians play based on cues and instructions given by the leader. The leader can change the cues and instructions at any time, and the musicians must adapt their playing accordingly. The game also includes elements of chance, such as the use of a random number generator, to determine certain aspects of the performance. Cobra allows a leader to guide the improvisation of a group of musicians while leaving room for individual creativity and spontaneity. Since its creation, Cobra has been played by many musicians, including Zorn himself, and has been used in a variety of settings, including concerts, festivals, and recordings (Figure 1.6).

Lastly, we must mention free jazz, a genre of music that emphasizes improvisation and the freedom of the musician to express themselves in any way they choose, rather than adhering to strict harmonic, melodic, or rhythmic conventions. The relationship between free jazz and gameplay involves a level of improvisation and spontaneity, as both require the participants to have a certain level of skill and knowledge in order to effectively participate. Free improvisation can be seen as a musical game in which the musicians are free to

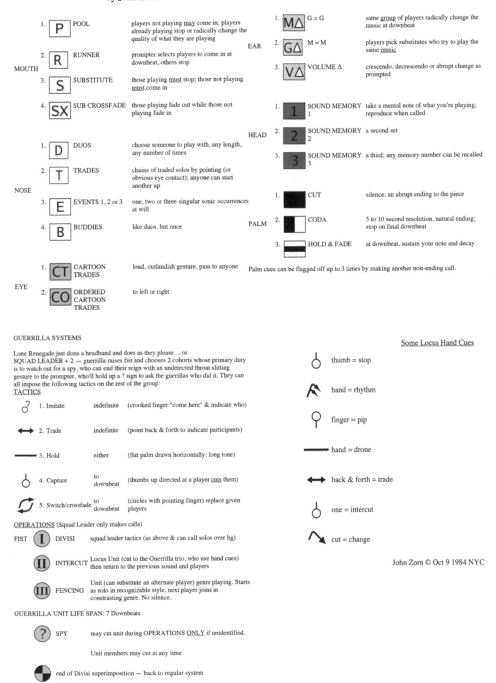

FIGURE 1.6   Cobra Score by John Zorn. (Used with permission.)

listen and react to each other in a democratic way. Free jazz and musical games share some similarities, in the sense that they both involve improvisation, spontaneity, and flexibility, but free jazz is more of an approach and aesthetic rather than a strict set of rules, similar to an open-form musical sandbox game.

The Big Takeaway: Awareness of the history of music and indeterminacy can only serve to help the modern composer develop a deeper creative understanding of what came before and how best to harness those ideas. The contention here is not that composers when working on a game are necessarily influenced by the music of the past or the exact examples given here. It is simply the realization that music for games exists by the very interactive and adaptive nature of the medium, on the same playing field. If form follows function, then the entire music system along with issues of timing, placement, triggering, files size, platform, gameplay dynamics and story all must be taken into account before writing even one single note. Perhaps these ideas will inspire you when working on your next project.

THE INSPIRATION OF LIMITATION: MUSICAL AND PHYSICAL

Philosophers have had a wide range of views on limitations throughout history. Some have argued that limitations are a necessary part of human existence and that they serve a purpose in helping us understand our place in the world. Composer Igor Stravinsky wrote, "The more constraints one imposes, the more one frees one's self. And the arbitrariness of the constraint serves only to obtain precision of execution." Stoics believed that limitations are an inherent part of the human experience, and that by accepting and embracing them, we might find peace and tranquility. They believed that limitations are a reminder of our humanness and that by accepting them, we can learn to live in harmony with the natural world. Others have argued that limitations are a form of oppression and that it is our duty to overcome them. Existentialists argue that limitations are a product of societal constraints and that it is up to the individual to break free from them and create their own meaning and purpose in life. The ancient Greek philosopher Aristotle believed that through self-discovery and the pursuit of knowledge, individuals could overcome their limitations and achieve their full potential.

Composers deal with limitations all the time. Without understanding the ranges and colors of individual acoustic instruments, we will have a hard time writing playable music. The same holds true for synthesizers and electronic instruments. Composers are often commissioned to write for a predefined set of instruments or band ahead of time, and then must adapt their musical ideas to that ensemble grouping. Many composers choose to work with a specific group of players for this reason, because they are well acquainted with their sound, idiosyncrasies, and limitations.

Music when applied to video games provides another unique set of challenges. With a game score, you might have no idea how long a player will remain in a certain location. You also frequently don't know what path that player will take to navigate through the game world. Time can be situational, and games can in some cases take a very long time to play. Considering that a film is usually about two hours, imagine writing music for a game that may last 100 hours! Yikes!

GAME ENGINES, PLATFORMS, AND STORAGE

Games come with a fair amount of basic technical definitions, and although it can seem daunting at times, it is important for composers to understand these concepts.

First, video games are made by designers and programmers, usually using some type of a game engine. This is a software tool that is specially optimized for creating games. There are a lot of these tools to choose from, but they will, in most cases, deal with recorded music as media files. Sound effects, videos, and even MIDI files are also considered to be in this category. These media files get processed and included in the final build of the game.

Games will also run on some type of device, whether that's a game console, a PC, a smartphone, or a VR headset. Each of these devices is called a **platform**. Different game engines often have very different technical capabilities when it comes to triggering music. Now add the fact that different platforms all handle sound differently as well, and you have many possible unknowns to deal with.

Another issue to confront is storage, which is how much room an asset takes up in a completed game build. Generally, you will import uncompressed music files into the game engine. WAV is a very common format, but there are many others that can be used. Whatever format you use, the file will take up storage space on the platform it's playing on. Uncompressed audio also takes up the most storage space. In terms of how much space, you can assume approximately 10 MB for a minute of stereo music saved as a 16-bit file playing back at 44.1 KHz (CD quality) and 11 MB for a file recorded and played back at 48 KHz. Multichannel music files are less common but can be found in more immersive games needing surround music tracks such as those that may be needed in VR games.

11 MB per minute doesn't seem like a lot of room – unless you start adding up the minutes of a typical film soundtrack which is usually at least 60 minutes of music. So if you were to do that, our storage space for music would be 660 MB. By today's standards of storage, that still doesn't seem like a lot, since we can easily buy tiny thumb drives with hundreds of times more space. But keep in mind that games can run on ANY kind of device from superpowered desktops to watches. Some social and mobile games for tablets and smartphones have data limits and are only a couple of hundred MB and many are much less. 660 MB of music is far too much to put in most mobile game titles. To address this issue in the past, hard choices would have to be made, such as reducing the sample and/or bit rate of the music or shortening the length of the music tracks themselves. This is why well-known music from classic games like *Super Mario Bros* are actually extremely brief.

Let's look at this classic musical example involving a beloved composer and game.

This example should help to show how music composition is, at its very heart, problem solving.

Koji Kondo is a Japanese composer and sound director who is best known for his work on the *Super Mario* and *The Legend of Zelda* series. Kondo was born in Nagoya, Japan, on August 13, 1961. He began taking lessons on the electronic organ from the age of five. Kondo studied at the Art Planning Department of Osaka University of Arts, but was never classically trained. Kondo is credited as being the first in-house composer at Nintendo and began working there in the 1980s. He is considered one of the most influential and respected composers in the video game industry.

Koji Kondo by Vincent Diamante. (CC BY-SA 2.0.)

SUPER MARIO BROS SCORE

In *Super Mario*, it is interesting to note that the composer begins the main gameplay loop with an ostinato introductory figure that then works its way into the main gameplay loop structure itself. Amazingly, there is only a total of 90 seconds of unique music for the entire game, with lots of repeating sections, but due to the clever arrangement, it sounds like more. Here's an excerpt from the main theme (Figure 1.7).

The composition in *Super Mario* is upbeat and fun. Looking at the Overworld theme, the main riff is built upon this harmonic structure, C-F-C-F-Am-G7. All the notes in the melody never stray too far from their root chord, and the rhythm provides a splendid and varied pulse. Triplets, off-beats, and swinging drum patterns keep the tune fresh and energetic. *Super Mario Bros* is one of the first games to repeat alternate sections before the entire song loops at the macro level. Rather than creating a large-scale loop by stitching together a series of repeated sections for example, ‖: A A B B C C:‖ For those of you familiar with song form, this style of notation will look familiar. Here Kondo incorporates out-of-order repetition into his basic looping structure, which creates the following pattern, ‖: A B B C A D D C D:‖ In this way, Kondo continually recontextualizes previously heard passages of music. These repetitions account for 72% of the Overworld theme, meaning that the 90-second piece contains just 25.5 seconds of unique content.

The music was written for the NES (Nintendo Entertainment System) which had an incredibly limited audio capability compared to modern consoles. Capabilities were limited in terms of polyphony (the number of voices or sounds that can be played simultaneously). Although the NES could manage a total of five voices, it was the two square/pulse wave and single triangle wave generators that were mostly responsible for the music in

Overworld Theme

From: *Super Mario Bros.*

Koji Kondo

FIGURE 1.7   *Super Mario Bros.* Score. (Excerpt – image: Jeff Neumann.)

Nintendo's early game titles, that's three voices available at a time. The fourth channel was a noise channel used mainly for sound effects, while the fifth channel allowed for very limited digital audio samples to be played back. It works by using low-resolution, one-bit audio samples and then modulating them on the fly to produce a high-quality sound. This last channel allows for basic percussive samples to be played, such as drums and other simple sounds. However, the audio quality is not very good. Also, it consumes a lot of memory, so it was typically used sparingly.

Koji Kondo used the NES's limited audio capabilities to write memorable and iconic music. He created a wide range of sounds by using clever programming techniques and compositional tricks. And he did all this to ensure that the music would sound good on the system and not exceed the limitations of the hardware. He later said:

> There was so much enthusiasm on this project because we were trying to create something that had never been done before. By changing the way I composed the four songs, the music had a lot of variety. It was like a puzzle for me, so it was a lot of fun.
>
> – KOJI KONDO

COMPRESSION

Nowadays, game engines will give you options to compress the data in the music file so that it takes up much less storage space in the final build, thus saving space, although it can sacrifice audio quality, especially at high rates of compression. Game engines commonly use the Ogg Vorbis format, as that comes with no licensing restrictions at all, although you will find MP3 or AAC/MP4 and others as well (Figure 1.8).

There are many different audio formats in use today; here are a few of the most common ones:

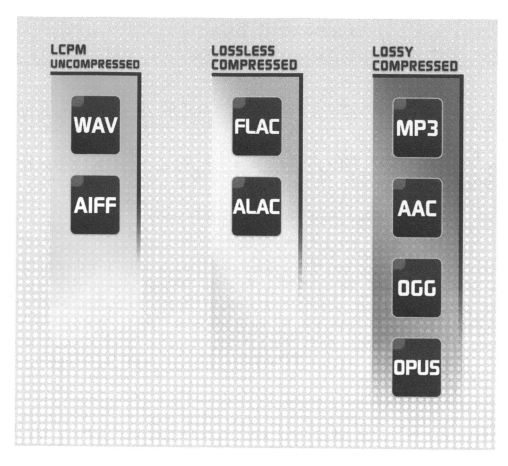

FIGURE 1.8   File formats and compression. (Image: Austin Smith.)

1. **WAV:** An uncompressed format that provides very high-quality audio but results in large file sizes. It consists of LPCM audio data.

2. **AIFF:** An uncompressed format developed by Apple, similar to WAV, but not as widely supported, especially after Apple began using Intel processors. Also uses LPCM data.

3. **MP3:** A widely used format that uses lossy compression to reduce file size and attempts to do so without significantly affecting audio quality.

4. **AAC:** A format that is similar to MP3 but is more efficient in terms of compression, resulting in smaller file sizes and higher quality.

5. **OGG Vorbis:** An open-source format that is similar to MP3 and AAC but is not as widely supported. Apple's iOS does not support it, for example, although all Android, PC, and Mac laptops/desktop can.

6. **OPUS:** An open-source, low-latency, high-quality audio codec from the same group that designed Ogg Vorbis. It is technically a replacement for Vorbis with better quality, but its popularity is not widespread. It does get used as a codec for spatial audio.

7. **FLAC:** The most popular lossless format, similar to WAV but more efficient in terms of compression. It's quite commonly used for distributing bootleg recordings made by 'concert tapers', but can be used by anyone. The compression ratio is nowhere near the level of lossy codecs like MP3 and AAC, however.

8. **ALAC:** A lossless format developed by Apple. It is similar to FLAC but is not as widely supported.

These are some of the most common, but there are many other audio formats as well. It's worth noting that some of these formats are designed for specific use cases, such as streaming or archiving, and may not be suitable for all types of audio contents.

Memory (RAM): Along with the storage of your music file, in order to play it back, the engine will need to uncompress the file into the active Random Access Memory or RAM of the game. RAM, like drive space, is not infinite. It is a separate storage limitation that needs to be taken into account and is much smaller in size than the storage space. There are various ways to uncompress music files. It can be uncompressed when the game level starts, or right when the file is called to be played. But the most common option for music files of any length (*anything over 10 seconds*) is that they are streamed, which means that the file is gradually uncompressed as it plays, which takes up far less memory. Less memory does not mean no memory, however. Keep in mind that the RAM has to hold **all** of the data in a game – textures, animations, 3d models, and sounds – as well as music. When it comes to smaller and less powerful platforms, this limitation can be much more severe.

Over the past three decades, video game composer and sound designer Michael Sweet has worked on more than 100 video games. His work can be heard on award-winning games from Niantic, Lego, Microsoft, Cartoon Network, Sesame Workshop, PlayFirst, iWin, Gamelab, Pogo, and MTV and on the XBox 360 logo. He has won the Best Audio Award at the Independent Games Festival, and been nominated for five Game Audio Network Guild awards. From 2008 to 2019, Michael led the development of the game scoring curriculum at Berklee College of Music, and is the author of *Writing Interactive Music for Video Games: A Composer Guide.*

Michael Sweet. (Used with permission from the artist.)

In this example, we get a first-hand view of how limitations can often result in innovative approaches to music.

Here in his own words, composer Michael Sweet details his strategy for dealing with significant limitations regarding the well-known casual game *Diner Dash*, published in 2005.

> The original game was built in Director (an application developed by Macromedia, then bought by Adobe) and intended as a game for the Shockwave.com platform by PlayFirst. This meant that we had to fit into a very small memory footprint. If I remember correctly, the audio budget for memory was about 500k, and we were not able to use MIDI at all (all compressed audio files). Everything was compressed at 24–32kbps mono swa files (which is similar to very low quality mp3 compression). There was a primary menu theme, and 3 gameplay themes (randomly picked), and approximately 30 sfx. We split up the music into 2–4 bar phrases and randomized these phrases during playback – doing our best to deliver something interesting while keeping the footprint small.

Now imagine something like the Mozart piece we discussed earlier, but with all of the sections decided by the game instead of by the player rolling the dice beforehand. By randomizing the loop order and progression, the composer managed to create the sense of a much longer piece of music with more variations available, while saving space at the same time. Note the use of mono files – in 2005 internet connections were pretty slow and stereo speakers were pretty uncommon so using mono files would save 50% of the space required.

PLATFORM LIMITATIONS

This is probably the most important issue to consider because in essence it's the last step in the chain. Regardless of what game engine you use or what operating system the engine will run on, the game build itself will run on some type of hardware platform, and the limitations for the platform can be considerable. There will be significant differences in storage and RAM capacity between a game created for the current Sony PlayStation and one created for the newest smartwatch or AR headset. In fact, this limitation can extend to the types of file support available. For example, due to Apple's focus on file types that they hold licenses to, an Ogg Vorbis file is not supported on iOS devices and those files are instead converted to MP3 format by the game engine if it makes a build on iOS. In many cases, the game engine can automatically convert files, but this is not always the case. Again this is why it helps to have some knowledge of each platform's capabilities before you start composing and potentially end up in a difficult situation.

Dealing with limitations in game music can be challenging. Here are just a few strategies that might help:

1. **Learn and Practice:** Acquiring new skills and techniques can help you overcome limitations and expand your abilities.

2. **Experimentation:** Trying different approaches and experimenting with new sounds and techniques can help you find new ways to express yourself.

3. **Collaboration:** Working with others can provide you with new perspectives and ideas.

4. **Use Technology:** Embrace advances in technology to create and produce music in new and innovative ways.

5. **Adaptation:** Be flexible and open to change.

6. **Be Creative:** Be creative with what you have, and try to find new ways to use the resources you have.

It's important to remember that limitations can also be opportunities for creativity and personal growth. Embracing and working with limitations can lead to new and unique artistic expression.

The Big Takeaway: Even though compressing your music files does save a lot of space, there can still be significant storage limitations imposed on you, especially in smaller social and mobile games, which is why game composers often have to be very creative when confronted with these situations and figure out ways of maximizing their music content using a minimum of musical assets. Since the logic of a game has to be programmed, it follows that music systems must also be programmed and come in all shapes and sizes. In many cases, the game that composers engage in is how to make music that won't drive the player crazy by being too short and at the same time won't drive the producers crazy by being too long and eating up coveted storage or RAM space. This is the kind of musical challenge presented to game composers on a fairly frequent basis, and the methods of solving these types of conundrums are as varied as the games themselves.

Discussion Questions: What is the difference between linear and non-linear music? What is the difference between interactive and adaptive music? How does indeterminacy affect music in games? Why do game composers need to use music loops? How does game music relate to the history of improvised music? What is game logic? How does gameplay influence the music choices a composer makes? How does the gameplay system influence the music choices a composer makes? How did Koji Kondo Deal with the limitations of the NES game system?

TERMS

- **Linear Media:** Forms of communication, such as television and radio, that are delivered in a linear, or chronological, format. Content is presented in a predetermined sequence and cannot be accessed out of order.

- **Non-Linear Media:** Forms of communication, such as the internet and video games, that are accessed in a non-linear or non-chronological way. Content is not delivered in a predetermined sequence.

- **Interactive:** Allowing a two-way flow of information between a computer and a computer-user; responding to a user's input.

- **Adaptive:** The ability or tendency to adapt to different situations. Adaptive media refers to forms that adjust and adapt to the specific characteristics, preferences, or behavior of the audience. This type of media uses algorithms and data to personalize the content, also known as personalized or dynamic media.

- **Music Trigger:** A specific event or action that initiates the playback of pre-recorded music. Music triggers can be used to indicate a change in the game's state, such as a change in level, a change in the weather, or a change in the player's status.

- **Dynamic Audio**: The use of sound that changes in response to the player's actions or the game's state. It can also change depending on the player's location, time, or other factors.

- **Dynamic Music:** The use of music that changes in response to the game's state or the player's actions. It can also change depending on the player's location, time, or other factors. Examples include music that changes in intensity and tempo as the player embarks on a quest, or changes to a more peaceful theme as the player enters exploration mode.

- **Indeterminacy:** The state or condition of being uncertain, unpredictable, or undefined. Indeterminacy can be found in various fields such as science, mathematics, physics, art, and music. In music, indeterminacy refers to the use of techniques that allow for a degree of chance, randomness, or improvisation in the composition or performance of a piece.

- **Clave:** A pair of cylindrical hardwood sticks that make a hollow sound when struck together, used as a percussion instrument in Latin music. They are usually used in a syncopated rhythm pattern of alternating phrases of three and two beats.

- **Raga:** A melodic framework for improvisation in Indian classical music.

- **Tala:** The term used in Indian classical music similar to musical meter, that is, any rhythmic beat or strike that measures musical time.

- **Concerto:** A piece for one or more soloists and orchestra with three contrasting movements.

- **Sonata:** A type of musical composition, usually for a solo instrument or a small instrumental ensemble, that typically consists of two to four movements, or sections, each in a related key but with a unique musical character.

- **Simulation Board Game:** A game played on a board that attempts to model actual events or situations and usually involves the movements of pieces.

- **Aesthetic:** A set of principles underlying and guiding the work of a particular artist or artistic movement.

- **Existentialist:** A form of philosophical inquiry that explores the issue of human existence. Existentialist philosophers explore questions related to the meaning, purpose, and value of human existence.

- **Sonification:** The process of using sound to represent data or information. It is a technique used in various fields such as science, engineering, and art, to make data more accessible and understandable to humans. The process of sonification involves mapping data to specific parameters such as pitch, duration, and timbre, to create a sound representation of the data.

- **Improvisation:** The act of spontaneous creation without prior preparation and involves making decisions and taking actions in real time. Improvisation can be guided by certain rules, forms, or structures, or it can be completely freeform.

- **Game Engine:** The software that a computer or video game is built upon.

- **Platform:** The electronic hardware or software system that can run games. Common platforms are console (PlayStation, XBox), PC, and mobile (iOS or Android).

- **MIDI:** Musical Instrument Digital interface is a technical standard that describes a communications protocol, digital interface, and electrical connectors that connect a wide variety of electronic musical instruments, computers, and related audio devices.

- **Digital Audio File:** A storable and editable collection of samples organized in a standard form that can be stored on computer drives, transferred to other computers or samplers, shared on the Internet to be downloaded, added to video files, or played-back in real time.

- **LPCM:** Linear pulse code modulation (LPCM) is a method for digitally encoding uncompressed audio information, where audio waveforms are represented by a sequence of amplitude values from a sample on a linear scale in which the values are proportional to the amplitudes, as opposed to being the log of the amplitudes. (*Commonly referred to as Digital Audio.*)

CHAPTER 2

Building Blocks

Topic: Game Design and Its Application to Musical Fundamentals

- Learning Outcomes
- Game Theory
- The Game Designer
- The Game Design Document
- Fundamentals of Game Music
- Game Music Form
- The Building Blocks of Music and Their Relationship to Games
- The Snowboarding Conundrum
- Transitions
- Structure and Form (*Horizontal and Vertical*)
- Game Composing Techniques in Action
- The Big Takeaway
- Discussion Questions
- Terms

Learning Outcomes

- Understanding Game Theory
- Understanding Game Music Fundamentals

DOI: 10.1201/9781003414728-4

- Differentiate the building blocks of music, and how they relate to games

- Analyze the basics of game form and function

GAME THEORY

In life, we play many different kinds of games. Drivers maneuvering in heavy traffic are playing a driving game. Bargain-hunters bidding on eBay are playing an auctioning game. When opposing candidates choose their platform in an election, they are playing a political game. Instrumentalists performing music together are playing a music game. In brief, a game is being played whenever human beings interact. In the case of video games, players may find themselves interacting with another human or a machine.

How games are regarded by their designers has an effect on how composers approach scoring. For example, **narrativists** argue that games are expressive due to their underlying story, and thus games can be interpreted like literary texts, albeit with many branching outcomes due to player decisions. On the other hand, **ludologists** assert that a game's rules and mechanics alone express a game's meaning. In practice, the game designer needs to acknowledge both of these viewpoints when positioning their game's approach. Like designers, composers must likewise take both of these points of view into account.

Remember the Architect character in the Matrix movies? Well, you can think of a game designer as an architect of sorts. They are responsible for creating and developing the concepts, mechanics, and systems that drive a game. They work with a team of artists, programmers, and other designers to turn their ideas into a fun and engaging player experience. A game designer's tasks may include writing game scripts, designing levels and puzzles, creating game mechanics and rules, and balancing game difficulty. They also play a crucial role in the testing, marketing and iteration process, making changes and improvements to the game based on player feedback. Even for the smallest of games, designers and programmers have a mountain of detail to manage and you can imagine how all of these little details might affect the form and structure of the music being composed.

Will Wright is a video game designer and co-founder of the game company Maxis. He is perhaps best known for creating the popular video game series *The Sims* and *SimCity*. Wright is considered one of the pioneers of the simulation genre in video games and has received numerous awards and accolades for his contributions to the industry. He is known for his innovative approach to game design, which blends elements of simulation and strategy with a focus on player creativity and choice.

Concerning his career as a game designer he says, "I love games because they collapse many different design fields into one thing. Games are probably the most interesting design object there is. You get aspects of environmental design, aesthetics, functional, storytelling. All of these are aspects of interactive design."

Another principle often governing a game's structure and development is **emergence** or more accurately, emergent design. Broadly speaking, this concept refers to the development of complex outcomes from simple ideas. A rough musical equivalent would be a composer like Bach or Beethoven writing an entire major work based on the inventive reworking of a simple musical idea or motif. Games that use this principle start out with a simple idea as well, and then build onto it in various ways, taking care to keep the game balanced as they go. In a role playing game like *World of Warcraft* where a human player is encountering opponents, they might gain more abilities or weapons that would enable them to defeat them quicker, but if the player gets too powerful, they might quit because winning is too easy. So the designers have to make the enemies tougher in response, but if they go too far, then the player might quit because it's too hard. A useful balance has to be maintained to allow the player to be challenged but not too much and not too little. Composers must certainly take these issues of balance and development into account.

How can we find these things out ourselves? In the world of games, it's always best to play the game and then make some decisions. However, long before prototypes get built or vertical slices and alpha builds made available, there is the Game Design Document (GDD) that will get created first. A game designer will work with the producer and other team members to gather all the necessary information concerning the artist and technical specifications of said game. They painstakingly compile this information into individual sections in the GDD.

THE GAME DESIGN DOCUMENT

You can think of this document as a road map or blueprint that describes everything that goes into a project. It typically includes information on the overall concept, gameplay mechanics, story, characters, art style, sound, music, and user interface. GDDs are often shared with investors, publishers, and other stakeholders in the process; they provide vital information to programmers, artists, musicians, and other team members.

GDDs come in all shapes and sizes. Some developers are super detailed right out of the gate and include drawings and system flow maps, while others use just plain text to get the information across. All of this information is important to the curious composer, and should help to spark the imagination. The GDD should be read carefully and studied before jumping on calls with team members, as it will serve to answer many questions and that can save you many hours before and after you start composing.

Every GDD worth its salt should have a music and sound section, but the sad truth is that many times these details are not included. It's up to the community of music and sound professionals to change this practice. We must be involved from the start to assure a more ideal result in the end. The music section of a GDD should provide information on the overall musical vision for the game, as well as specific details on how music will be implemented. It should provide a clear and detailed description of all aspects concerning the music, and how it will contribute to the overall player experience.

Things to include:

- **The Overall Tone and Style of the Music:** This could include information on the genre, instruments, and other elements that will be used to set the mood and atmosphere of the game.

- **Audio Production Information:** Such as how the music will be produced, including whether it will be composed by an external composer or in-house team, and whether it will be recorded with live instruments or created using software.

- **Music Cues/Asset List:** This is a list of the tracks or pieces of music that will be used in the game, along with notes on how they will be triggered highlighting specific moments in the game where music will be used, such as during gameplay, cutscenes, and transitions.

- **Technical Design:** Include as much information as you can on the music system itself and how the music will develop in each section of the game. File size and type should be included here as well.

Games can be a bit overwhelming when it comes to information overload. But we have to be cognizant of the emotional quality, story, and function as they all help to inform the nature of our soundtracks. The musical choices we make deeply affect player perception. That is why it is vitally important that we strive to understand the basic tenets of game design. For more information, here are a few highly recommended books on the subject. They cover a wide range of topics from mechanics and systems to player experience and storytelling. They will give you a solid foundation in game design principles and techniques.

1. *Game Design Workshop: A Playcentric Approach to Creating Innovative Games* by Tracy Fullerton

2. *The Art of Game Design: A Book of Lenses* by Jesse Schell

3. *A Theory of Fun for Game Design* by Raph Koster

FUNDAMENTALS OF GAME MUSIC

The complexities and requirements of the game environment raise many questions:

- If you don't know how long the player will stay in a game location, how long should you make the piece of music for that location? Should the same piece of music play each time the player enters that location?

- If the action and intensity speed up as the player goes further into the level, should the music speed up and slow down as well? If yes, how?

- At what point in time can you declare victory or defeat in a game? How do we move from section to section? And how can we make that musical transition a smooth one?

- Since I am using looping music, how can I keep things fresh and interesting over a long period of time?

These are just a very few of the questions and thoughts that come up as you start to compose even before you put a note on paper or enter it into your DAW. In general, the practical answer to these questions is "let's find out." We can do that by asking the creators, reading a game design document or by playing through the game ourselves. Remember, composers are problem solvers, and in the end, it is our responsibility to figure these things out.

GAME MUSIC FORM

These general categories are found in most games:

- **Cinematic Music**, accompanies various video clips within a game—whether they are cutscenes, introductions, endings, or story transitions. These pieces of media are usually linear and help propel the storyline forward or signal the end of a game level.

- **Gameplay Music**, from menu selection and instruction screens, game backgrounds and loops, to victory and defeat fanfares, music plays a huge part in defining mood during gameplay.

What are some other things that we must consider as we start to compose? Well, music helps create an emotional connection that makes for a satisfying experience; it is deeply missed when it is absent. Music can completely change the pace, mood, and feel of a game. Let's review some of what a good musical soundtrack for a game can accomplish.

- **Set the Mood and Overall Tone of a Game:** From a catchy title theme to a spooky background, music helps set and maintain the player's emotional connection to the game.

- **Identify Time and Place within the Game:** Music helps set the time and place of the game—whether that be medieval England or the cold void of space—as much as any costume piece or scenery.

- **Identify Locations and Settings in a Game:** Is your character on the beach or in the bustling streets at rush hour? Music helps players identify their surroundings.

- **Identify Characters within a Game:** Like a music theme associated with a role in opera, specific musical passages associated with a character can subconsciously clue a player into what is happening in a game.

- **Establish the Pace of Gameplay:** Fast beats can elevate already heart-pounding action. The pace of gameplay is highly influenced by music.

You may also recognize that these characteristics are also similar to the traits of good film or television music scoring. This is logical since these are also visual mediums, so a lot of the same characteristics apply. Either way, as we take all this into account, we start to realize that music really is a driving force in immersing the player into the game world that is being created. Music aids immersion by providing the emotional underpinning to the whole experience; music creates and can manipulate emotion.

THE BUILDING BLOCKS OF MUSIC AND THEIR RELATIONSHIP TO GAMES

So, how can we apply the fundamental building blocks of music to games? There is no doubt that game music composition is very special, but as with all forms of music composition, the fundamentals still apply.

These are:

- **Melody:** A group of notes of various pitches (*high or low*) which are played in sequence one after another.

- **Harmony:** A combination of simultaneously played pitches that produce intervallic relationships, chords, and chord progressions.

- **Rhythm:** A systematic arrangement of musical sounds set according to duration, tempo, or periodic accents.

- **Timbre:** The character or quality of a musical sound or voice, separate from its pitch and intensity.

- **Form:** The structure of a musical composition.

The special nature of interactive media makes it possible to allow all musical characteristics to stand alone or be tied to events in the game. Because of this, we have the opportunity of associating any or all of these elements in the game in real time. By tying music to single triggers or random arrays, or associating them with parameters, a series of numbers, or an algorithm that is being generated by the game engine, we begin to create interactive and adaptive soundtracks that provide a truly immersive musical experience.

What might this look and sound like?

For example, in Figure 2.1, let's take a balloon game where your goal is to move up and down on the screen to collect items hidden in soft puffy clouds. The game engine

FIGURE 2.1   Balloon game parameter – changes over time. (Image: Austin Smith.)

most likely will be tracking the position of the balloon as it moves. This gives us the opportunity to tie any one of the building blocks of music mentioned above to that same parameter or series of numbers that is being generated. If we associate melody with this action, we can imagine a piece of music where the melody rises and falls in real time as the balloon goes up and down. Alternatively, we could associate tempo with the motion of the balloon in the same way and then our music would speed up or slow down as the balloon rises and falls.

This example is predicated on the fact that we have a programmer behind the scenes helping us with the **implementation** of our idea. We might be able to make the musical part of this work by ourselves using what is known as audio middleware, but that's a discussion for another time. For the moment, let's assume we only have the tools of a composer working with a DAW at our disposal.

THE SNOWBOARDING CONUNDRUM

Here is another interesting thought puzzle to consider. In this game scenario in Figure 2.2, you are a world champion snowboarder ready to set a new world's record at the top of a steep course. As the snowboarder heads down the run, music starts to play in a loop. Why do we use a loop? Well, since we have no idea exactly how long this run will take, we have to have a way to create music that can accommodate the structure of this game and then transition to other music clips.

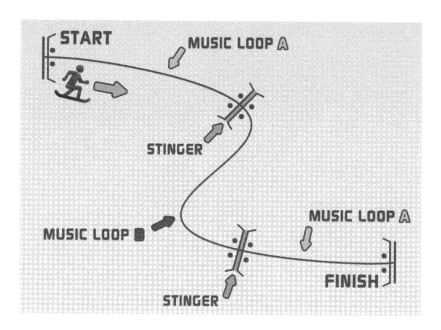

FIGURE 2.2 Snowboarding conundrum. (Image: Austin Smith.)

Looping means going around and around, repeating the same material after a certain time. If the music to be looped is too short, it might drive the player crazy, but if it's too long we might never hear the entire track. Additionally, a long loop may take up more storage space than the developer allotted. In the case of our snowboarder we have composed seamless loops and by playing through the game we have decided on a duration that makes sense using the least amount of space. For example, if the whole run takes 120 seconds, we might choose to make our loops 30 seconds in length figuring that we would probably hear any given piece of music for 30–60 seconds or two repeats. That should keep the music fresh to the player and not take up too much file size. For the moment, let's think of music loop A and B separate from any specific genre. Let's just say they are upbeat and energetic. For argument's sake we'll say Loop A is in the key of C major and Loop B is in the key of A minor.

So, returning to our game – our snowboarder barrels down the hill gaining momentum, and because of the way the game is programmed, a power up will appear at some point in the run. We have no idea exactly when that power-up will appear, but it will make the snowboarder go much faster. The arrow in the middle on the left shows us where it will occur in this instance and in this instance only.

When the player gets to this power up transition point, the music will generally need to change, since we're now going faster. But now we need to ask ourselves "how should the music respond?" Will it get faster? Will it get slower? Louder? Will it change key? We have lots of choices in this regard but, in this case we're going to assume that it does get faster because that would be very exciting, after all when you grab a power up one might expect the music to change and going faster is a good choice that matches the gameplay dynamic. The change of key from the relative major to the relative minor also helps delineate this turbo section of the game and also serves to change the emotional quality for the player.

Now back to our snowboarder, as they plummet downhill and the player arrives at the agreed upon transition point, boom! Power up engaged, turbo mode activated and our faster music loop B starts playing. As the run continues, the power up ends, maybe the character starts flashing to visually signal that, and we return to music loop A until the end of the run.

TRANSITIONS

Musical transitions like the ones we have just described are used all the time to move smoothly from one music cue to another. A disjointed score leads to a disjointed experience for the player; however, if well handled, transitions help to maintain the continuity and the flow of gameplay.

Now, since in this example we are composers, not programmers, how can we deal with the very simple yet challenging transition? How do we create a smooth transition when the power up hits? If we're in the key of C in loop A and we don't know when the power up is going to be grabbed, perhaps it would be in the middle of a beat or worse yet, in the middle of a bar or in the middle of a chord suddenly we'd hear loop B, which would be in a different key and that would be quite jarring to suddenly go between those two pieces of music. What can we pull out of our musical bag of tricks? How can we solve this puzzle purely compositionally using only digital audio files?

FIGURE 2.3   Musical transitions. (Image: Austin Smith.)

The first observation is that you really can't do any kind of untimed transition without a programmer, because some code has to tell one loop to switch to another or to control how the loop is playing. Unless you know **exactly** how long a loop is needed, you cannot automate the changing of a loop to another one. Those of you who are experienced with audio middleware may argue differently (and we'll cover its benefits soon), but let's say we don't have that option in this case (and keep in mind this is still a reality – some game developers do **not** use audio middleware). What can we ask our programmer friends to do? Here are some options:

In Figure 2.3 Example A on the left, **Cue-to-cue transitions trigger musical phrases end to end**, so as one piece is ending, the next piece begins. The problem with this approach is that the composer never knows when the player will trigger a new segment of music during gameplay and it is possible the transition may take place in the middle of a bar or musical phrase. Not the best sounding solution, as you can well imagine. To the player, this type of transition has the potential to sound jarring and sudden and break the flow of gameplay. A programmer might be able to determine a point to cue and wait for a musical length of time before changing, but that's a pretty sophisticated request. In this example, we'll assume we don't have that option.

As Figure 2.3 Example B in the middle shows, **you can also fade the main loop out**, which is to say, fade the first loop before starting the next one. Obviously you can't bake the fade out into the loop asset itself, unless you know the exact time you'll be traveling before you encounter the power up. If it's in the loop and too short, then music will fade out and start again. If it's too long, then it will also sound wrong as you have already moved past the powerup. So the loop's volume in the game engine has to be programmed to fade out whenever the power-up is encountered. But this is going to affect the intensity a lot – you just encountered the powerup and are increasing speed, and the soundtrack fades out briefly and the next track starts up. It's probably going to be a bit jarring and disjointed and not as satisfying. In short we're part way there, but we need something else to make this transition work and keep the intensity high or even increase it.

SOLUTION – USE A STINGER

Finally in Figure 2.3 Example C on the right, we have a decent solution. To cover a transition like the one in our example, a composer may use a special piece of music called a **stinger**. Musical stingers are non-looping musical phrases that act more like musical sound effects. They play over transitions to make the changes between tracks inaudible. For example, to obfuscate the transition from slow music A to fast music B and back again, we might stop

FIGURE 2.4   Music maze game lesson. (Image: Game Audio Institute.)

and fade the slow piece of music at the same time that you trigger a stinger and then play or trigger the faster piece of new music for the duration of the power-up. The stinger smoothes over the transition between the slower and faster music by functionally suspending time with a short or long burst of notes ascending or descending. As the player listens to the stinger, they don't even realize that loop A has stopped and we are already well into loop B. We've successfully covered that transition compositionally. We have fooled the player's ear as if by magic. We do need to tell our programmer friend to trigger the stinger as well as the fade out, followed by the playback of the second faster loop – remember, none of this happens by itself and we can't time it precisely (Figure 2.4).

Here's an example that helps to demonstrate this technique. This is from a Game Lesson developed by the Game Audio Institute called the Music Maze. In this example, the player starts with a basic drum music loop, and then walks into a trigger object. This object plays a stinger, and at the same time the current music crossfades with another loop with added instruments at a more intense level. A crossfade is when one part fades out as the other fades in, but the stinger is still doing its job – covering up and smoothing the transition between the two loops. A simple but very effective system that is used in many popular games.

STRUCTURE AND FORM

Now, let's take a look at some overarching compositional methods that are more advanced tasks for a programmer to have to manage in a game's soundtrack. Using either (or preferably both) of these methods will enable a composer to get a lot more versatility out of their existing music assets (Figure 2.5).

Branching is conditional music based on actions in the game. Different actions lead to different musical results. In other words, music can be triggered horizontally in pieces. If the character goes left, play music A; if the character goes right, play music B. You can think of these expanding structures as leaves on a tree. The music unfolds with the action on the horizontal plane. Some composers can also refer to it as horizontal sequencing, and

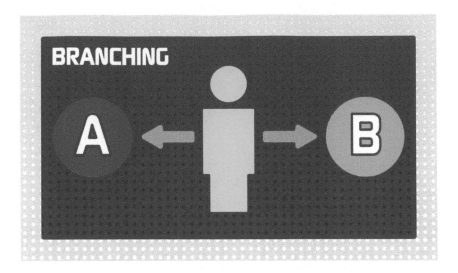

FIGURE 2.5   Image: Austin Smith.

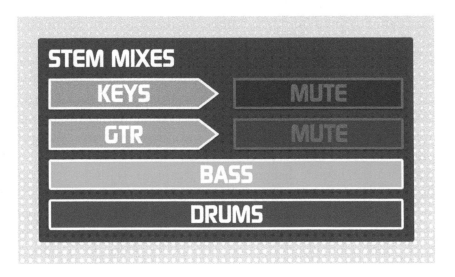

FIGURE 2.6   Image: Austin Smith.

there can be a lot of successive branching. Narratively oriented games often have branching storylines to them so this is a musical example of that in action (Figure 2.6).

Stem mixes (or stems) are the individual parts of a piece of music. Stems are created by exporting each instrument or sub grouping of instruments in a piece of music. A programmer can use these multiple layers by muting them on and off and re-combined them in a variety of ways to increase musical variation. This can also be referred to as layering, sometimes called vertical orchestration. Although this is a great way to get more mileage out of existing musical materials, it can end up being less interactive, as it has a limited amount of choices available. Also, timing between layers may not be the most responsive or as timed to gameplay events as one might prefer. However, using layering combined with several different variations can extend the usefulness of this method.

Now, let's take a look at just some of the ways that these techniques are being used by composers in the field.

GAME COMPOSING TECHNIQUES IN ACTION

Red Dead Redemption (2011, Rockstar Games) – Woody Jackson/Bill Elm

This composing team was tasked with creating an iconic and immersive soundtrack for the open world Western-themed game *Red Dead Redemption*, published by Rockstar Games in 2011 (Figure 2.7).

As discussed, composition is by nature problem solving. The problem that this composing team faced was to write a score that matched not only the mood of the game, but also the action. Not an easy thing to do in an open world game where the player has a variety of options available at nearly any time – they could decide to attack a train, explore the wilderness, capture some cattle rustlers, and more. The score that Jackson and Elm produced is a great example of making choices and solving these problems. By making all the music stems based on 4/4 time signature in A minor at 130 bpm, the soundtrack stays locked in tempo, key/mode, and time, regardless of activity. Then once they had all of the individual

FIGURE 2.7   Woody Jackson was one half of the composing team that recorded the soundtrack to *Red Dead Redemption*. Image by Jeriaska (CC BY-SA 2.0).

stems ready, the developers and composers worked out what combinations of instruments and what variations would be associated with different actions the player takes in the game, or where they go on the map. More intense activity like robbing a train results in a more densely orchestrated sound with timpani and distorted guitars, whereas traveling in the open country results in much sparser instrumentation. At all times though, they did a great job keeping the music fresh and non-repetitive. Ultimately, they found a way to use period instruments in a modern way to create music appropriate to the genre, that was adaptive, and could change in terms of density no matter what the player decided to do. Using stems as they did is an example of vertical resequencing in action.

Composer Chase Bethea, a NYX award-winning and VGMO nominated Composer and technical audio designer, is known in the industry as the "swiss army knife of video game composition." His schooling includes an AA in audio engineering from The Los Angeles Recording School, an AA in Music Theory and Composition from Moorpark College and a BM in Media Composition from California State Northridge. Chase has received many accolades throughout his career, the soundtrack for the game *On the Peril of Parrots* won the 2023 NYX Award *(Gold Winner)* for Best Original Soundtrack.

Used with permission.

For this game, Chase was tasked by the developer/programmer Glen Henry from SpriteWrench studio with creating a Bossa Nova based score to go along with hundreds of levels of increasingly complex puzzles. He took the challenge seriously and jumped right into doing extensive research into the genre, paying homage to composers like Antônio Carlos Jobim and João Gilberto. He even went so far as to teach himself to play an old mandolin he had lying around the studio. Here he describes his process in his own words:

> I grew up listening to bossa in my childhood, but never thought I would have to write a full soundtrack based on the style. I filled a sketch book with my ideas and research into the origins of the music. From the start, the idea was to make the score interactive. Musical elements, like percussion and flutes develop as you progress through the game's levels. There are also title and menu screens that pop up and must be accounted for. Throughout the process, I was really focused on how this was going to work with the gameplay. I asked myself if

Jobim was alive today, how would he score this game? I worked closely with the programmer on a daily basis, to make sure that the music system was properly implemented. The programmer would make a puzzle a day and send it my way. I worked in my DAW to match and produce tracks that transitioned seamlessly from section to section. It was a painstaking process but, I think that this kind of one to one development paid off, I feel it really works and people have responded very positively.

– CHASE BETHEA

The Big Takeaway: Music when applied to interactive and adaptive situations poses a lot of new questions and presents unique compositional challenges. Where linear media ends, interactive composition begins. Understanding forms and structure and how it applies to each individual project is essential to success. Yes there are standards, but that being said you will find that style and form is changing all the time. What worked yesterday might not work tomorrow. Developing a syntax and vocabulary of how game design manifests is part of the gig. We cannot compose in a vacuum, we have to meet the game on its terms and bend the music to fit. Transitions are especially challenging as unlike linear forms they are a moving target and often bridge disparate things together. Mastering this aspect of music composition is not to be seen as a limitation, it is simply structure, a path that opens a doorway into further creative dimensions.

Discussion Questions: Why do composers need to understand game theory and design? What is the purpose of a game design document (GDD)? What is the relationship of technology to game music? How does technology influence the creative choices composers make? Why do composers need to use music loops in games? How can the basic building blocks of music be applied to game logic and architecture? Why are transitions so hard to compose for? What are some creative musical and technical strategies composers can use to create smooth transitions? What techniques did the composers for *Red Dead Redemption* use in their score?

TERMS

- **Game Theory:** A branch of mathematics concerned with the analysis of strategies for competitive situations, where the outcome of a participant's choice of action depends critically on the actions of other participants.

- **Narrativists:** Central to the narrativist philosophy is the idea that in playing a game, you are essentially following a perceived storyline, albeit with branching outcomes and multiple endings.

- **Ludologists:** The study of games and other forms of play. Central to this philosophy is the idea that gameplay mechanics are the most important element in video games.

- **Environmental Design:** Is the process of addressing surrounding environmental parameters when devising plans, programs, policies, buildings, or products.

- **Game Design Document:** A game design document *(GDD)* is a highly descriptive living document that describes the entire system and elements for a video game. A GDD serves as the blueprint from which a game can be built.

- **Vertical Slice:** A type of milestone, benchmark, or deadline, with emphasis on demonstrating progress across all components of a project. The term vertical slice refers to a cross-sectional slice through the layers that form the structure of the software code base.

- **Alpha, Beta, and Gold Master Builds:** Alpha means an earlier version of the product. Alpha versions are often very different from the final product, have bugs, errors, and in general, the product has just begun to be created. Beta versions are more thought out and developed. A gold master is a release candidate milestone which passes all of a publisher and platform's requirements. It is considered the finished game, locked and ready to be reproduced and sold.

- **Music Loop:** A structure, series, or process, the end of which is connected to the beginning.

- **Cinematic Music:** Is music written specifically to accompany the linear movie clips or cutscenes in a game.

- **Gameplay Music:** Is music written specifically to accompany the interactive sections of a game.

- **Pace:** A general term related to tempo which can be defined as the speed at which a section of music is played. Tempo is a more exact measurement in comparison.

- **Mood:** The overall feeling or emotion of a piece of music in relation to gameplay.

- **Triggers:** Activate scripted sequences; pre-defined series of events that occur when triggered by player location or actions that play out in the games engine.

- **Random array:** A list of similar items where elements are randomly chosen, often used to provide more variety or variation to musical tracks.

- **Game Parameter:** A numerical or other measurable factor forming one of a set that defines a system or sets the conditions of its operation.

- **Algorithm:** A type of formula that represents the rules of a game, a collection of which comprises a game system.

- **Musical Transition:** A musical behavior that occurs whenever one music object, called a source, stops playing and another starts.

- **Musical Stingers:** A stinger is a short musical phrase that's played on top of the music to signal a game event to the player. Stingers are often played when a goal is reached, a player dies, or treasure is found.

- **Implementation:** It is the execution or practice of a plan, a method or any design, idea, model, specification, standard, or policy for doing something. Implementation is the action that must follow any preliminary thinking for something to actually happen. In the case of audio, it is the placement and execution of each sound in a game.

- **Audio Middleware:** A tool set that sits between the game engine and the audio hardware. It provides common functionality that is needed on each project such as randomizing pitch or volume, fading sounds in or out, and picking sounds randomly from a set of sounds for example.

- **Power-Up:** A bonus that a player can collect and that gives their character an advantage, such as more strength or firepower.

- **Game Audio Institute:** A game-based learning company dedicated to game audio education.

- **Branching:** Conditional music based on actions in the game, music that is triggered horizontally in pieces.

- **Stems:** The individual parts of a piece of music, exported out, grouped, and layered together.

- **BPM:** Beats Per Minute.

CHAPTER 3

The Composer's Toolbox

Topic: Understanding and Applying the Tools of the Trade

- Learning Outcomes
- Preparations and Considerations
- Words of Wisdom – Matt Levine
- Orchestration
- Digital Audio Workstations
- Working in the Box
- Working with Humans, Notation, and Notation Programs
- Stereo Editors
- Music Middleware
- The Big Takeaway
- Discussion Questions
- Terms

Learning Outcomes

- Recall different tools and techniques for creating and applying game music
- Review DAWs and their function in games
- Develop an Understanding of Orchestration
- Learn about different audio tools and their relation to music
- Review different middleware tools for music implementation

DOI: 10.1201/9781003414728-5

PREPARATIONS AND CONSIDERATION

Previously, we covered just some of the definitions, overarching concepts, practical techniques, and approaches that composers use every day to structure music for games and interactive media. Since every game is unique, you can see how a composer must organize their music so that it is tightly related to the structure of the game itself. And as we discussed earlier, this structure is going to be different for each game.

Your composer's toolbox is more than just a list of stuff you need to buy, or stuff that you think you need to make music. It is also a conceptual thing – understanding what tools fit your aesthetic, and how best to employ them to develop your sound. It is true that at some point, in fact, at many points in a project, you will have to consider things final and make a delivery or update an asset under a pressing deadline. Defining your toolbox ahead of time can help speed up your workflow tremendously for these situations.

WORDS OF WISDOM

Matt Levine is a talented and diverse musician and long-time industry professional. He has worked in the music department at SONY and teaches at the San Francisco Conservatory of Music. A very experienced composer, producer, and educator, Matt divides his time between his students, composing, producing, and developing his own sound immersion applications. Be sure to check out Tone Pool®, a sound immersion app for iOS and Android.

Matt Levine. (Used with permission.)

Here he shares his perspective on the creative process.

Most people who want to get into game scoring ask me what tools they need to learn. It's a valid question, but it isn't the most important one. The fundamentals of game scoring change very slowly over time, so I think a better question would be, "what is the creative process for scoring a video game?" Scoring a game can in many ways be similar to scoring a film. In both cases, the music helps to tell the story and support the emotional subtest. Games require an additional phase of implementation that accommodates different styles of gameplay. The implementation phase requires the use of tools that tend to change more quickly than the tools of traditional music production. That is why the tools question is valid; you do need to learn new tools every year or so, but they are generally doing fancier versions of the same basic things. There are only a handful of adaptive music techniques that are used in the vast majority of game scores. If you understand these techniques thoroughly, it is easy to figure out how to do them in next year's tools. A good place to start is to ignore the tools. Look at what you want the player's experience to be, and then use the fundamentals of storytelling and adaptive music to design an emotionally compelling score. Once you have figured out the "why," it is much easier to figure out the "how."

– MATT LEVINE

We begin this section with a disclaimer. We have tried to provide, to the best of our knowledge, the most commonly used tools in the industry as well as explain how they are uniquely used in the context of scoring for games. Our goal is to provide resources and give answers to the most common questions that students ask concerning what tools are essential to working on games. But it is the nature of such recommendations in the world of technology that once given, they are soon (or even already) out of date.

ORCHESTRATION

Music orchestration is the art and craft of arranging music for live or virtual ensembles. Orchestration involves assigning all the parts of a musical composition to the various instruments or sections tasked with performing each part. Orchestration can also involve adapting or arranging existing music for instruments or ensembles that are not associated with the original composition. It involves choosing instruments, adjusting dynamic levels, adding or removing harmony parts, and making other changes to personalize the sound, meaning, and impact of the music. Orchestration is a complex and wonderful art form unto itself. We could write a whole book on orchestration. However, others have already beaten us to it, and luckily many great books are available. Highly recommended is *Instrumentation and Orchestration* by Alfred Blatter. It is listed below along with a couple of others commonly used by composers over the years for reference.

- Alfred Blatter, *Instrumentation and Orchestration*

- Walter Piston, *Orchestration*

- Samuel Adler, *The Study of Orchestration*

A good orchestration book should provide you with all the information you need to compose for each instrument family, strings, brass, percussion, keyboards, and the like. It will also explain things like score order, range, transpositions, common, and extended techniques as well as providing useful score examples and hands on exercises. The Blatter book is recommended as it is written in a very direct style, well organized, well written, and easy to understand. There are also a lot of resources for learning the art of orchestration online, also a great way to go.

The study of orchestration is a lifelong endeavor and one that will sharpen your composition skills. The longer that you apply yourself, the more adept you will become. The art of orchestration is creative, and a very special part of being a composer. It cannot be stressed enough how important good orchestration is to your music. Orchestration is the reason that the same chords and same rhythms played on a slack key guitar makes us think about Hawaii, and if you just change that one instrument to a pedal steel guitar, suddenly we're in Texas. Orchestration is just that powerful.

In game music, we apply the art of orchestration in two main ways:

- **MIDI orchestration,** the creative use and combination of sampled instruments triggered by MIDI. These techniques you will apply inside of your DAW blending and mixing to create musical color and timbre.

- **Live Orchestration,** the traditional study and application of instrumental combinations for live players.

In many cases, you may find yourself combining these two techniques; it is a very common practice in music for visual media. Many times you will find yourself creating complex and rich MIDI orchestrations that you will then blend with real humans. This technique creates hyperreal and satisfying textures by allowing the composer to blend in a few live instruments to create a sense of realism. The truth is, no matter how much we fall in love with the sounds of our samples, nothing beats real musicians who have spent many years of painstaking practice mastering their instrument.

The ability to have live players deliver all sorts of complex articulations not only sounds great, but can also save a ton of time. Creating complex articulations in MIDI using controllers is quite detailed and painstaking work. Lastly, always remember that sample instruments many times are not mapped to the actual ranges and possible techniques that can be achieved by the real thing. This is not a problem and in fact can be used to great effect if you are only using samples. Once you give parts and scores to live players, however, any misunderstandings between live musical requirements and sampled instrument libraries can cause a lot of problems that will make you look both unprepared and unprofessional.

In the case of MIDI orchestration, you're going to have to deal with sample sets of one kind or another. The good news is that you can get into doing this for free with reasonably good sounding sampled orchestras as well as numerous other libraries to start with, which is great as a starting palette and the list of free resources keeps growing.

The bad news is that if you're really trying to be a professional in this field and you're after the most accurate and believable orchestral libraries, they do cost money. There are many commercial sample libraries available, made by many different companies, and you will find that many are not cheap and often require significant computer hardware resources to run efficiently. Our advice here would be to do your research, listen to the offerings, watch tutorials, and then pick these up as you need them. There are often sales and educational discounts as well which can help take some of the bite out of your wallet. Additionally, most digital audio workstations already come with instruments included. Logic Pro, for example, has way more bells and whistles than Pro Tools, and for a much lower price.

Now, having established that the priority of a game composer is how to imagine your goals for the score relative to the game's story and the player's experience, we still cannot ignore the fact that you do need hardware and software tools to accomplish this task. Even traditional classical composers had to utilize pen and paper to realize their music, and since then even composing "traditionally" now can involve music sequencers, notation programs, and much more. And game music adds extra elements of indeterminacy, interactivity, and adaptive design that will require even more specialized tools for the job.

Given that, let's start with the basics and take a look at some of the practical nuts and bolts aspects involved with game composition. Before jumping into that first project, it's a good idea to set up your studio ahead of time. Many of the tools and programs we will discuss are universal to the art of composition in general, regardless of the medium, while others are more specific to games. All of these tools have specific applications and will become an important part of your knowledge base and composer's toolbox.

WORKING IN THE BOX

The term "working in the box" means that the composer is working within a DAW. For those unfamiliar with the term, A DAW or digital audio workstation is a software application (or occasionally a hardware device) used for recording, editing, and producing audio. Software-based DAWs can use the computer's hardware or external hardware to convert analog sound into digital audio (PCM), which can then be edited and manipulated in various ways with a graphic user interface (GUI). Today, DAWs can be found in studios of all levels. You can safely assume that a vast majority of music released today has been recorded or edited using a Digital Audio Workstation.

The number of DAWs has spiked in recent years. Hard to imagine that back in the day, there used to be only two or three commonly used. Here is a short list of some popular programs:

- Pro-Tools
- Logic Pro
- Ableton
- Reaper
- Nuendo
- Cubase
- FL Studio
- GarageBand

Some of these names may be familiar to you and there are always new ones emerging, while older ones fade. But what we are interested in with a DAW is that they have a roughly universal set of tools available to composers to create, edit, mix, and master music.

Q- What is the Best DAW for Composing Game Music?

Whether you use a Mac or PC, at the moment, there is no one DAW that is more functional for game music. The hope is that in the future, commercial digital audio workstations will natively offer more built in interactive and adaptive composing features. These tools could aid all composers interested in extended behaviors, regardless of the platform that music ends up on. So, knowing that and understanding that this is not a course on using a DAW (that would be a whole other book), our advice in this regard is always the same (Go get that book!). Do your research, find a workstation you like, and watch a ton of videos and tutorials to see what you find most appealing and conforms to your workflow and budget. Maybe even try downloading a free trial version (if available) and playing around with it. Then read the manual, watch more videos, and keep asking questions till you understand the full feature set and start to get results you are happy with. Using a DAW to effect can take time, but it will be time well spent and will pay off greatly over the course of your career.

For the purposes of composing for games, any DAW you choose needs to allow the composer to do the following tasks:

- **Record and Edit Music:** DAWs feature audio sequencers that let users record multiple tracks and play them back simultaneously. You can then cut, copy, and paste audio waveforms much in the same way you can move text in a word processing program. Tracks can easily be muted and cross faded into one another. At any point during the editing process, the digital files can be played back as analog audio through speakers or headphones.

- **Play Virtual Instruments:** Using MIDI commands, you can control virtual instruments that mimic any sound under the sun or provide completely new never before imagined tones. Some virtual instrument libraries specialize in replicating the sounds of acoustic instruments like the piano, violin, cello, clarinet, guitar, bass, and drum sets, while others provide various synths from classic models to modern day. All of these sounds can be controlled by MIDI keyboards or other user interfaces.

- **Mix and Master Audio Tracks:** Digital audio workstations typically offer various ways to process and music. Effects such as delay, reverb, compression, and EQ, tend to come standard. Some composers also make extensive use of third-party plugins for particular effects.

PREPARING YOUR AUDIO

Now you may be asking, "How do I use my DAW to get my music ready for use in a game?". As you start composing, you can follow the basic steps shown in Figure 3.1:

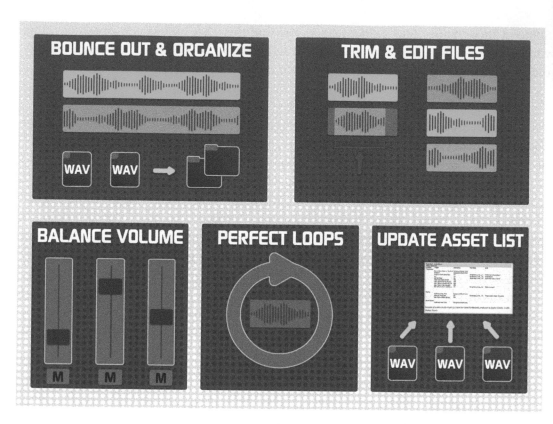

FIGURE 3.1   Preparing your audio. (Image: Austin Smith.)

- **Bounce Out and Organize**
  All music files will be exported as separate assets that need to be triggered at the appropriate time. Because of this it is conventional to bounce out individual instrument parts or full mixes of the various music cues in the game from your DAW. Organizing your music cues for the right level or section of the game is best done by placing them into individual clearly labeled folders. This will make for easy import into the game engine.

- **Trim and Edit Files**
  All audio files in a game generally will need to play immediately when triggered. Use your DAW to trim and edit your music files before you bounce them out of your workstation. Improper edits may result in delayed cues, clicks, and pops or the abrupt cutoff of a piece of music. For one shot music transitions such as fanfares and stingers it is important to not leave too much silence at the start or end of a file. Silence equals wasted space and increases file size for no reason. Attempt to edit as closely to the first sample in a piece of music as possible. Even 100 ms of silence may cause problems. The ending can trail off in a natural way and you might not have to be as strict as you are with the start of a piece, again remember this is just for non-looping tracks!

- **Make Perfect Loops**
  Since we are dealing with scenes and game levels of indeterminate length music tracks must loop seamlessly. To some extent it is the most vital skill in every game composer's arsenal. Do not be discouraged if you don't get this to happen perfectly right away, creating seamless loops takes time and skill to master. You must trim the beginning and ending of a music track down to the sample level, use your eyes and ears to find the proper loop point. It is also wise to check your loops in a separate stereo audio editor after you bounce them out of your DAW. And of course you should always check if the loop sounds correct in the game as well.

- **Volume Balance Files**
  This is especially important. All your music tracks should be at the same volume level so no tracks stick out in the mix when triggered inside the game. When creating Stems for vertical or horizontal combinations, if you just normalize all of your music stem parts in a mix you've essentially forced yourself to remix the entire piece in the middleware or the game engine – not fun. It is conventional to normalize volume to 90% of maximum volume, but if you're combining your music with sound design, other sound effect assets, especially ambiences, you will probably be working at a much lower volume. As always this will depend on the game's requirements.

Not all DAWs are created equally so you have to do your research on which might be best for your particular usage. Features and prices will vary depending on your budget. In general, if you are interested in composing, you should prepare yourself for spending money along the way. It is a simple fact of life that new programs and features are coming out every day and in many of them you will find useful or essential features and they will in turn find a way to tap into your pocket book. This is all part of the sad fact that as a composer, you find yourself in competition with other composers, and the quality and dependability of your tools do matter.

Sample Libraries

Choosing sample sets is a fun and personal thing. Custom sample libraries are a great thing to consider developing on your own. Every time you record a real live instrument, edit it, and include it in your custom library. Over time you will find yourself with an original batch of sounds that nobody else has. This brings us back to the idea of using tools in creative ways, finding and creating your own unique sound as a composer. Simply cut up your new samples and import them into the sample player in your workstation.

Here is a short list of some popular sample libraries and players. Again there are just too many to list them all but, these are a few of the popular and well-known libraries.

- **Native Instruments (NI) Kontakt** is a very common standard for sample-based instrument libraries. This is partially due to its power, flexibility, and customizability, allowing other developers or individuals to make their own instruments besides NI. There are also two versions of the program available – those composers less interested in making their own instruments can use the free **Kontakt Player** version and simply purchase their desired instrument from NI or other developers.

- **IK Multimedia** is also a major player in the sample game. They specialize in the development of software, hardware, and mobile apps for music production, recording, and audio processing. They have a wide range of products, including virtual instruments, effects processors, amplifiers, and recording interfaces, aimed at musicians, producers, and audio engineers.

- **East West** started out originally offering Kontakt-based orchestral libraries, but has since transitioned to its own custom and proprietary format, called Play and now more recently a format called Opus. In addition, they have also created a subscription – only based service where composers can have access to any of the 42,000 instruments they've created.

- **Spitfire Audio** Although this company started like many others, offering Kontakt-based instrument libraries, Spitfire has since struck out on their own with their own design, offering a huge array of instrumental and sonic goodness ranging from free options, like the BBC Discovery Orchestra and the 30+ and growing LABS instruments, all the way up to premium library collections fetching several hundreds. One other amazing resource of note is Pianobook.co.uk, started by Spitfire co-founder, composer Christian Henson and featuring a growing 900+ instrument collection of sampled instruments, most of these available for free.

Notation Programs and Working with Humans

As for orchestrating for live instruments, as discussed you are way ahead of the game to get yourself a good orchestration book or online subscription. There is one more thing you may need and that is a good notation program. Of course you can do all this by hand with pen and sheet music paper as well-old school for sure, but you never know when the power might go out! Seriously, the conventions for composers of writing by hand is a good skill to master, or at least try out. It slows down the process and forces composers to pay attention to every little detail when creating scores and parts. This knowledge will only make your computer scores more complete and professional.

So, you've written your awesome music and it's sitting inside of your digital audio workstation. At this point in the process if you have only recorded live instruments and there are no MIDI tracks, you are ready to start mixing. However, if you are working on a MIDI score, you may think about adding live instruments. In fact, adding a live instrument or two to a sampled orchestra is one way to get a better and more convincing level of musical realism than just using the sampled orchestra by itself.

When you need to have live instruments involved, you may at that point find that you need a separate notation program. DAWs often come with some notation features already. These may be good for use under pressure when last minute preparation of scores or parts is necessary, but experience tells us that you will probably find this feature lacking in most DAWs. It would seem to make sense that the DAW companies would spend a bit more time making this feature more robust and useful to composers but, like we said earlier, in most programs this is just not the case. In fact, we are hard pressed to mention one that we think is adequate for score and part preparation.

Thankfully there are several dedicated score notation programs available and worth mentioning. The basic toolset for these programs is pretty much all the same; they can create, edit, and print sheet music. Users create music using symbols like notes, rests, clefs, and key signatures, as well as features like chord symbols, lyrics, and extended techniques. These applications are widely used in the music industry. Many of them also offer tools for collaboration and sharing music files, which is good for projects that require teamwork. All of them can also play notated music back using sample libraries, and some (but not all) can play back video as well. Each one has its idiosyncrasies. All of them will do the job and have varying pros and cons. Many mentioned here also offer student discounts.

- **Sibelius** is produced by Avid Technologies, the same company that makes Pro-Tools. It is currently the world's largest selling music notation program. Named after the Finnish composer Jean Sibelius, the company was founded in April 1993 by twin brothers Ben and Jonathan Finn. In 2006, it was acquired by Avid. You would think that because they are part of the same company that the integration between the two would be seamless, this however is not the case. Importing a Pro-Tools MIDI file into Sibelius is pretty much the same as all the others. However, it does have a reputation for being a bit more intuitive and user friendly than the others listed here.

- **Finale** is produced by MakeMusic, Inc. and has been around the longest of all the notation programs. It was first published in 1988. Finale, like the others listed here, is very feature rich; it also has the reputation of having a steep learning curve. Finale offers composers more features that make it possible to produce scores that use extended techniques and unconventional or abstract notation. Finale is the only program here that does not include the playback of synced video along with the score.

- **Dorico**, released in 2016, is a recent newcomer to scoring apps, and was developed by most of the team that was associated with Sibelius, and who were forced out when they were acquired by Avid in 2012. It is published by Steinberg, makers of Cubase and Nuendo and claims it has a more intuitive workflow, though there are differences of opinion on that. Although the software is designed to be user-friendly, in actuality, just like Finale and Sibelius, it has a relatively steep learning curve and logic flow of its own that requires patience to adapt to. Dorico does have its own vision of bringing DAW functionality and notation workflow closer together. Additionally, there are several levels of Dorico available-SE is a free version with limited staves, the budget conscious Elements version currently allows up to 24 players/parts, and the top of the line Pro version is unlimited. Dorico also offers a version running on iPad, with subscription or one-time payment options to extend functionality in their Premiere version.

- **MuseScore** is a bit different from the others; it is free and open-source under the GNU General Public License. Created in 2002, when Werner Schweer, one of the

MusE developers, decided to remove notation support from MusE and create a stand-alone notation program from the codebase. It is not as full featured as the others mentioned here and in general is a good starter program but not considered to be fully up to professional standards. However, the most recent version (version 4) has overhauled the entire UI, and provides a sample set that is much improved. And we did mention it was free, so for those on very tight budgets this is a great option.

Combinatorial Workflow

Since it is possible to export the MIDI data from your DAW into a notation program, this can be a good way to work. However, you should be aware that MIDI files exported from DAW sessions/projects don't always open up in your notation program looking very good, and a lot of the time they can be a complete mess. Your MIDI files will likely need to be cleaned up first before you export them. What do we mean by cleaned up?

In your DAW's MIDI track, some MIDI notes will trigger instruments that may sound great in that DAW but are hanging over the beat or the bar and as a result when you get them into your notation program it will interpret all those slight variations as rests or incorrect durations and the whole thing can then become unreadable. Some octaves while sounding good on your virtual instrument may not be in the correct register for the real instrument, and the notes themselves might not be in the correct transposition, such as a Bb clarinet or trumpet for example.

One method you can employ when you are finished with your composition is to do a save as and save a new copy dedicated more for score preparation. Then spend some time editing each duration ahead of time, both the start and end point of each note quantized to the nearest 16th note. By going through this process and cleaning things up ahead of time you'll save yourself a lot of effort, and in some cases confusion, as you start to work inside your notation program.

Some composers will work directly in their notation programs and do not use a DAW at all. This can be quite effective when working with live instruments in the concert hall, studio, or on a scoring stage and is a completely different pipeline than working first in a digital audio workstation and exporting a MIDI file. If you work directly in your notation program no export is needed and you can go right to printing your music.

A Note on Music XML

There is also a format that can be imported into notation programs and exported from DAWs and this is called MusicXML. Essentially it is a way of encoding notated sequencer data or sheet music via XML (eXtended Markup Language) in order to be compatible with notation programs. This means that if you had notation capability in your DAW-like Logic Pro or Cubase for example, and you worked on it a bit, adding score markings – that data can potentially be exported to a notation program to work on it further. Or you could export MusicXML to your sequencer, possibly to get better quality instruments to play the parts for a future mixdown. You might also use it to get around blockages that might happen between different notation programs or even incompatible versions of a program. In practice, of course, new standards solve some problems and often create others which also have to be solved or worked around, but it does show promise in terms of standardizing a type of data exchange for music engraving.

Programs like Finale, Sibelius, or Dorico cost a bit, and others like Muscore are free to use. Much like your DAW, you may find that the free versions are functional to a point and that you need to spend some money to get a more in-depth, reliable, and feature-rich program. We hate to sound like a broken record/tape loop/sampler (pick your media) here, *but* do your research, watch tutorials, and download free trials and you'll be well on your way. Once your MIDI tracks are completed in your DAW, you can export those tracks as a MIDI file and open them into a notation program. Then you can commence with the tedious process of cleaning up parts or score to make them presentable for live performance.

Stereo Editors

A good stereo editor is a good thing to have. Why do we need a stereo editor when we have a digital audio workstation? Good question. As we're exporting our final mixed files from our DAW, we need to be absolutely sure that any loops we've created do not skip or pop. The truth is that sometimes when a loop sounds perfect in our DAW after we export it, that same file may not be played in exactly the same way. This can be due to the fact that many DAWs often smooth out those things while in the editor, but the actual bounced file still has a discontinuity. So, in this case, having a good dedicated stereo editor is a great way to test your loops and make sure they are seamless.

Many of these apps can also come with mastering plugins which allow you to balance out all of your files, double checking that they're all at the same level and in general checking that there are no glitches. And batch processing is another great feature that's often found in stereo editors and allows you to apply multiple processes like compression, reverb, normalization, and volume balancing to hundreds or even thousands of files at the same time, which can be a huge help when you're under a tight deadline.

Here is a short list of just a few stereo editors we recommend:

- Twisted Waves
- Adobe Audition
- Steinberg Wave Lab
- Audacity
- SoundForge Pro

MUSIC MIDDLEWARE

Until now, the tools and techniques we've described are common to composers in linear media as well as games. For this next set of tools, we find ourselves firmly in game composer territory. The tools we are about to discuss are, for the most part, mainly used in games and interactive media. These tools are all examples of middleware, specifically audio middleware – although they can definitely handle music. Middleware is a tool that an artist can use to make their job easier as it provides more control. It generally sits in the middle between individuals that create content and the game engine itself (see Figure 3.2). In games, there are middleware tools for just handling optimized 3D models, video, or physics. And of course there are dedicated tools for composers and sound designers to get more control over their content.

Below is a list of well-known audio middleware that game composers use frequently. These tools have become a staple in the game industry, and many job postings require at least some level of knowledge working with them. Keep in mind that larger developers will often code their own custom in house solutions. Yes, this may be re-inventing the wheel to some extent, but it is an individual business decision and may be more economical to do so than pay a licensing fee to a third party company.

- **FMOD Studio**
  Firelight Technologies introduced FMOD in 2002 as a cross platform audio runtime library for playing back sound for video games. Firelight has since continued its innovation, releasing a brand new audio engine in 2013 called FMOD Studio with

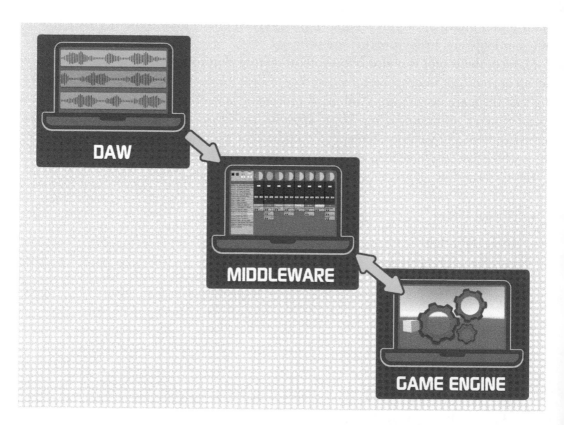

FIGURE 3.2 Audio middleware in action. (Image: Austin Smith.)

significant improvements over the older FMOD Ex engine, such as sample-accurate audio triggering, better file management, and a more advanced audio mixing system allowing busses, sends, and returns. Music can be configured within FMOD Studio using tempo-based markers and timed triggers. FMOD can be downloaded and used free for educational purposes. FMOD is a widely adopted audio middleware choice and continues to be a major player in today's game development environment. You will find FMOD used in many types of games. Since it runs natively on Mac (as well as PC computers) it is commonly found in educational institutions. The user interface is quite friendly and often reminds one of Ableton Live in look and feel.

- **Audiokinetic Wwise**
  Introduced in 2006, the Wwise (Wave Works Interactive Sound Engine) and toolset provide access to features of their engine that has become a desired standard for many development houses. The Interactive Music Engine in Wwise is highly regarded as well, enabling unique and unpredictable soundtracks from a small amount of existing music material. Their commitment to consistently providing new features and improvements has led to their adoption at publishers both large and small, although it tends to be the tool of choice more for AAA developers making large and complex games rather than smaller indie games. Wwise is like FMOD, widely used on all sorts of games. The user interface looks more like a game engine and has been developed for PC computers. It will run on a MAC, but some shortcuts and key commands may not be available. Due to its deep and customizable tool set WWISE comes with a bit more of a learning curve then others on this list.

  While FMOD and Wwise are the most frequently mentioned middleware apps in North America, there are many other middleware tools that are used for various purposes by game developers, so this is just scratching the surface. However, one worthy of special mention was created entirely as a music middleware originally.

- **Elias Studio:**
  This middleware got its start and earned its reputation as a tool solely for game music and composers, but has since announced an audio component in its new 4.0 version, while still keeping the music engine's workflow intact. Recent updates have focused on adding new features and even bringing back some older ones like re-integrating MIDI as a production tool along with custom high-quality sample banks. Elias can handle streaming audio files and various types of audio conversions. With the re-introduction of MIDI-triggered music, Elias also includes a VST plugin: the Elias Sampler, along with a premium sound library. Elias is unique in the middleware space as it is a music-first tool.

- **CRIWARE/CRI-Middleware:**
  One of the most popular and used audio middleware engines in Japan, CRIWARE consists of audio and video solutions that can be integrated with popular game engines such as Unity, Unreal Engine, and Cocos2d-x and supports more than 20 platforms,

from all major consoles to mobile devices. The company has recently started to move into the North American market and follows a similar paradigm to FMOD and Wwise in terms of the audio development pipeline. The authoring tool called ADX2 looks in many ways similar to other middleware engines. It allows for the creation of complex sound behaviors to the composition of interactive music, from digital sound processing and mixing to dialogue localization. ADX2's sports several proprietary codecs (ADX, HCA, and HCA-MX) and also comes complete with plugins for Unity, Unreal, PC, iOS, Android, PS4, Xbox One, and Switch.

The Big Takeaway: Well that's a lot of stuff that we've gone over but remember, the most important tool in your composer's toolbox is your creativity, passion, and ear. As composers we now have the option of combining sampled instruments, live instruments, and all the colors of the musical rainbow together. The sky is the limit and applying your individual creativity to the entire recording, composing, mixing, orchestration, and even implementation process will help you to develop a personalized and professional sound.

Discussion Questions: Why do I need to know so much about music technology? What are some essential tools composers need to work on games? What are some of the pros and cons of audio middleware? What is the best notation program? What is the best orchestration book? Do I need a stereo editor? Can I use my DAW for music notation? Why can't I edit my music in a game engine? What is Middleware and why do I need it?

TERMS

- **DAW:** Stands for Digital Audio Workstation. It is software used for recording, editing, mixing, and producing audio.

- **GUI:** Graphical user interface is a system of interactive visual components for computer software. A GUI displays objects that convey information, and represent actions that can be taken by the user.

- **PCM:** A method used to digitally represent sampled analog signals. It is the standard form of digital audio in computers, compact discs, digital telephony, and other digital audio applications.

- **Audio Middleware**: A tool set or code base that sits between the game engine and the audio hardware. It provides common functionality such as randomizing pitch or volume, fading sounds in or out, and picking randomly a sound from a set of sounds.

- **Virtual Instrument:** A software application that emulates the sound and behavior of a real musical instrument. Some virtual instruments use samples of real instruments to create accurate sound reproduction, while others use mathematical algorithms to generate new sounds.

- **User Interface:** The means by which the user and a computer system interact.

- **Sample Library:** A collection of recorded sounds, typically in the form of digital files, that can be used to create music or sound design. Sample libraries can range from small collections of sounds to large, comprehensive libraries that include multiple variations and articulations of the same instrument.

- **Notation:** A system of symbols and signs used to represent musical sound and structure.

- **MIDI:** Musical Instrument Digital Interface is a protocol for communicating between digital devices, such as computers and synthesizers. MIDI data consist of messages that specify events, such as notes being played, their duration, and their velocity, as well as control changes, such as adjusting the volume, panning, and modulation.

- **Orchestration:** The process of arranging a musical composition for live instruments or virtual ensembles.

- **Score:** A written or printed document that represents a musical composition using musical notation. It is a visual representation of the music that includes information about the pitch, rhythm, tempo, dynamics, and other musical elements.

- **Parts:** A part refers to the written music for a specific instrument or voice within a composition. When musicians perform a piece of music, they read and play from their respective parts in the score.

- **MIDI Orchestration:** The process of creating an arrangement using MIDI data. It involves assigning MIDI data to different virtual instruments, such as sample libraries or synthesizers, in order to produce the desired sound and performance.

- **Transposition:** Changing the clefts and pitches of a musical work, but not altering the relationships between pitches (or notes).

- **Mastering:** The process by which a music track or asset is finalized for publication or for use in a game engine or middleware.

- **Normalization:** A destructive digital audio process where the selected audio is analyzed, the loudest point found and the amplitude of the selected audio is increased to a desired level.

- **Compression:** A process whereby dynamic range is reduced and usually made up by increasing gain, resulting in a louder signal level.

- **EQ:** Short for equalization, a process where certain frequencies are increased or decreased to affect the overall timbre of a track or a mix.

- **Bouncing:** The act of rendering an audio file from a DAW, often including sound effects or different plugins.

- **Batch Processing:** A technique used to apply a set of operations or effects to multiple audio files simultaneously.

CHAPTER 4

Music as Information

Topic: Form and Structure in Game Music

- Learning Outcomes
- Music as Information
- Music Characteristics
- Orchestration In-Depth
- Don't Forget the Mix
- Game Music Form and Structure
- Applying Creativity
- The Big Takeaway
- Discussion Questions
- Terms

Learning Outcomes

- Understanding music as information
- Differentiate music characteristics
- Differentiate form and structure
- Analyze and critique effective orchestration

DOI: 10.1201/9781003414728-6

MUSIC AS INFORMATION

Music for games cannot be weighed, measured, or appraised like a bag of cookies. Composers for games and interactive media must rely on a keen eye for details and a well-developed ear. Composers speak in a personalized language that serves to enhance and highlight the emotional and functional qualities of visual media. Music for pictures brings us face to face with the idea of music as information.

When sitting down to compose for any visual media, we meet, on the most fundamental level, with the challenge of matching eye and ear. Music and games share some common principles, in that both are playable and take place in real time. The art of composing to picture is one of the findings some fundamental truth within the visual imagery, and enhancing or bringing out that aspect. Things like depth of field, overlapping images, character, motion, graphic accents, and color patterns all must be taken into account. Composers manipulate and change elements in a game score to create varying moods and interactions. Music directs the viewer's expectations in many interesting ways that can often be hard to quantify. Nonetheless we need to start to develop a syntax for explaining and understanding its effect.

MUSIC CHARACTERISTICS

The basic building blocks of music itself can be harnessed and manipulated by creative composers. These of course should be familiar to any musician, but let's review them in the context of a game.

RHYTHM

Our first and most fundamental characteristic is an important element of music that refers to the arrangement of sounds and silences in time. It is the timing and placement of the various elements of music, including pitches, melodies, and harmonies, and it is an integral aspect of musical structure. Rhythm can be used to create a sense of momentum, tension, and release, and it can also be used to establish a sense of groove or pulse in a piece of music. Rhythm can have a significant impact on the overall feel and character of a piece of music. In addition to its role in shaping the character and emotion of a piece of music, rhythm is also an important element of musical form and structure. It serves to create patterns and repetition, and it can help to establish a sense of coherence and unity within a composition.

Nobuo Uematsu by Sharon Nathan. (CC BY-SA 3.0 DE.)

Nobuo Uematsu is a game music legend. He is most well known for the extremely popular and groundbreaking Final Fantasy series of role playing games and is extremely well respected in the industry. His music is, without a doubt, integral to the popularity of the series. Nobuo started out very early in game scoring – trained in classical piano from an early age, he also has a background in jazz and rock. He studied music composition at the Junior College of Music in Tokyo, Japan and his diverse musical background has influenced his work and helped to shape his unique style. Over the years, his work has contributed much to the development of video game music as an art form.

Uematsu's score for *Final Fantasy VI* is especially notable for its diversity, as it includes a wide range of musical styles, from grandiose orchestral pieces to emotional ballads. To explore how rhythm can prominently affect game music, let us look at "Another World of Beasts" from *Final Fantasy VI* in Figure 4.1. Here Nobuo uses rhythm in a very creative way; he puts the music in

Another World of Beasts

From: *Final Fantasy VI*

Nobuo Uematsu

FIGURE 4.1 "Another World of Beasts". (Excerpt – image: Jeff Newman.)

the ⅞ time signature, grouped as 3-2-2. The use of arpeggios develops that steady ⅞ pulse while the upper melody clearly delineates the rhythmic structure by accenting the downbeats over time. This punctuated rhythmic structure along with the unaccented arpeggios creates a rolling feel, much like a creature walking. The chromatic falling 16th note triplets that start at bar 23 in this example, further serve to accent the mysterious quality of the post romantic harmony, in this case the mixing of minor thirds with major 7ths. Overall, it's a great example of how odd time signatures can help to support and enhance unique musical moods (Figure 4.1).

Yoko Shimomura graduated from the Osaka College of Music in 1988 and joined Capcom the same year. She also composed the music for *Street Fighter II* and *Super Mario RPG* among many other well-known games. She has won many awards for her work and is considered one of the prominent female video game composers. Shimomura often combines classical, folk, and rock elements to create lush and beloved soundtracks.

Yoko Shimomura (https://www.flickr. com/photos/nick_fong/466147401/in/ photostream/)

Another example worth highlighting for interesting rhythm is from the game *Kingdom Hearts* composed by Yoko Shimomura. The music for "Hollow Bastion" accompanies the level of the same name, which is one of the original worlds in the *Kingdom Hearts* series. Here in Figure 4.2 Shimomura employs the use of the 5/4-time signature broken into a pattern of 3-3-2-2 in the bass combined with a steady accented syncopation in the treble on beats 1, 4, 6, and 9. This fast 5 beat pattern combines weak and strong beats in the percussion and bass parts that strongly emphasize beats four and five, while steadily moving accented runs in the strings add to the overall chaotic feel. This type of disjointed syncopation enhances the suspenseful feeling that accompanies the dark and brooding visuals.

TEMPO

The tempo of a piece of music has a huge effect on the pace and tension of gameplay. By speeding up or slowing down the tempo, composers can achieve many different psychological effects. Slow tempos may sound ominous and foreboding and fast tempos may give the player extra energy. Tempo changes are often attached to the speed of the gameplay

Hollow Bastion

From: *Kingdom Hearts*

Yoko Shimomura

FIGURE 4.2 "Hollow Bastion", Yoko Shimomura. (Excerpt – image: Jeff Neumann.)

itself and when properly matched or contrasted, they help to increase a player's feeling of immersion in the game. Using varying kinds of rhythmic patterns can also have different effects on the player's perception. Tracks with steady rhythmic pulses can bring a feeling of forward motion, or by contrast, stasis, while the use of odd time signatures and tempo changes together might provide a more unsettled or chaotic feeling to match the visuals.

The music for *Batman Arkham City*, written by Nick Arundel, is a superb example of the use of tempo to create suspense. His music is characterized by its ability to evoke a sense of tension, drama, and atmosphere. In this example from the opening of the game, he uses sparse low strings along with light held synthesizer pads and subtle rhythmic pulses that crescendo and decrescendo in time, leaving a bar of silence in between re-attacks. This regular pulsation serves to build tension and anticipation as Batman explores the city at night. Once Batman finds the bad guys and engages them, electronic drums, low toms, and 16th note string patterns all enter the fray. This bubbling and insistent percussive under-pinning exposes the music's underlying tempo and drives the action forward. Then as the last baddy is subdued, a stinger plays on the next down beat and we go back to the original orchestration as described earlier. This simple use of contrasting slow and fast tempos takes the player on a pulse pounding ride that perfectly accompanies gameplay. The use of silence and space is also a nice compositional device that provides a super effective solution for creating smooth transitions between cutscenes and gameplay.

MELODY

Melody is a sequence of pitches that form a distinctive and recognizable musical line. It is a fundamental element of music and is often the most memorable and influential aspect of a piece of music. Melodies are typically composed using a specific scale or mode, and they often follow a set of rules or conventions in terms of their structure and progression. Melodies can be simple or complex, and they can be used to convey a wide range of emotions and moods. They can be played by a single instrument, or by a group of instruments or voices. In addition to their role in shaping the overall emotion of a piece of music, melodies are very frequently the most important element of musical form and structure, and often play a central role in defining the shape and direction of a piece.

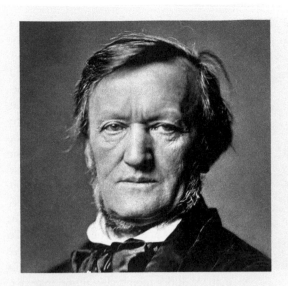

Richard Wagner by Franz Hanfstaengl. (Public Domain.)

Melody can be applied to visual media in many ways and forms. Wilhelm Richard Wagner was a German composer, theater director, and conductor chiefly known for his operas. Unlike most opera composers, Wagner wrote both the libretto and the music for each of his stage works and developed the idea of **leitmotif**, a musical device that associates a melodic phrase or figure with the reappearance of an idea, person, or situation. This concept has been continued through films, where composers like John Williams created unforgettable themes, on through to games, as in many well-known titles when we hear a specific melody this might make us think of a certain character, action, or location.

In *The Legend of Zelda: Ocarina of Time*, a heroic melody based on the whole tone scale (shown in Figure 4.3) is played when opening a treasure chest. The music rises chromatically in pitch, dynamics, and tempo. The last bar is a chromatic fanfare that acts as a final statement or cadence. Tied to achievement in the game, this leitmotif builds emotion and

Chest Opening Motif

From: *The Legend of Zelda: Ocarina of Time*

Koji Kondo

FIGURE 4.3   "Chest Opening Melody". (Excerpt – image: Jeff Neumann.)

Steve Kirk. (Used with permission.)

Known as a stunt guitar player, Steve Kirk has written some really memorable music for some very popular games. His compositional work is characterized by a colorful, intricate, organic, and sometimes psychedelic style. Some of his projects include, *Thimbleweed Park*, *Voodoo Vince*, and the cantina music for the *Star Wars* MMO *The Old Republic*. Steve also wrote the music for the game *Farmville*, the mobile hit, which after launching on Facebook in 2009, became the most popular game on the site, and held that position for over two years. At its peak, in March 2010, the game had 83.76 million monthly active users. Daily active users peaked at 34.5 million. This means that Mr. Kirk's memorable music may perhaps be one of the most listened to pieces of music on planet earth!

anticipation. Throughout the game, it serves as a musical reward to the player, reminding them of their success every time it triggers; although since you open a lot of these in the game, it can get a bit annoying after hearing it dozens of times.

The *Farmville* melody fits into a long tradition of title themes and title screens. For many reasons, it seems that melody is one of the key ingredients that is needed when creating music that grabs you right from the get go. Laidback and friendly, the tune takes us right back to the farm and the American west, with some jazzy bits mixed in to modernize the song for a new *(at the time)* platform. It has all the elements that a great title theme needs. It is memorable, emotionally impactful, and most importantly recognizable, making it synonymous with the game. By having a strong melody, a title theme is more likely to stick in the mind of the player, making it easy to recall the game, even after a long period of time. If you are looking for an unforgettable earworm, then melody is a great place to start.

These are just a few short examples of the power of melody, the hold it has on a listener's ear and the ways in which it can be used in games. You can likely come up with many more instances from your own experience. When overused, players often will become fatigued and want to turn the music off, as the melody has essentially overstayed its welcome. This overwhelming feeling results from in game music that is melodically heavy handed, and not based on the structure and flow of the narrative. However, when used by a sensitive composer in the proper amounts and in the right moments, it can be magical.

HARMONY

Harmony refers to the combination of pitches and chords played or sung at the same time to create a sense of vertical structure. It adds depth, color, and interest to a piece of music. Harmony is typically created by combining different pitches in a specific scale or key to form chords. Different chords can be played in sequence to create chord progressions. Harmony is used to create a sense of tension and release, and to establish a sense of tonality or tonal center.

Music that has little harmonic development is often used in loading screens or during times of relaxation or cool down from more intense gameplay. Music that uses lots of chord progressions and harmonic development lends themselves to a feeling of transformation and movement, as if the character or story is going somewhere and moving toward a goal. Harmony is created using key centers based on scales or modes that an individual piece of music is in. Music in a minor key/mode often has a sad feeling while music in a major key tends to sound happy. Take these characterizations as generalizations; there are many ways to manipulate keys and modes to conjure different emotions. For example, a knight headed out on a quest might be best served by heroic music in a major key with chord progressions that emphasize the tonic and fifth relationship, if these chord changes start to develop and also include minor chords and then the music returns to the tonic or home chord, this can create a feeling of epic transformation giving the character a feeling of substance and complexity.

Phillip Charron composed the original soundtrack for the 2010 video game *Naughty Bear*. The game's music has a dark and comedic tone, blending elements of orchestral and electronic music to create a unique and unsettling atmosphere. The soundtrack has received quite positive reviews for its fitting accompaniment to the game's over-the-top use of dark humor.

Naughty Bear is an off the wall, irreverent game about a homicidal teddy bear hell-bent on revenge on his fellow bears for failing to invite him to a party. The story centers around this sad and disturbed teddy and well, needless to say, things get strange and go downhill from there. Here we are presented with a very functional and effective interactive score as well as a great example of the use of harmony, in this case very dissonant harmony to help tell the story of the inner emotional life of our main character. Mr. Charron's music starts out in a very happy and child-like manner in all its major key glory as the player walks around on an idyllic tropical island. However, as Naughty's emotional state deteriorates the music transforms and we are presented with jagged minor second intervals. You can imagine the effect, this use of harmony takes us inside the main character's inner turmoil and serves to give the player vital information all at the same time. We should also note that these transformations in the harmony are tied to triggers in the game which helps the music to match the action on screen. Lastly, it is important to point out that no real teddy bears were hurt during the making of this game.

VOLUME/DYNAMICS

Dynamics refer to the loudness or softness of a piece or a specific musical passage. Loud dynamics and high volume can create a sense of energy and excitement, while soft dynamics and low volume can create a sense of intimacy and introspection. Dynamic shifts are often used to create contrast and variation, and to highlight specific melodic, harmonic, or rhythmic elements. Many acoustic instruments have very different timbres when played loudly versus when they are played softly. Brass instruments in particular increase in both volume and timbre at loud dynamic levels. Drums sound different when played at lower intensity versus higher intensity of dynamics. The entire family of strings have physical mutes they can insert that not only lower their volume but also provide a specific texture well loved by composers across generations.

The proper use of dynamics depends upon the music genre and type. Older game music in particular suffered historically from a significant lack of dynamics for its first couple of decades, as the chips that were generating the waveforms often had very little in the way of smooth dynamic control available. As game systems became more powerful the use of dynamics also became more prevalent. That original game music aesthetic still retains its popularity in its own genre called **chiptune**, since it uses sounds or techniques from the older non-dynamic game music, and typically does not usually have much dynamic range.

Something as simple as turning up the volume can seriously affect how a player will react to a given situation. A sudden rise in volume or intensity can trigger a special moment of excitement that gets players to jump out of their seat, or highlight an important game play clue. Our ears are highly tuned to this, and it can be used to great effect when composing soundtracks. Keep in mind that this change in volume can be related to mixing but its effect can be different, depending on the instrument.

This compilation of jump scares from some popular titles might help to illuminate the point. In each case you can see how regardless of the style of music being used, an increase in volume is employed to trigger a response from the player. Usually a jump scare starts from silence or a very quiet background, so it's definitely not a subtle approach.

ORCHESTRATION

As we mentioned before, orchestration is the art and craft of arranging music for live or virtual ensembles. Let's dive into this more fully to explore how it can be effectively used in composing game music.

Using effective orchestration techniques, we can change the emotion and effect of a piece and subsequently of a game simply by changing the instruments that are playing. Trumpets can often make music sound noble and proud – but bassoons not so much. Creative orchestration is the secret sauce of composition. When we look at game images to design music for, we have to ask ourselves, is this a natural setting or a cartoonish environment? Is it set in space or in the ocean? What is happening with the story and sound design? The answer to all of these questions will help to determine the best instrumentation for that particular game or scene. If the image is very futuristic, synths and sequencers might serve best. If set in a natural open world, acoustic instruments may sound better.

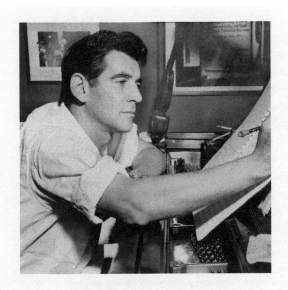

Leonard Bernstein by Al Ravenna. (Library of Congress – No Known Restrictions.)

Leonard Bernstein was an American composer, conductor, and pianist. He was one of the most influential figures in classical music in the 20th century. He served as the music director of the New York Philharmonic, a position he held for 11 seasons from 1958 to 1969. Bernstein's work as a conductor and composer spanned a very wide range of styles, including classical, jazz, and Broadway, he was known for his innovative and energetic approach to music making. Most remarkable was his deep understanding of the principles of orchestration, with which he molded an orchestral sound that was unparalleled and immediately recognizable.

Garry Schyman. (Used with permission.)

Garry Schyman is an American composer, known for his work for the *Bioshock* series, *Praetorians*, *Destroy All Humans*, Dante's *Inferno*, and *Middle Earth Shadows of Mordor*. Very early in his video game career he composed and conducted the score to *Voyeur*, where he uses live instruments to great effect. In fact, this score is one of the first if not the first orchestral recordings for a video game. Developed for the Phillips CDi system, notable for featuring live-action video, *Voyeur* is widely considered a pioneer of interactive movie games. Released in 1994, it is an adventure game developed and published by Censor Design. The story is set in a luxurious hotel, where the player takes on the role of a journalist named James Ransome, who is investigating a murder that occurred in one of the hotel rooms. The player must gather evidence, interview suspects, and solve puzzles in order to uncover the truth behind the murder.

The score calls for flute with piccolo and bass clarinet double, 2 french horns, tuba with bass trombone double, percussion, harp, and strings. The music perfectly matches the mood and atmosphere of this interactive noir experience that was based on the Alfred Hitchcock film *Rear Window*, with score by Franz Waxman. This cue, shown in Figure 4.4, is from

FIGURE 4.4   Schyman *Voyeur* Score – M53 cue (Pages 1&2). (Used with permission.)

the opening of the murder sequence. Note the use of well-timed crescendos in the horns doubled by strings creating a dark forbidding sound as well as the use of sul ponticello in the string divisi in bar 8. The opening string gliss serves not only as a detailed and effective extended orchestrational technique but also to unsettle the player; from the start, we know that something unusual is going to happen.

Looking in more detail on page 2 in bar 11 and 12 the sforzando minor second stabs combine high flutes, brass, violins, and violas along with a metal plate being struck in the percussion. The flutes and strings in the high register serve to create a satisfying blend with the mid-range french horns, demonstrating a master's orchestrational touch and understanding of instrumental registration.

In this ending cue shown in Figure 4.5a b, the effective use of the lower registers in the french horns and tuba along with the cellos and basses serves to create a dark and

FIGURE 4.5A   Schyman *Voyeur* Score – End Credits (Pages 1&2). (Used with permission.)

FIGURE 4.5B   Schyman *Voyeur* Score – EndCredits (Pages 3&4). (Used with permission.)

emotional underpinning that is reminiscent of film composer Bernard Herrman, another longtime collaborator of Hitchcok, a master of murder, the macabre, and suspense.

A further look at the opening bars gives us a repeated pizzicato ostinato figure in the violins that later in bar 15 is taken up by cellos and doubled with percussion. This ostinato serves as an underpinning for the brass swells and melodic figures that further develop a sense of suspense and danger.

In bar two we see immaculate attention to detail as the pedal position for the harp is provided and not left to the player to figure out. Lastly, the ending bars of the piece conclude with an extended harp gliss, doubled by bell tree percussion along with a slowly rising flute melody in the upper range. This serves to create a well-developed sonority and use of the full orchestral range.

Austin Wintory by Simon Sorted. (CC BY-SA 4.0.)

American Composer Austin Wintory composed the hauntingly beautiful and highly interactive music for the hit game *Journey (as well as its predecessor Flower)*. *Journey* was released for the PlayStation 3 via PlayStation Network in March 2012 and ported to PlayStation 4 in July 2015. Both were developed by That Game Company. Mr. Wintory has also penned music for *Assassin's Creed Syndicate*, the underwater exploration game *Abzû*, and the turn-based tactical *RPG The Banner Saga (1 and 2)*. His work is far ranging and he is credited with the scores for over 50 video games. The score for *Journey* was nominated for a Grammy award, making him the first video game composer to receive a Grammy nomination. Wintory has also composed music for films, television shows, and live performances. He is known for his use of a wide range of instrumentation, including live orchestras, choirs, and solo instrumentalists.

Abzû is a 2016 video game developed by Giant Squid Studios and published by 505 Games. The game is an exploration-based adventure game set in an underwater world. The player controls a diver who must explore the depths of the ocean and uncover its secrets. The game features a minimalist narrative, with no dialogue or text, allowing players to interpret the story for themselves through the visuals and music. *Abzû* received generally positive reviews from critics and was praised for its immersive atmosphere, beautiful art design, and hauntingly beautiful soundtrack. It was nominated for several awards, including "Art Direction" and "Music" at The Game Awards 2016 as well as a BAFTA award in 2017.

The music of *Abzû* very successfully evokes the feeling of being underwater and exploring the ocean. It features a mix of orchestral, choral, and electronic elements. One of the most remarkable features of the score is its bold orchestration. Austin employs the use of seven grand harps to create a vast underwater musical landscape along with oboe, a full string section, percussion, synthesizers, and a choir of soprano, alto, and tenor.

Looking more closely at the first page of the score shown in Figure 4.6a, the first thing that is quite striking is the orchestration of the harps all in unison in the low register. But is it unison?

FIGURE 4.6A Wintory – *Abzû* Score – To Know Water Pg 1. (Used with permission.)

FIGURE 4.6B   Wintory – *Abzû* Score – To Know Water Pg 3. (Used with permission.)

Upon further examination one sees this note "Repeat, out of time" followed by squiggly lines. This indicates that the players are not to try and sync up but rather to try and not listen to their fellow harpists and the line indicates repetition as fast or slow as they want. The result of this simple and clear orchestrational note is a complex and beautiful web of shimmering raising and falling arpeggios that create the sonic effect of water. No surprise then that this cue is called "To Know Water."

Looking at the choir parts on page three shown in Figure 4.6b, it shows the entrance of diatonic stepwise melodic motion combined with warm synthesizer chords blended into the texture. This kind of orchestral layering acts as an additional coloration, like water riding on the waves, caught between the angelic voices high above the surf, and the deep sea harps below the surface. It is remarkable how much the orchestration is tied to the game's narrative. The use of the oboe to represent the games main character and the harps to represent water, all of this creates a delicate and intimate relationship that rides along with the ebb and flow of the narrative.

> *Abzû* was a score for which I composed and discarded enormous amounts of music in comparison to the final output. As much as 50 minutes of music were tossed out for five minutes of music that actually made it into the game. The orchestral recordings were done in Nashville. Seeing the musicians chew through these more active, playful, dancing parts was such a joy. In the background is the main theme, consistently appearing to remind us that all of this is still the diver's journey. This game gave me the freedom to craft the regions of the game with far more musical distinction than my other scores so far.
>
> – AUSTIN WINTORY

Destiny 2 is an online multiplayer first-person shooter game developed by Bungie and published by Activision. It was released in 2017 for multiple gaming platforms. In *Destiny 2*, players create a character known as a Guardian, who is tasked with exploring the solar system and battling against various alien races and other hostile forces. The game features a mixture of story-driven missions and open-world activities as well as player-versus-player (PvP) multiplayer modes. The music was composed by Michael Salvatori, Skye Lewin, and C. Paul Johnson, and it features a blend of orchestral and electronic elements. The soundtrack was recorded with live orchestras and choir, and features a sweeping, epic sound that is well suited to the game's sci-fi setting.

The cue "Lost Light" shown in Figure 4.7 features the Kronos String Quartet, considered one of the most innovative and influential string quartets of our time. The music here is sublime, delicate, and infused with emotions of sadness and loss. The first page, shown above, is extremely well orchestrated.

FIGURE 4.7   Michael Salvatori and Skye Lewin's "Lost Light" score.

THINGS TO NOTICE ABOUT LOST LIGHT

- The use of not only dynamic markings but also dynamic curves, crescendos and decrescendos written in to give the music a breath-like quality
- The use of the descriptive words "like a ticking clock" along with the use of a playing technique "Con Sord" short for con sordino, meaning played with mute (*A mute is a device that can be attached to the bridge of a string instrument, to alter its tone. Mutes are often used to reduce the volume of a particular instrument or group of instruments, or to produce a softer sound.*)
- The use of Accent Marks (*side carrots and dots*) to denote long and short beats
- The liberal use of legato phrase markings, for example in bars 3–12

All of these details right from the start give the player an understanding of how the composer wants the music to feel so they can interpret that onto their instrument.

Now take a look at the opening page and page 4 of "Battle Stations," as shown in Figure 4.8a and b, another cue from the same game. This cue calls for a much larger orchestra featuring 3 flutes, 2 oboes, english horn, 2 clarinets in Bb, Bass Clarinet in Bb, 2 Bassoons, contrabassoon, 6 french horns in F, 3 trumpets in C, 2 trombones, bass trombone, tuba, a rather large percussion ensemble, harp (optional), piano, choir (SATB), and string orchestra. In looking over the score, you might notice an almost complete absence of any of the same care and detail given in the previous example.

THINGS TO NOTICE ABOUT BATTLE STATIONS

- The sparse use of dynamic markings (*only given upon entrances, very little in the way of internal dynamics*)
- The sparse use of phrase markings and articulations (*information is given on some instruments not all*)
- The lack of information in the timpani (*no indication at the start of the score how many drums are involved*)
- The lack of sectional information in the strings (*since no forces are given for the strings we really have no idea how many are in each section*)
- Lack of information as to flute divisi (*we know how many flutes we have not what notes they should take when called*)

Perhaps the most noticeable thing in the orchestration of this piece is the number of bars that play without any variation or coloration. For example, the cellos enter in bar #1 playing a staccato quarter note E and continue to play that exact same phrase over and over unchanged until bar 31. The Violas enter in bar 5 and do the same. This kind of orchestration is uninspired,

FIGURE 4.8A   Michael Salvatori, C. Paul Johnson, and Skye Lewin's "Battle Stations" Score.

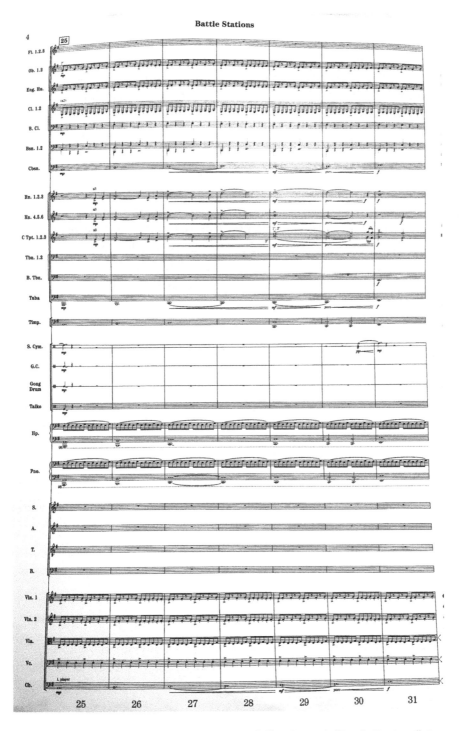

FIGURE 4.8B   Michael Salvatori, C. Paul Johnson, and Skye Lewin's "Battle Stations" Score.

laborious, and boring not only for the players, but for listeners as well. Frankly, the score looks as if large numbers of bars were simply copied and pasted over and over again, without consideration for the many ways in which we can use the orchestra to develop robust variation. This lack of detail gives the music a flat uninspired sound, missing out on the chance to breathe creative life and energy into the music and as a result, the game itself suffers.

Don't Forget the Mix (*And how it applies in games*)

An important aspect that is often overlooked and that must absolutely be considered relative to orchestration is the quality of the production and overall mix. Although somewhat related to dynamics, a proper mix is vital when the acoustic dynamics of certain instruments might create timbres that cannot compete with inherently louder timbres that are happening at the same time. When blending live and virtual instruments, great things can happen. Well produced tracks bring all the elements discussed above together and create magic. The quality of the samples, the quality of the recording, the use of reverb, EQ, and compression – all of these and more are vital tools. An ideal music mix allows every part to have an important place in the sonic field. Great mixes make every individual element shine or sing in its own way, sometimes in a way that you don't quite understand but still affects you emotionally.

Here is a short list of the things you want to consider when mixing:

- **Balance:** Maintaining a balance between different elements of a mix (e.g. vocals, instruments, drums) to ensure all elements are audible and don't overpower each other.

- **EQ:** Adjusting the tonal balance of individual sounds and instruments to make them fit better in the mix.

- **Compression:** Controlling the dynamic range of individual sounds and the overall mix to make it sound consistent and professional.

- **Reverb:** Adding space and depth to the mix by simulating the acoustics of different environments.

- **Delay:** Adding echo and spacing to elements in a mix to enhance the soundstage and create a sense of depth.

- **Imaging:** Creating a sense of width and depth in a mix by using stereo and 3d panning.

- **Implementation:** How will the music be triggered and played back in the game and how will this affect how you break up your tracks as well as all of the instrumental choices and elements you use?

Mixing for visual media is often working to bring out or enhance one or more of the elements discussed above in an attempt to enhance the action on screen, games have their own set of unique considerations as well. Many times as composers, we are asked to deliver finished pieces of music that will be put directly into a game. We may deliver fully produced tracks that will simply play when triggered. Other times we may be asked to break our music into a bunch of individual parts, recombining them in game in real time. For that reason, it is vital to understand each game's music and audio system in order to use it to the best advantage. Once the music sounds fantastic, we must then take into account how we deliver our tracks and the subsequent changes that may occur once tracks move from DAW to engine. There are in general two ways to think about mixing a game, either inside or outside the engine.

Pre-Mixing/Mixing outside of the game engine: Working outside the game engine is quite common. You simply mix and balance all your tracks. For example, you may have a music loop that is broken up into three levels of intensity, with the drum part alone as the lowest, adding bass creates the second, and the addition of a saxophone for the third and highest intensity. In your DAW, once you are satisfied with the overall balance and blend of these three instrument parts, you simply highlight all tracks, making sure they are exactly the same length, and proceed to bounce them out one at a time into a clearly marked folder, and into the prescribed delivery format (.wav, aiff, etc.). This means that the balance will be maintained and whenever the game music intensity changes, the other parts are added, and create an effective mix balance without having to manage the volume in the game itself.

Post-Mixing/Mixing inside of the engine: Working inside the game engine or middleware, you still follow the steps above to bounce out individual tracks. However, in this case, you can either normalize these tracks in your DAW or use a separate stereo editor to normalize everything to 90%. It is not recommended to normalize your music tracks to 100% as when combined, they may peak over 0 db and create clipping or distortion. The tracks are then brought into the game engine or middleware, and fully volume balanced and blended there as needed.

Which one to use and why? Good question! And as always the correct answer is "It depends!"

Normalizing your tracks before sending them over for implementation provides the highest quality and produces less noise in the system. It also requires the game developer, implementer, or technical sound designer, whoever is doing the implementation, to re-balance the music. Depending on their level of expertise, this may be out of their field and may not sound as good as you might prefer. Pre-mixing your tracks gives you potentially more noise in the system, but it also gives you more control over the final product. Keep in mind that things will change once tracks are downsampled and compressed inside the game engine or middleware, but in general this method will give you a significant head start to ensuring that your mixes are at least in the ballpark and playing as you had hoped. A general rule of thumb is to find out what the audio capabilities of the developer or implementer are on the team, speak with them about their pipeline and process, and make your decision based on your assessment of how likely it is that they have the tools and expertise to successfully incorporate the music into the game, taking into account sound effects, ambient tracks, voice over, and other audio elements.

Lena Raine spins up a lovely synth based texture that echoes the best of early game music but with a new and fresh approach. She got her start in music singing in choir, then through a Sonic fan community, later making MIDI triggered arrangements of songs she knew, and then transitioned into composing her own music, while at the same time being interested in game development as a whole. She graduated from Cornish College of the Art and has worked for ArenaNet on *Guild Wars 2* for six years as an in-house composer. In 2018, Raine released her own text adventure game called *ESC* which she also wrote the music for. Raine released a solo album in 2019 called *One Knowing*.

Lena Raine ("Kuraine") by Sara Ranlett. (CC BY-SA 4.0.)

In the game *Celeste*, Lena was tasked with not only composing the soundtrack, but also mixing and mastering all of her music. In this quote she explains her working process and how she had to adapt and change over time to get a final music mix that was functional and also something she was happy with:

> From the start, it was primarily down to budget and experience. Because I am a fairly DIY composer, I don't really have a production crew, regular collaborators, etc. I was hired as a composer whose only experience was mixing and mastering her own music. I worked in tandem with the developers, scoring each level as it was being designed, and so I would often mix and master as I went, delivering as close to the final stem as I could. Of course, doing this meant that eventually everything felt a bit uneven, and so at the end of the project I went back and did one more final mastering pass on everything to make sure the levels, dynamics, and overall sound felt as uniform as possible across the entire game. It got to a point where I had to go back to the very first series of cues I'd written, and actually give them a second pass to bring them in line with my own new standards.
>
> – LENA ("KURAINE") RAINE

GET CREATIVE!

By harnessing the power of music and varying all these different elements, a deft composer can foreshadow events and alert the player both consciously and unconsciously to actions taking place within the game. Furthermore, all of the elements above can be tied to triggers and events in the game adding an extra interactive or adaptive element. For example, when the character starts running faster, the music gets faster to keep pace, or as the player's point total rises, so does the pitch or key. By using audio middleware or programming, all of this is possible. In the end, great music becomes indelibly linked to the game and serves to increase fun, emotion, and player immersion.

There are many creative techniques that can be used in music scoring, depending on the context and the desired effect. Some examples include the following:

1. **Using Non-Traditional Instruments or Sound Sources:** This can include incorporating unusual or unconventional instruments, such as household objects or found sounds, into the score to create unique and interesting sounds.

2. **Experimenting with Structure and Form:** This can include using unconventional structures or forms for the music, such as using irregular time signatures or playing with the expectations of the listener.

3. **Layering:** This involves adding multiple layers of sound on top of each other, such as adding percussion or ambient sounds to a melodic line to create complex textures.

4. **Using Electronic Processing and Manipulation:** This can include using software or hardware effects to manipulate the sound of traditional instruments or sounds, such as using reverb or delay to create an otherworldly atmosphere.

5. **Using Unconventional Playing Techniques:** This can include using unorthodox techniques to play traditional instruments, such as using a bow on a guitar or playing inside a piano.

These are just a few examples. The key is to be open to experimentation and to think outside the box to come up with unique sounds and structures.

The Big Takeaway: We cannot stress enough – there is no right way to score a game! In all cases, it's up to the composer to look at an image or animation and decide what elements to bring out and how best to enhance what they are seeing on the screen. It is easy to think that composition is all about you, when in fact the minute you start writing, the music and the image will ask something of you as well. It's a two-way street with a message that we must remain open to hearing; we have to accept and adapt to it. In the end, there's no right or wrong, just solutions that feel good or right or satisfying to you, producers, and the player. These kinds of terms are by nature subjective. One person might love it, and the other hate it; it is just the nature of the art form.

Discussion Questions: How does music give information to players in a game? What are some of the ways that composers can use Rhythm in game scores? What is leitmotif? What are some ways that composers use leitmotifs? What are some of the ways that Orchestration ties into animation? Is learning classical orchestration necessary? What are the building blocks of music and how can we use them in games? What is Syncopation? How do composers use layering in game scores?

TERMS

- **Rhythm:** Refers to the pattern of sounds and silences in time. Rhythm is created thru the variation of sound and silence, known as beats that go together to establish a tempo.

- **Meter/Time Signature:** Refers to the underlying pulse or rhythm of a piece of music. It is established by grouping beats into regular patterns and determining the number of beats in a measure. The number of beats in a measure is indicated by a time signature, which is a fraction written at the beginning of a piece of music. The top number of the fraction represents the number of beats in a measure, and the bottom number represents the type of note that gets one beat. For example, a time signature of 4/4 means that there are four beats in a measure and a quarter note gets one beat.

- **Odd Time Signature:** Refers to a meter where the number of beats in a measure is not divisible by two. In contrast, a meter with a time signature where the number of beats is divisible by two, such as 4/4 or 2/2, is considered regular or even.

- **Melody:** Is a linear succession of musical tones that creates a recognizable and distinct musical phrase.

- **Harmony:** Is the use of multiple musical notes played or sung simultaneously to create a vertical simultaneity.

- **Libretto:** The text of an opera or other long vocal work.

- **Earworm:** A catchy song or tune that runs continually through a person's mind.

- **Orchestration:** Is the arrangement of musical compositions for various live or electronic ensembles. It involves deciding which instruments will play which parts and how they will be used to bring out the desired sound, texture, and balance in a piece of music.

- **Tonal Center:** Also known as the tonic, is the central pitch or note around which a piece of music revolves. In Western music, the tonal center is typically determined by the key signature of the piece.

- **Dynamics:** Refers to the loudness or softness of a sound and how it changes over time.

- **Syncopation:** Refers to a rhythmic pattern where the accent or emphasis is placed on beats that are normally unstressed.

- **EQ:** Refers to the process of adjusting the balance between different frequencies in a sound or audio signal. It is used to shape the tonal balance of a sound, making it brighter, warmer, or more bass-heavy.

- **Reverb:** Is a type of audio effect that simulates the natural decay of sound in a room or other space. It can help to add depth, dimension, and atmosphere to a recording or mix.

- **Music Mix:** Is the process of combining and balancing multiple audio tracks to create a cohesive and balanced sound. Mixing involves adjusting levels, panning, equalization (EQ), and adding effects such as reverb, compression, and delay, to each track.

- **Timbre:** Refers to the unique character or quality of a sound that distinguishes it from other sounds. It is sometimes referred to as the "color" of a sound and encompasses all the sonic properties that determine how a sound is perceived, such as its tone, texture, and overtone content.

- **Articulation:** Refers to the way in which a musician performs the attack and decay of a sound, and can be expressed through a variety of techniques, for example, staccato (short and detached) and legato (smooth and connected).

- **Sul ponticello:** Indicates for strings that the bow should be kept near the bridge so as to bring out the higher harmonics and thereby produce a nasal tone.

- **Divisi:** A musical direction indicating that a section of players should be divided into two or more groups each playing a different part.

- **Ostinato:** A continually repeated musical phrase or rhythm.

- **Staccato:** A dot placed over a note that signifies short duration and separation from the next note with silence.

CHAPTER 5

Cinematic Transitions

Topic: Cutscenes and Cinematics

- Learning Outcomes
- Cinematic Traditions in Games
- Cutscene Nuts and Bolts
- Cinematic Categories
- The Art of Composing to Moving Picture
- Composers in Action
- The Big Takeaway
- Discussion Questions
- Terms

Learning Outcomes

- Understanding cinematic traditions in video games
- Differentiating between different types of cinematics
- Understanding the art of composing to moving picture
- Analyzing music for moving pictures
- Understanding the difference between linear and non-linear media

DOI: 10.1201/9781003414728-7

CINEMATIC TRADITIONS IN GAMES

It is understandable that composers get very excited and focused on the possibilities of interactive music. However, we must not forget that games also frequently include the playback of plain old linear media. We call these videos cutscenes or cinematics and they have much in common with film and television. There are, in fact, composers and companies that specialize exclusively on cinematics in games and many story based games can have a tremendous amount of linear media that needs original music. Over the years, as games have grown in size, so have the opportunities for composers to focus on this growing market.

As a recent example, let's look at *Death Stranding*, the 2019 action game from director Hideo Kojima, which is chock full of cinematics. The score was composed by Ludvig Forssell and Ryan Karazija. It begins with simultaneous explosions around the world. The "Death Stranding" is the result and the world of the dead and living become intertwined, with drastic consequences for human society and the ecosystem. The longest opening sequence without player inputs is a whopping 31 minutes long and the ending cinematics easily last, in stages, for around two hours. The game in many ways expands the idea of narrative design to such a point that much like the "Death Stranding" itself, it essentially bridges the worlds of games and film. The production company, much like in film, actually released an expanded and remastered Director's cut. As Kojima himself says: "The human body is supposed to be 70 percent water. I consider myself 70 percent film."

Days Gone, developed by SIE Bend Studio with score by Nathan Whitehead, is a post-apocalyptic survival horror that follows protagonist Deacon St. John. Set in the ever-changing landscape of the Pacific Northwest, zombies known as "Freakers" roam the world, and the surviving humans have learned to adapt. Thanks to an interview with the designer on the Denmark-based site GameReactor, we know that *Days Gone* features six full hours of intense cinematics.

Both of these games present the modern day composer with amazing opportunities to use their chops to underscore and develop long form narrative.

So, how did this all get started? Well you might be surprised to discover that a game made in 1966, the *Sumerian Game*, built on an early mainframe computer designed by Mabel Addis, introduced the first known cutscene (Figure 5.1). The game was made for elementary school children and was created through a partnership with IBM to explore the idea of using games in the classroom. The opening was an introduction to the subject matter and the gameplay; it featured a slideshow synchronized to an audio recording, essentially a rather long introductory cutscene.

In 1980s, *Pac Man* from Namco had short interludes that essentially told a simple story, but Shigeru Miyamoto's *Donkey Kong* (1981) advanced the concept by using cutscenes to connect different levels. As time marched on and as technology advanced, other games started to use the same device.

Then as CD-ROM and increased storage capacity debuted in the 1990s, full motion video burst onto the scene with games like *The Daedalus Encounter* (featuring actress Tia Carrera) an interactive movie puzzle adventure game.

FIGURE 5.1   A child playing the *Sumerian game*. (Image credit: Gamehistory.org.)

However, as with all new technologies, there can be a tendency for designers and producers to focus on it to the detriment of other equally important factors, like gameplay.

Such was the case with *Cadillacs and Dinosaurs: The Second Cataclysm*, a driving and shooting game, which made extensive early use of cinematics, while gameplay seemingly was an afterthought (Figure 5.2). Developed and published by Rocket Science Games in the time of Sillywood (the merger of Silicon Valley and Hollywood) the story was based on the American alternative comic series *Xenozoic Tales*, by Mark Schultz and set in a post-apocalyptic future. It was released in the USA in December 1994. Disclaimer here, one of the authors of this book early in his career actually wrote all the cinematic music for the game, and had a lot of fun doing so. After the gameplay music was composed, there was even a live studio re-recording of several of the main themes from the game scheduled for a soundtrack release that never actually made it out to the general public.

The games from this period generally receive mediocre to terrible reviews, with the gameplay taking a back seat to this shiny new cinematic toy. As you can imagine, this did not go over well with audiences and critics, who at the time, were more interested in fun, inventive and challenging gameplay. Jeff Sengstack of NewMedia wrote that *Cadillacs and Dinosaurs* "bombed miserably." Its sales apparently were below 20,000 units. "The graphics are quite good, but the overall theme of the game isn't very thrilling," said Mike Weigand of Electronic Gaming Monthly. Scary Larry of GamePro agreed that the game was dull, remarking "there's not much else to do here but shoot and steer."

As we have seen, time progresses, technology improves, and directors and designers develop their craft. This has cemented the role of cinematic elements as a useful and even essential part of the games we play today.

FIGURE 5.2 A cutscene moment from *Cadillacs and Dinosaurs*. (Image: Game Audio Institute.)

CUTSCENE NUTS AND BOLTS

Cinematics can be triggered in many ways. Let's break down some of the more prominent ways they are represented in games:

- **Pre-rendered cutscenes** can be quite sophisticated these days and take advantage of a full array of techniques from computer generated animation to full motion video capture. Like live-action shoots, pre-rendered cutscenes are often presented in full motion video and read just like any other linear medium. Most commonly found at the start, they can take place anywhere in the game. Historically these types of cutscenes had a much higher production value and quality than the gameplay itself, but the gap closed significantly as visual rendering tech improved in the 2000s and 2010s to the point where it has now become nearly indistinguishable and it's now more of an artistic choice for the developer rather than a technical limitation.

- **Real-time cutscenes**: Real-time cutscenes are rendered in game on-the-fly using the same game engine as the graphics during gameplay. This technique can also be considered a type of **Machinima** – essentially that's cinema done within a game. Real-time cutscenes can adapt to the state of the game. For example, some games allow the player character to wear several different outfits, and appear in cutscenes wearing the outfit the player has chosen. It is also possible to give the player control over camera movement. Depending on how it's applied, this approach can blur the line between cutscenes and regular gameplay.

- **Mixed media cutscenes**: In the past, many games would use both pre-rendered and real-time cutscenes in combination. The difference in quality between each of these was usually obvious, but over time as technology has improved, the quality of the live action cutscene's imagery has closed the gap significantly. In the remake of *Final Fantasy VII*, it has several scenes in which real-time animations and rendering are alternating with scenes done with pre-rendered full motion video and the difference is much less noticeable than in previous titles. However, using these two methods together in a game can present additional compositional challenges.

- **Interactive cutscenes**: Interactive cutscenes involve the computer taking control of a player's character while prompts (such as a sequence of button presses) appear on screen, requiring the player to follow them in order to continue or succeed. These are fairly common in story driven games.

Everything listed above will tap into your creative powers and task you with composing music that underscores the action and emotion on screen. It will certainly also challenge your technical understanding of how the music functions.

Now let's break down some of the general categories you may encounter.

Categories of Cinematics

Introductions/Intros are animated or live-action video sequences that serve as an introduction to the game's story and characters. They are used to set the scene, establish the mood, and provide background information to the player. They can be used to convey the game's narrative, introduce the game's characters, or provide a context for the player's actions. They are an important aspect of narrative design and serve to immerse the player in the game world. These scenes can be quite involved and will frequently feature the music prominently. You will find them used to keep the narrative moving forward and although they are often found at the beginning and end of a level, they may also be found intertwined throughout the experience.

Outros/Conclusions are equally important and traditionally used to wrap up loose ends, provide closure to the game's narrative, and give the player a sense of resolution. Ending cutscenes often depict the consequences of the player's choices as they conclude their journey through the narrative. Again as with the Intro, there can be big or small conclusions, and the emotional quality can vary widely.

Significant Story Points are cinematic moments in a game that may or may not involve music; it just depends on the game. There are a lot of permutations and forms that these can take, so there is just no way to list them all; however, here are just a few examples.

- The introduction of a significant non-player character (NPC) or a place the player has arrived at.

- The completion of a goal.

- The completion of a chapter.

- The death of a NPC in the game.

Bridging/Connecting cinematics fundamentally rely on the narrative and events players encounter to determine their overall function and character. Short segments may trigger during game play in a variety of ways in order to expand the narrative and guide the player. Longer segments may help further define background characters and plot lines. These cinematic segments all serve the function of providing the player with context and information vital to success or failure in the story. Music is of course a huge part of that narrative.

Credits are important, we can't forget the credits! This is the moment for the folks who made the game to be acknowledged and for the composer to shine. It usually takes quite a large village to produce a game, as result credit rolls tend to last quite a while. With luck, players will actually watch them and listen with undivided attention.

Directors Diss-Cussion

Apparently, not everyone is a fan of cinematics. Directors Steven Spielberg and Guillermo del Toro, and game designer Ken Levine, all of whom are avid video gamers, have all criticized the use of cutscenes in games, calling them intrusive. Spielberg states in a 2013 interview published on the Verge: "I think the key divide between interactive media and the narrative media that we do is the difficulty in opening up an empathic pathway between the gamer and the character — as differentiated from the audience and the characters in a movie or a television show." He opined that his objection is mostly centered around the use of the game controller which in his mind then turns a story into a sport and that making the story flow naturally into the gameplay becomes a challenge for future game developers as long as the controller is involved. In a somewhat similar critique, Hollywood writer Danny Bilson called cinematics the "last resort of game storytelling," as for him, a person doesn't want to watch a movie when they are playing a video game. Of course there are certainly fans of cutscenes in games out there who would disagree with that assessment, as *Death Stranding* alone has sold more than 5 million copies as of 2021 and is still quite popular.

The Art of Composing to Moving Pictures

Regardless of whether you love them or hate them, cinematics are part of the landscape and a rapidly growing part of what you will encounter in the industry. As such, there is a lot of crossover with the creative decision making process found in film. Music and film, as we know, have a long history together. From Bernard Hermann to Jonny Greenwood, the art and craft of film scoring have been well codified and documented. Since music is able to evoke memories and awaken feelings, it may help to explain why it's such an impactful element in the cinematographic world. Soundtracks influence our brain, and in turn manipulate our emotions. Music can influence metabolic rates, blood pressure, energy levels, and digestion. When we look at moving images on screen, we need to be cognizant of the ways in which our music may affect the viewer.

We are used to the idea that music can help to highlight specific actions or motion on screen, building a bond between eye and ear. In 2015, University of Helsinki researchers carried out a study, and concluded that classical music went so far as to affect the genes related to pleasure. In fact, in the study, those who listened to Mozart during the experiment showed increased brain activity and synaptic activity. Composers can use music to trigger a multitude of feelings – one could even say they are manipulative creatures brazenly harnessing the power of music to lead the audience so as to express their point of view.

When composing for cinematics, take a good look at the visuals and then consider all of the aspects below asking yourself what effect they might have on the viewer/listener.

- **PACING (*Rhythm and Tempo*)** Rhythm and tempo can be used to match or contrast action on screen. Tempo refers to the speed at which the music is played. Rhythm refers to the pattern of strong and weak beats. Pacing is an important aspect of the soundtrack and can help to enhance emotional impact and support visual storytelling. Keep in mind that rhythmic development does not have to be over complexified when scoring. Smaller divisions of a beat can appear to make the music speed up, conversely, larger multiplications of a beat and the use of sustained notes can appear to slow the pacing whatever tempo is used.

- **EMOTION (*Harmony, Melody, Orchestration*)** Harmony, melody, and orchestration can all be manipulated to great effect. Harmony refers to the combination of different pitches played at the same time. A memorable melody can help to anchor the music and create an emotional connection with the audience. Orchestration refers to the arrangement of different instruments and their parts in a piece of music. All of these combined establish the mood or atmosphere of a particular scene and are all key elements that help to enhance emotional impact on screen.

- **DIRECTION/MOTION** This larger category refers to how music ultimately relates to the story being told, either visually or with the aid of dialogue. There are many different methods a composer can use to control this relationship; here are a few things to consider:

  - **PARALLEL (*Going with the narrative*)** When a composer follows the action on screen in a one to one relationship and uses music to reinforce what the viewer is seeing we define this as moving parallel with the story and action.

  - **CONTRARY (*Going against the narrative*)** When a composer contrasts the action on screen and uses music to go against what the viewer is seeing on screen we define this as going contrary to the story. For example, in a gigantic space battle scene, if the music's motion stays slow and somber it would be contrasting the visual storytelling.

  - **NEUTRAL (*Not giving any clues*)** When a composer uses music to neither reinforce or contrast what the viewer is seeing on screen, we call this going neutral and it can be used to great effect to help develop mystery.

  - **IMPLICATION (*Leading the narrative*)** Somewhat similar to parallel direction, a composer can in effect lead the narrative and provide musical clues or foreshadowing. Employed by a deft hand, a composer can, with music alone, lead the audience. The music can provide clues about how characters are likely to feel and respond by anticipating events on the screen and even help to keep the viewer guessing, if it serves the story line.

Keep in mind that a composer can change their approach from moment to moment – they aren't stuck with needing to follow the narrative absolutely and inflexibly or constantly go against it, although they do need to work closely with the director, producer, and screenwriter. The trick is to manage this in a way that is emotionally satisfying whatever the approach.

- **SETTING/IDENTITY** Music can evoke a sense of time and place, and certain pieces of music may be associated with specific periods or events in history. For example, a piece of music from the Renaissance may evoke a sense of that time period, while a piece of modern electronic music speaks of the present. Music is related to time in many ways, and it can help to shape our experience and memory.

The connection between the cinematic musical world and the gameplay world is something important to consider. The use of any of the techniques above as applied to cutscenes might make for a powerful relationship and connection when also heard during gameplay. For example, the use of a **leitmotif** or **leitmotiv** (a musical theme or idea that is associated with a particular character, place, or idea) when heard in the opening cutscene of a game, which is then brought back to represent our main character during game play, represents a powerful way to create unity and cohesion over the entire scope of a score.

Now let's take a closer look at a real world application of music and cinematics in games.

Winifred Phillips is a BAFTA-nominated video game composer who writes music for games such as *Assassin's Creed*, *God of War*, *The Sims*, and *LittleBigPlanet*. She has received numerous awards, including a D.I.C.E. Award from the Academy of Interactive Arts and Sciences, six Game Audio Network Guild Awards (including Music of the Year), and three Hollywood Music in Media Awards.

Winifred Phillips by Ehtonal. (CC BY 3.0.)

Winifred penned the score to *Call of Champions*, a 3 vs 3, 3D MOBA (multiplayer online battle arena) game casual/competitive gameplay; it also features cinematics. Here are her own words describing the process of composing for a tutorial cutscene:

> As the composer of music for a tutorial cinematic for *Call of Champions*, it was my job to support the visual explanation and try to make it easier to follow. I started with a musical style that called to mind the competitive bravado of a top TV sports program. Then I strategically shifted the tonal center of the music to help facilitate player comprehension. Just as a printed manual might break up paragraphs with boldface headings, I broke up the music with these harmonic shifts. This gave the long explanation a sense of organization and flow, which made it easier to follow. Finally, in order to add extra emphasis to an important point, I let the music momentarily stop dead when the player is warned about being shot by enemy towers.

She was also responsible for the music in the VR game *Shattered State* and describes its introductory cutscene here as well:

> ...The backstory of the game features terrorist attacks, a civil war, peace talks, the resignation of a popular general, the founding of a new nation, and the establishment of a new intelligence organization. It's a lot of information to convey in a very short time.
>
> As the composer of the music for *Shattered State*, I had to make sure that players were able to absorb all these details. Like the *Call of Champions* cinematic, I employed harmonic shifts here as a tool to reinforce topic divisions and help things feel organized. However, since a lot of the content is presented very simply using text and simple images or stock video snippets, I made sure the music incorporated world-building elements that would help bring things to life. This included grim military rhythm during warfare discussion, and slick synth arpeggiation when describing the elite intelligence agency.

THE BIG TAKEAWAY

Composing cutscenes and cinematic moments in games shares a lot with writing for more traditional linear media like film and television. For our purposes, cinematics are another important piece of the puzzle for the well-rounded composer. How we tie the music together with music from game play is an interesting and worthwhile compositional challenge. Thinking about their relationship to the whole game as well as how to support the development of story and character. As we are quick to point out, we have only scratched the surface of this topic and have concentrated mostly on the specifics of how cinematics relate to the musical world of games. If you are interested in diving deeper into the craft of composing for linear media, there have been many great books written on the subject that cover all aspects as well as marvelous composers like Bernard Herrmann, Shirley walker, John Williams, and more.

One book we recommend is *Film Music – The Soul of Cinema*, written by Larry Timm, a veteran Hollywood studio musician, producer, and university professor. This volume provides a historical timeline of relevant film music with information about the composers and their scores. The book in very clear terms addresses the many functions of scoring.

TERMS

Cinematic: A gameplay cinematic is a cutscene or event scene (*in-game cinematic or in-game movie*) that is not interactive, and often interrupts gameplay at key moments.

Cutscene: A non-playable animated or live-action sequence in a video game, usually employed as a storytelling device, and typically following established conventions of cinema.

Machinima: A method of making animated films using the same or similar software used in the game industry.

Narrative Design: The creation of gameplay elements and systems that define how players interact with the story.

Leitmotif: A recurrent theme throughout a composition, associated with a particular person, idea, or situation.

Arpeggiation: An arpeggio is a type of broken chord in which the notes that make up a chord are individually and quickly sounded in a progressive rising or descending order.

Harmonic rhythm: The rate that chords change in a progression over time.

Harmonic shifts: The interplay between chords that help to create a sense of movement, either dynamic and/or static.

NPC: Non-player character.

MOBA: Massive Online Battle Arena.

CHAPTER 6

Living in Limbo

Topic: Form in Interactive Composition

- Learning Outcomes
- Defining Form
- Defining Style
- Time Is of the Essence
- Trigger Happy
- Transitions Are Hard, Gameplay Analysis of *Ori and the Blind Forest*
- The Big Takeaway
- Discussion Questions
- Terms

Learning Outcomes

- Defining musical form
- Defining musical style
- Understanding various types of music transitions
- Creating and understanding music asset lists
- Creating and analyzing music for basic interactivity

DOI: 10.1201/9781003414728-8

DEFINING FORM

As we start to tackle the idea of working interactively, we must bring all the skills we have learned from previous chapters and exercises to bear; however, now we must also start to think differently. We need to question time (When) and implementation (How). We need to understand overall form as well as transitions and how they manifest. We must take the first exciting steps into thinking interactively. Exact timing is not the most important issue, as that will more than likely change in real time as the game is played. Instead, we need to figure out how to move from one piece of music to another in a satisfying and seamless manner that matches the way the game moves from section to section. It requires us to think about how the game is built and how the music system works, otherwise our music will not be successful.

In game music, form follows function. Before you start any game project, you should know the scope of what is expected of you. If we can't start to write music for a game until we understand it, how do we go about familiarizing ourselves with the form and structure of a game? Music for games can be a complex endeavor and there's a lot of preparatory work you need to do before starting out in earnest.

DEFINING GAMEPLAY STYLE

Although video game genres were once fairly clear cut, that's simply not the case these days. There's a growing variety of genres and subgenres out there as developers mix and blend different types of games in new and unexpected ways. That means the video-gaming landscape is constantly evolving. Studios work on tight schedules and tend to follow trends when the opportunity arises.

Composers need to be fluent in all sorts of gameplay styles. The style of a game describes how it delivers its experience. Understanding these styles of games can help you define your overall musical form, structure, and direction. Keep in mind that many genres have some degree of overlap with each other.

You may have come across game terms like FPS (First-Person Shooter), TBS (Turn-Based Strategy), or MMO (Massive Multiplayer Online). Although these abbreviations are often types of games, these terms can also refer to things like camera mechanics, how the game will progress, or larger categories of games. In an FPS for example, the first two letters denote the camera mechanic as it looks from your perspective (first person), but none of that relates much to how you're going to organize the music. Even the last initial doesn't mean that the game has combat. This is because games evolve and change over time. For example, the game Firewatch is considered an FPS but has no shooting, whereas a game like *Call of Duty* is a much more typical example of a first-person shooter. Over time the last initial was included for any first person-based game regardless of whether the game had combat or not. The first two letters of TBS are "turn based", and turn-based mechanics in games are incredibly common across all genres. The last letter S denotes strategy which again has a lot of open meanings from completely abstract settings, on up to realistic scenarios. So overall these terms don't really help a huge amount. And MMO just means thousands or more players will be playing the game at one time; it doesn't even have a defined style, though it's not likely to be a 2D-oriented game.

What does help in terms of looking at music systems is looking at and analyzing how specific games and game genres handle music playback, bearing in mind that even this can result in a wide variety of music system approaches.

TIME IS OF THE ESSENCE

As we have seen, time functions differently in interactive media. It's quite often unpredictable. Leaving cinematics aside and just concentrating on gameplay, time, or to be more accurate, timing, are vital. Every type of game design has various actions and routines that engage the player. These actions can often be open ended – however, many have a time limit – it's not necessarily an absolute, but it is a common practice in game design.

For example, let's look at a sports game like *NBA 2k*, a series developed by Visual Concepts and released annually since 1999.

NBA 2k emulates the sport of basketball, and more specifically, the National Basketball Association. As per the rules, each team possession is governed by a 24-second shot clock. That means that a team's actions within the game are limited by that clock, and after each change of possession, the clock is reset. Often in arenas during the game, music can be heard playing in the background. In basketball, music is often used to motivate the crowd. This type of emulation mechanic tasks the composer with understanding when music will and won't be triggered, and most importantly figuring out how long the music needs to be within the prescribed time. It might necessitate composing short loops, 5–10 seconds each, because a longer piece of music might never be heard in full, and eat up storage space unnecessarily. Also, since these music segments are meant to accompany the action while at the same time being as authentic as possible to the real thing, that information must certainly inform the style of the music.

The music is built around percussion instruments (mimicking the sound of a marching band in the arena) and only triggers when the home team has the ball. This builds up excitement and pace for the locals, and drops out when the visiting team has the ball – an effective compositional choice to motivate the player, as long as you're playing the home team!

Another example is combat in a first-person shooter game like *Doom Eternal* (2020 by id Software/Bethesda) vs combat in an open world setting like the third-person open-world game *Mad Max* (2015 by Avalanche Studios/WB Games). In *Doom Eternal* combat never seems to stop, whereas in *Mad Max* you have large stretches of desert to travel in your car in order to get to the next combat location. In the case of our FPS, as we play through the game we can measure how much time is spent exploring vs fighting basic enemies as well as time spent in boss battles. It's usually assumed the bigger the boss, the longer the fight and as a result the longer that the music will likely be playing. This is used as a basic yardstick so that you don't compose a five-minute piece for fighting normal enemies, because chances are good you won't even hear the vast majority of the music since the enemy will be dispatched in a much shorter time. In this scenario, you'll be back to hearing the exploration music before you ever hear the rest of your magnum opus "EnemyFight01.wav!"

Understanding gameplay mechanics and making basic estimations of actions over time should absolutely be part of your compositional process. Some games might involve composing long form pieces. Combat music for example, might start small and get bigger over time, adding more and more layers of complexity, reinforcing the idea that the longer you're in battle the more tension should be added. Others will jump from scene to scene and precipitate the use of small loops connected by stingers in order to traverse transition screens. The thing to keep in mind is that there isn't really a right or wrong way to compose, but there are more or less efficient uses of your resources, and of course it totally depends on the game as to how those resources are spent.

TRIGGER HAPPY

The next question to ask will be "how?" How will the music be triggered exactly? This is probably the most important thing to keep in mind after timing. We can make music happen right from the start when we load up a map, or when we receive the Champion's Cudgel (one of the powerful enchanted weapons in the game Skyrim). But how does that happen exactly? The accurate but glib answer for this is, of course, the time-honored "it depends," but we can at least look at some of the methods of interaction we're likely to encounter:

PHYSICAL TRIGGERS

A physical trigger in a game engine uses a physics component called a collider. A collider acts as a solid surface that you can stand on, like the ground, or run into, like a wall. But it can also be configured as a transparent object to act as a simple switch. These triggers come in many shapes (a box is quite common) and are usually invisible in the game itself. The player can pass through them, but doing so can make any kind of action happen, including playing music loops or stingers. Even if our game is a 2D-based platformer, programmers can use this option. For example, if there's some location on the game map that counts as the beginning of the level, then when the player passes this point the music will start. If they enter the boss room the music suddenly changes to the boss fighting theme, and if our brave adventurer manages to get to the end of the level, a trigger placed there can play the fanfare announcing that they have emerged victorious. Additionally, any object that triggers a stinger, like a powerup or bonus, can be played by picking it up. A pickup just means that the object will disappear after being encountered; disappearing is an action that can also trigger an event.

Triggers placed at various locations play a huge role in determining the form and function of the music and how it might develop. *Monster Hunter World* (Capcom 2018) is an open world with jaunty exploration music. In it you fight large monsters, usually one at a time, and the battle music is quite energetic. In the game you can choose to stand and fight or you can run away. That's good news, as discretion in the face of huge monsters can many times be the better part of valor. When and if you do decide to turn tail and flee, you'll notice the music system as it gently crossfades back to the exploration music. Turn around and head back to the trigger area that has been programmed around the monster and the music increases in intensity again. Interactive music in action!

The previous examples might seem pretty obvious. In reality, nearly everything in a game is based on some kind of action, even if it's not obvious at first. Let's call this an event for simplicity's sake. So, what are some less obvious triggers? The answer to that question is based on the structure of gameplay. Nearly every game out there is going to be based on a number of game states. A game state is a collection of variables, values, and data that define the state of the game at any given moment. The game state can be thought of as a snapshot of the game's current situation, including the positions of game objects, player scores, health and other attributes, game rules, and any other relevant information that affects the gameplay experience. The game state is constantly changing as the player interacts with the game and as the game processes events and actions. Game states are usually global in nature meaning that they affect the entire game.

Here's an example – take a fantasy RPG (Role-Playing Game) like Skyrim where you have to manage inventory frequently – sometimes even during combat! This is an opportunity to also manage the music. In the game, inventory management is a global state that pauses gameplay while you say, find the Elixir of Potent Health and drink it before you battle the evil ice wizard. And it's a game state that can control many other things, like reducing the music volume, or cutting it out entirely. What action controls this? In the case of Skyrim, it's 100% player triggered because you pressed the I key on your PC or a button on your controller which opens up the inventory window. Pressing it again toggles you back into the real world and resumes normal gameplay, along with whatever music was reduced in volume.

Events can also be internally part of the game's structure, where they are neither part of the physical world nor manually triggered by the player via a keyboard key or controller button. If we return back to the *Monster Hunter World* game, or *Shadow of the Colossus*, we stated earlier that a triumphant music stinger will play once you defeat the enemy. But what triggers that music exactly? It isn't under manual or physical control in the game or globally via the controls. In this case, and speaking generally, the game has a way of tracking the existence of the monster. A very obvious visual indicator of this is that, as you're battling the monster, its health bar will usually be gradually reduced over time. So the game is aware of the monster's health level and once it reaches zero it will decide that the monster is vanquished, usually with some type of dramatic animation, which might have a musical stinger as accompaniment. As with all games, it depends on how the developers choose to implement this moment.

In RPG games, it is also common for the game to track the player's own statistics. When the character moves up a level, after much grinding and slaying of monsters and other miscreants, the game acknowledges this with a prominent musical stinger or sound effect. Note that this music may play completely independent of whatever music may be happening in the background.

Although there are many different ways that games can be organized, there are patterns that can be discerned based on genre. Bear in mind though that genres are always evolving and changing, with constant cross fertilization and grafting of gameplay mechanics from one style to another, creating new genres.

Here's a short list with some brief descriptions of how a game genre might relate to the music system's structure:

- **Sandbox** games are open world and much less strictly structured, allowing for a lot of personal freedom to do or be whatever you want. As a result, it's often difficult to discern the function of the music. By playing through the game and analyzing the form of gameplay, we start to understand how the music functions. Below we take a general view and closer look at some popular genres, and through observation, break down the way the music is expressed.

  - *Minecraft* – During gameplay, we hear floating, relaxing, ambient, and romantic music from Daniel Rosenfeld (aka C418) while performing various tasks in a huge voxel-based world. Music doesn't really progress here very much based on game events – it's more of a playlist than anything else, but those playlists can change as you enter different locations. Music becomes part of the scenery and changes in ways that may go with or against what is happening on screen. Playlists can be tailored to specific environments as well. For example, you sometimes find yourself underground, which tends to trigger more unsettling music.

  - *Grand Theft Auto* – The last initial should give you a clue that a lot of the action in this game revolves around driving, although you do have the freedom to just walk around if you want. The cars all have stereos and you can tune into a variety of stations playing licensed music as playlists in a number of genres while cruising the town. In this case, music becomes a diegetic part of the environment and serves to help heighten the overall sense of realism. There are also storylines and quests to follow that trigger highly structured musical moments during cutscenes and confrontations with other gangs or the law. These serve to increase the emotional drama in these sections of the game.

  - *The Sims* – Is an incredibly popular series, and very open to allowing players to do or be whoever or whatever they wish. The music system is a bit of an odd beast though. There are menus with background music, like in setup mode where you can buy and place items in your house. In this mode, a pre-selected music loop plays in the background. This track will vary the orchestration and intensity, and fades out when you go into live mode. In live mode, you might have a music producing device like a stereo that plays diegetic music, like a playlist in the background when friends come over. Many of these tracks are remixes of popular songs re-recorded by the original artists singing in Simlish. Simlish is a made up nonsense language and quite funny. During moments of achievement pre-selected stingers play. These are non-diegetic short musical tags that highlight specific in-game events. Overall, the music system for *The Sims* seems much more complex and varied than the other sandbox systems we've covered.

- **Real-Time Strategy** games often have a lot of continuous music, which is occasionally interrupted by in-game events. Examples of this type include *Age of Empires, Command and Conquer, and Warcraft* (not *World of Warcraft* which is a MMORPG). In this case, the music systems don't track any kind of storyline or emotional development, and the sound effects and VO tend to dominate at times. *Age of Empires* for example, has elements of crafting and construction of economic and military resources, but the overall gameplay tends to unfold on one main screen. Events and actions may occasionally be interrupted with cinematics that help to move the game forward. Campaign-based transitions are significant moments where cinematic storylines and dialogue are present. In this case, music tends to serve the function of relating emotion to the player. When blended with all the other sound elements, it provides a welcome underpinning for on screen events and clues the player into important gameplay developments.

- **Shooters (Such as** *Halo, Gears of War, and DOOM Eternal*) are generally very high-intensity games, whether done in first or third person, where, as the name implies, you do a lot of shooting. As a result, you can expect the music intensity to be generally quite high. This serves to get the players adrenaline pumping and increase engagement for much of the game. However, they often tell a story and often have cutscenes that move the plot along. Music in these moments is likely to be more subdued and serves to give the player time to relax and reset between rounds. Because campaigns and chapters can be very complex and multi-staged, the music will often be scripted to respond in a one to one fashion. As the numbers and strength of various enemies are encountered the music can also change to reflect these varying degrees of intensity and resolution. There will likely be occasional moments of brief rest while you pick up ammo, health, and anything else you need to smite the enemy, who is likely hiding just around the next bend.

- **Multiplayer Online Battle Arena** games can have tens or even hundreds of thousands of players online at one time, though they are broken up and placed into thousands of unique game sessions that will only allow a limited number of players at any one time. Games that fall into this category are *DOTA (Defense Of The Ancients) 2, League of Legends, and Smite*. All three of these feature teams of five players pitted against each other 5×5, on a relatively compact game map. One of the most prominent features in this genre is the availability of dozens of characters that players can use, each with unique attack and defense characteristics, sound effects, and of course, their own identifying music, like a modern day leitmotif. During gameplay, there's not likely to be a lot of low-key or introspective moments. It's fairly high action with lots of moments of drama as characters fight for ultimate supremacy. Prominent moments trigger one shot stingers and the final win at the end of a round will usually culminate with a victory stinger for one team while the other gets the defeat stinger.

- **Role-Playing** games tend to allow a lot of player actions other than running around and killing, such as crafting, alchemy, and enchantment. Games that cover this category are *Elder Scrolls V-Skyrim, Fallout 4, and The Witcher 3*. As the name implies, you are playing a particular role, but that can be either player defined, as it is in the first two examples, or preset, as it is in the *Witcher* series where you play the role of Geralt (mostly). These are usually large open world games with lots of exploring to do, as well as enemies to fights and quests with cutscenes (fairly common in *Witcher*). The music system in these games needs to be able to support significant moments in the quest storyline while also being able to adjust dynamically to combat situations, and provide different clips for varying locations and location types. The music itself will tend to be quite varied and support emotion as well as provide vital information to the player.

- **Sports** games can be as varied as the sports themselves. Some simulations tend towards extreme realism, as if you're watching it in the venue (like a stadium) or on television. Game examples here are (*Forza Motorsport, Madden NFL, FIFA, and NBA2K*). In other cases, they can be cartoony and artistic recreations of the sport. In the case of realistic stadium games, the audio design and music tend to be more diegetic. They often utilize marching band or percussion tracks triggered to build suspense and tension when the visiting team has the ball or short stingers that pay when the home team scores a basket or touchdown. The music clips triggered here will be fairly short; full pieces of music aren't usually found, except at the start and end menus, in UI or at the start of a season. Oftentimes tracks will be mixed with chants, cheers, and other crowd sounds. As for racing games, a similar paradigm holds true. The music and sound effects are usually designed to hold true to the television or track experience. This means that music is mostly mixed with ambience and SFX to recreate a realistic view experience.

- **Puzzle** games of course can be as varied as the games themselves, but in general tend towards slower and more introspective play, though of course this can also vary and tension can certainly be added if there's a countdown mechanic as the player races to finish.

HERE'S A FEW DIFFERENT EXAMPLES OF PUZZLE GAMES

- *Cubism* **(2020, Thomas Van Bouwel/Vanbo)** is a 3D puzzle game where you attempt to move and rotate various 3D blocks inside an outlined volume of differing shapes. It uses a very sparse and quiet musical texture throughout with only solo piano playing. In early levels the piano notes act as stingers when you make certain movements, but as you progress and it takes longer to make your move the music more fully develops. It's a beautiful example of utilizing only musical elements for all in game events. This kind of musical sound design is quite common in puzzle games where the player needs sound to provide specific information for both interface (UX/UI) and gameplay. Using music for both is a dynamic challenge for any composer and a musical puzzle unto itself. When done well, it brings a satisfying level of sophistication to the game.

- *The Talos Principle* **(2014 Croteam/Devolver Digital)** is a third- or first-person puzzle game that involves your character solving puzzles in a surreal garden maze with ruined architecture, sentry robots, and other obstacles. Ambient and relaxing music plays in the background, and when a player clears a puzzle, a synth laden success stinger plays. Overall it's a relatively simple, but effective music system, mostly driven by game events. Certain cutscenes and story driven moments get more dramatic treatment, but there's little in the way of adaptive music happening. The music for *The Talos Principle* is atmospheric and reflective, with a mix of electronic and orchestral elements. It features a variety of instruments, including piano, strings, percussion, and synthesizers. The soundtrack is composed of over 30 tracks, which are used to great effect throughout the game to set the mood and enhance the player's emotional connection to the story.

- *Portal* **(2007 Valve Software)** is a highly unique first-person puzzle game that uses music in unique ways. The main character Chell is armed with the Aperture Science Handheld Portal Device, a high-tech gun that can create portals on flat surfaces. Using this device, Chell must solve a series of increasingly difficult puzzles to progress through the game and ultimately confront GLaDOS, the devious AI conducting the tests. The music in Portal is mostly ambient and electronic, with a minimalist style that fits the game's sterile and futuristic setting. One notable aspect is how it is used to enhance the player's experience of the puzzles and challenges they must overcome. Certain pieces of music are triggered when the player completes a puzzle or reaches a milestone in the game, creating a sense of satisfaction and progress. The game quite unusually has diegetic music that is heard from with the Aperture Science testing facility as well as moody ambient non-diegetic music. The most recognizable track from the game is the ending theme, "Still Alive," which is sung by GLaDOS (the game's antagonist) and features humorous lyrics that have become iconic among fans of the franchise. Overall the music system is not geared to be tremendously musically reactionary to player outcomes. There are no stingers upon successful completion of a level for example.

- **Action-adventure** games tend to be heavily story driven and directed, however they do take place on large maps and there is a lot of exploring going on. Music in this setting needs to respond to different levels of combat intensity as well as achievements. In addition, there are also numerous cinematics to manage. Games in this category include *Star Wars Jedi: Fallen Order, The Legend of Zelda series, Uncharted, Sekiro: Shadows Die Twice,* and the *Assassin's Creed* series and can encompass a wide range of sub genres and styles, so the music in these games can vary quite a bit. However, there are a few common themes and characteristics that tend to pop up. Many feature epic orchestral music that is inspired by film scores, with sweeping, cinematic orchestral arrangements. These scores are often heavily influenced by classical music and can incorporate a wide range of instruments, from strings and brass to percussion and woodwinds. In addition to the more bombastic orchestral pieces, many action-adventure games also feature atmospheric ambient music. These tracks often use synthesizers, electronic effects, and other sound design elements to create moody and immersive soundscapes. In games with well-defined characters, the music may incorporate specific themes or motifs that are associated with those characters. For example, a heroic character might have a triumphant and upbeat theme, while a villainous character might have a more ominous and menacing theme. Many modern action-adventure games also feature music that can adapt to the player's actions and choices. This means that the music can change based on factors like the player's location, the enemies they are facing, or the actions they are taking. This kind of a dynamic music system helps to create more immersive and reactive game worlds.

- **Horror** is the genre where music and ambience often meet in a sort of unholy union, and where dissonant and jagged music can be found. It's also the most likely to have sudden event driven jump scares that are tied to musical stingers. Games in this category include *Dead Space, Silent Hill,* and *Resident Evil:Village.* In this case, composers have more of a tendency to use music sparingly. One reason being that hearing just sound effects and breathing already takes up a lot of sonic real estate and creates a lot of tension. Combine that with significant moments where something horrific happens or appears and the music matches that moment with even wilder ambience and weird effects and you have an excellent audio cocktail of extremes appropriate for the genre. The systems are largely event driven and there can be quite a few cutscenes. Intensity management is the name of the game and must be controlled especially at denser and climatic moments in order to create a dynamic score. Similar to action-adventure games, some horror games use dynamic music that can adapt to the player's actions or the game's events which can help to create a more immersive and reactive horror experience.

- **Platformer** is a genre where gameplay approaches can be wildly different, so it's difficult to make many blanket statements or precisely quantify how a music system will behave. Examples include *Super Mario Bros., Sonic the Hedgehog, and Donkey Kong Country.* There's usually a map and usually some kind of goal to reach (whether it's visible or not). Many platform games feature music that is upbeat and energetic, with catchy melodies and fast-paced rhythms. Many modern platform games also incorporate music that is inspired by the classic 8-bit soundtracks of *Days Gone* by. These chiptune-style tracks often feature simple, catchy melodies and the distinctive sound of old-school synthesizers, and sound chips. Platformers are in some ways the bread and butter of gaming; classic, familiar, and new all at the same time.

HERE'S SOME BRIEF EXAMPLES

- *Crash Bandicoot 4* (**2020 Toys for Bob/Activision**) is a 3D platformer that is the latest in the ongoing series, and has deceptively simple music driven by the various sections of the map. The music is heavily influenced by the music of the original trilogy. This update uses the same instruments and musical motifs, but adds an original flair to create a new, modern sound. The score is primarily orchestral, with a focus on percussion and brass instruments. The composer also incorporated themes and motifs from the game's story and characters into the music. For example, each of the game's playable characters has their own theme that plays when they are on screen, and the music for each level is tailored to match the environment and challenges that the player will face. Arriving at the end of each section can alter the music on beat, but there's no winning stinger at the end of completing a level. There are some short cutscenes as well, but the emphasis seems mainly focused on gameplay.

- *Celeste* (**Matt Makes Games**) is a challenging story driven 2D platformer with a romantic chiptune-inspired soundtrack. It is obvious that the designers really want you to hear the main theme, which essentially plays uninterrupted throughout gameplay, while you try and fail numerous times to clear its levels. As you progress, each level features its own unique soundtrack. The music in Celeste is designed to reflect the game's themes of struggle and personal growth, with the theme becoming more intense and urgent as the player progresses. As for function, the music doesn't pause much, except briefly for big achievement moments where it fades out and back in. It also changes in unexpected ways as the player gets to certain parts of a level or after meeting certain characters. There are occasionally cutscenes that sometimes feature the same theme.

- *Bit.Trip Runner* (**2010 Gaijin Games**) is a rhythm-based platformer that uses a very basic retro art style reminiscent of early Atari 2600 games. The music is a fusion of chiptune and rock, characterized by upbeat electronic melodies, heavy use of 8-bit sound effects, and frenetic drum beats. It is designed to match the fast-paced gameplay, with the rhythm and tempo of the music often dictating the timing of the player's jumps and other actions. Bit.Trip forces you to jump, slide, and duck your way to victory as your character sprints at hypersonic speeds fiendishly in sync to the background track. The game literally runs on music and interactively rewards the player by adding additional instrumental parts and timbral layers as they pass various obstacles and stages. As you run, the soundtrack becomes larger and fuller, and even adds distorted encouraging VO clips to keep you moving forward. Player actions also trigger notes that harmonize in time to level themes. You literally build the music as you play the game. Levels get progressively harder and more involved as the game unfolds and when you reach a new world the soundtrack transforms with it. Each level is not tremendously long – when you fail (and you will), the game will fade down the music, place your character at the beginning and start the music again. This style of melodically and rhythmically timed gameplay is addictive and truly places the music at the center of design. It also provides composers with a unique and fun challenge.

TRANSITIONS ARE HARD

Moving from place to place in a game can be a challenge for composers. In fact, dealing with transitions is one of the major differences between linear and non-linear music. As you can see from all the different genres and styles listed in the previous section, there are a myriad of ways to design and program a game, and each one will change the way the music is triggered. Computers often have to load all sorts of data as we play. Programmers must figure out how music will be delivered and stored for each gameplay scheme. Music loaded up all at once may overtax the CPU and cause the game to crash. Streaming music into the game in the background can help to alleviate this problem but may also cause the CPU to hesitate and leave bits of silence. Understanding how music is fed into the system brings the composer face to face with understanding form, structure, and transitions.

To proactively address this, solving problems compositionally (*IE without programmers*) is a great first step. Instead of someone else figuring out how to create smooth transitions from your music, it is always best for the composer to wrestle with the issue first and compose tracks that will work naturally and organically.

Music Analysis – *Ori and the Blind Forest*

It's a good idea and an excellent practice when playing a game or watching it, to analyze how the music system behaves. This is done by observing the frequency, function, and length of transitions, and creating a document that clearly delineated the sequence of musical events. Doing this will not only increase your appreciation of the fine work taking place in your favorite games, but will also give you the tools you need to analyze your own game projects and communicate your ideas clearly and effectively to developers.

Let's take a closer look at *Ori and the Blind Forest*, a superb and stunningly beautiful 2015 platform game developed by Moon Studios and published by Microsoft Studios. Ori is actually specifically classified as a "Metroidvania" which is a subgenre of platform games combining elements of the games *Metroid* and *Castlevania* into a portmanteau that uses both RPG and adventure elements. It features a strong storyline, leveling up, a large map, and platform mechanics. The game is a great one to analyze, as it features a cascade of transitions that deftly move between in game cinematics and game play.

The soundtrack was wonderfully composed by Gareth Coker, and implemented by the team at Moon Studios directly inside the Unity game engine, and with no audio middleware involved. Now as discussed, in this case, we're not going to analyze the musical nature of the score. Here, our interest is on how the music changes from place to place, and section to section based on in game events.

Here's a breakdown of the first 10–15 minutes of gameplay. Note that this analysis is formulated from watching the gameplay only, and may not completely accurately reflect how the designers organized the music system:

Ori and the Blind Forest – *Beginning of the Game – Music Only*

1. The game opens with a cutscene of a large luminescent tree in a storm. Words appear on the screen detailing the story as a remembered event, all part of a prolog before the gameplay actually begins in earnest. The storm's violence blows a bright object out of the tree, through the clouds and flutters its way, eventually sailing past a lone creature sitting on a rocky outcropping. The creature gets up to investigate this strange object.

2. At this point, roughly 57 seconds in, gameplay begins and the user can take control of the creature, called Naru, but can only move it to the right towards the resting place of the object. This is a nonlinear moment, but we're not in full game mode, as the game only allows limited player control (there are several such moments of semi-control in the prolog, as you'll see). The player could move slow or fast, or even potentially pause for several seconds. To work within this indeterminate time frame, the music needs to loop until some action or event makes it change. What's really cool about this transition is the fact that while the first piece of music is dying out, the interactive piece of music begins. This is a quite elegant compositional technique that uses the very nature of the music itself to create smoothly overlapping transitions. The opening cutscene music is rubato and the use of the ending decay on the last note leaves the perfect amount of space for the gameplay music.

This change from the cutscene to the loop can be indicated in a shorthand like this:

- **0:00 Opening cutscene music plays until ending at 1:01**

- **0:57 gameplay_musicLoop01 (starting before cutscene music finishes).**

3. The gameplay music loops for as long as it takes Naru to get to the spot where the object lands, which is revealed to be Ori. Then at 1:22, the next music section begins and the game's control of the cutscene resumes. If you listen very carefully, you will notice that the cutscene loop gets cut off as it changes to the next cue, which finishes around 1:35.

   We can indicate it like so:

- **0:57 gameplay_musicLoop01 continues until 1:22**

- **1:22 on trigger, cue loop quick crossfade to discovery_endTheme > scene end at 1:36**

- **1:36 crossfade to opening_cutscene_musicloop01**

4. The screen fades to black, and we transition back into a scene of Ori lying in a bed in Naru's burrow. Ori wakes up and jumps down, and at 2:01 player control is resumed, this time over Ori, as the light, floating music that started the scene continues. Again as the player moves Ori to the far right entrance of the burrow, the scene fades out and as it fades back in, control is given back to the game, and the music transitions with a cymbal swell into a full-fledged sunny theme at 2:08 as Ori greets Naru happily and jumps on his back. It is possible that player control of Ori happens until jumping on Naru but it's not clear.

   This looks like this:

- **1:38 opening_cutscene_musicloop01**

- **2:07 On trigger cue, fade opening_cutscene_musicloop01 >**

- 2:07 transition_stinger_cymbal01 >

- 2:09 sunny_musicLoop01

5. At 2:22, we find another brief window of open ended player control with Naru and Ori together. This time they must walk to the right, and at 2:35, there is another change, this time we hear percussion that transitions into another part of the main theme as Ori and Naru together cross the water, to get to the trees to gather nuts. This goes on for a while as night falls and the music slows, and a new pensive theme emerges. This new music is melancholy and features a flute line.

Here's the shorthand:

- 2:09 sunny_musicLoop01 > location trigger at 2:35

- 2:35 on trigger, cue transition_stinger percussion1 >

- 2:36 sunny_musicTheme > ends at 3:07

- 3:04 on scene downward pan, overlap with treeCalling_music_loop

Take a moment to consider how much mileage the music gets from overlapping various sections together, where they elide so well with each other. The composer has carefully constructed moments like this by having the music fade out naturally and since the previous section was a cutscene, we know exactly how long that music section needs to be.

6. At 3:16 player control of Ori resumes, as Ori walks away from Naru carrying a load of nuts, answering the call of the tree. Now the player needs to walk Ori to the left, and once in the trigger area near the top of the hill at 3:42, the music transitions with a huge swell as the old tree calls out to Ori with a burst of light. Ori drops the nuts, and is soon picked up by Naru, who is frightened of the tree and perhaps a bit possessive of Ori. They both enter Naru's burrow as the scene closes.

Here's the event:

- 3:42 treeCalling_music_loop > fade out

- 3:42 on trigger cue, transition stinger huge_swell01 > ends at 3:45

- 3:43 end theme > scene end at 3:56

7. The cutscene fades back in at 3:57, this time in a montage of sorts indicating that time is passing and the food is running out. At the same time, the music gets slower, sparser, and more wistful as Naru tries and fails to forage for more food. Naru comes back to give the last nut to Ori and falls asleep. Ori then jumps down and tries to look for food.

Event:

- **3:56 somber_musicTheme > ends at 4:23**

- **4:23 hope_never_came_musicTheme (no pause) > ends at 5:36**

- **5:36 oriGoesOut_musicTheme (no pause)**

This whole section is set and perfectly timed. Nothing interactive is happening here, but it's obvious that the first theme returns and drops in intensity from the previous scene. It seems to end followed by the even more somber music accompanying the montage of Naru searching for food and then Ori going out starts a third and more hopeful theme.

8. Eventually Ori manages to find more nuts, high up in a tree that Naru failed to reach earlier. At 6:04 limited player control of Ori resumes. Again, this is limited to walking towards Naru's burrow with a brief ghostly flashback of happier times. Once in the burrow, the scene shifts and as Ori gets closer, a small transition to quite sparse music triggers as Ori slowly realizes that Naru has passed away and curls up to sleep as the scene fades out.
   Event:

- **6:07 on trigger cue crossfade to oriBringsNuts_musicloop >**

- **6:45 on trigger cue, transition to percussion_stinger ending 6:50 >**

- **6:49 naruDies_ending > scene end at 7:22**

9. We fade back in on a bereaved Ori under complete musical silence. The text indicates that Ori must leave Naru, an orphan once again. The scene fades out, and at 7:54, the cutscene fades back in playing a delicate and melancholy theme as Ori struggles and gives up. Another theme emerges, gains momentum and comes to a huge climax, as the camera pulls out to show the entire location with the tree in the background. The scene fades out again and then more text appears, recounting to us that Ori was revived in a new age. As Ori passes, the music ends, and then the last track with a huge crescendo plays.
   Event:

- **7:55 ori_searchingForMyLight > ends 9:26**

- **9:30 panOut_hugeTheme scene end at 10:15 >prolog concludes**

10. A musical ambience starts at 10:15 as the gameplay fades in. After a brief moment where Ori spawns in, the main theme begins and player control of Ori is fully enabled. The player moves Ori around, running into obstacles and there's a point at 11:05 where Ori dies but the music does not respond. Platformers require a lot of

coordination and running into obstacles or missing jumps and dying is a very common occurrence, and rather than discouraging players with a negative stinger, the game instead fades out and in a while the music stays constant.

Event:

- **10:15 ambienceIntro01 > overlap to gameplayMain_musicloop01**

11. At 11:35, our first genuine achievement: fanfare/stinger comes in over the top of the music bed as Ori finds an Energy Cell. Note that the music doesn't pause or change during this moment, the stinger is musical and correspondingly harmonizes with the music loop.

Event:

- **11:35 energycell_stinger**

Keep in mind here that the game is NOT concerned with timing here. It plays the stinger on an action. The times given here are just for reference.

12. At 11:54, the first combat happens in the game and very quickly the music crossfades to battle music. This transition happens in a fairly jarring way. No stinger is heard here, as the player is defeated, the game starts again from the last save point and does repeat the same sequence of musical events. Then the creature attacking is defeated, and a quick stinger plays.

Event:

- **11:53 on combat, fade out gameplayMain_musicloop01 >**
- **11:53 start battleMain_musicloop01**
- **12:12 on monster dead, fade out battleMain_musicloop01**
- **12:13 play deadStinger01 > ends at 12:15**

13. Immediately after the monster is defeated, Ori picks up another item, a bit of Spirit Light. The transition here is either tied to the end of the music when the monster is defeated, or the pickup item makes its own sound when it spawns before it's picked up. Either way the pitch of this item is designed to harmonize with the key center of the gameplay loop, which continues roughly where it left off. The stinger is overlaid on top and is louder in volume, with a decay that smoothly leads in, without transitioning, to the music loop. There's not really much of a need to notate this as no transition actually happens. But it does show the desire of the game developers to make many of the sound effects in the game musical in nature.

Event:

- **12:17 play Spirit Light pickup**

14. At around 12:26, a subtle transition takes place to another loop as Ori gets close to the area where a very important item the player will need will be discovered.
Event:

- **12:26 gameplayMain_musicloop01 >**

- **12:26 on trigger cue crossfade >**

- **12:27 gameplaySeinPickup_musicloop01**

    Note that music is sort of hovering here, as if it's waiting for something.

15. At 12:38 the player picks up another item, which turns out to be Sein, the light and eyes of the Spirit Tree. The previous loop fades out, and a long triumphant stinger plays.
Event:

- **12:38 gameplaySeinPickup_musicloop01 >**

- **12:38 on trigger cue fadeout >**

- **12:39 stinger03_seinPickupTheme (ends at 12:55)**

16. At 13:06, as the text intro for Sein comes to a close, a quick intro stinger leads into much more intense combat music. Since Ori now has Sein as a companion, the player has gained a significant attack capability since Sein can attack and defeat monsters. This happens until 13:30, where a percussion stinger announces the victory, as the combat music crossfades back to the main gameplay loop. Event:

- **13: 06 on seinIntro end > stingerIntro_combat02 (ends 13:09)>**

- **13 :08 battleMain_musicLoop02 >**

- **13:30 on monsters dead, playdeadStinger02 >**

- **13:32 crossfade to > gameplayMain_musicloop01**

17. There aren't any more significant events that transition the music in the rest of the playthrough for this video clip, but there are several moments when the player opens the map or the skill tree window and the music drops down in volume considerably. This is a directly player controlled event, as a button or key is pressed to activate the window and upon return to gameplay, the music returns to its original volume level.

This type of detailed analysis will help to hone your awareness of transitions and how they manifest during gameplay, and you'll notice that even in well-regarded games like this one, the systems involved may not result in completely smooth transitions every time. Nonetheless, it is a valuable tool for understanding how music unfolds over time. The more of this you do, the more you will relate to the ebb and flow of gameplay and start to create music that fits hand in glove with the game's architecture.

The Big Takeaway: As we begin composing for an interactive environment we must not only take into account all the issues we have discussed previously but we now enter into a realm where our music must match the way the game is designed. Form follows function and composition must not happen in a vacuum. Transitions can be hard to navigate; getting from point A to point B can be a challenge but, by using the analytical tools at our disposal we begin to understand how to construct music that fits hand in glove with the game itself. As we have discussed previously, interactivity and indeterminacy are fundamental to game music, as a result we come up against a whole host of new and unique problems to solve. These are the fundamental issues that separate the art of game composition from film, TV, and other forms of linear media. Just like in film, our music must highlight key moments and support the action on screen, we must also at the same time support the system on which it is built. It is always best to solve these problems compositionally, through the structure and form of your music. The more we do that, the less we will have to rely on audio post editing and implementers to make things right. Let us try our best to get it right the first time and not have to "Fix it in the mix."

Discussion Questions: Why does form follow function in game scoring? How does a game's style affect its music? How do transitions work in games? Why are transitions hard to deal with? What are some practical solutions for dealing with transitions? Why does a composer have to know about all these game play styles? Why is analyzing a game's music system important?

TERMS

- **Form:** The visible shape or configuration of something.

- **Form Follows Function:** Is a principle of design associated with late 19th- and early 20th-century architecture and industrial design in general, which states that the shape of a building or object should primarily relate to its intended function or purpose.

- **Style:** A distinctive appearance, typically determined by the principles according to which something is designed.

- **Narrative:** An account of connected events; a story.

- **Sound Design:** The craft of creating an overall sonic palette for a piece of art.

- **Diegetic:** Sound that occurs within the context of the game and can be heard by the characters.

- **Programmer:** A person who writes computer programs.

- **Algorithm:** A procedure used for solving a problem or performing a computation. Algorithms act as an exact list of instructions that conduct specified actions step by step in either hardware- or software-based routines.

- **Transitions:** To make a change or shift from one state, subject, place, etc. to another.

- **Game Music System:** Is a code base or set of instructions that define the behavior of how music is triggered.

- **Gameplay mechanics:** The rules that govern gameplay within a video game.

- **Game State:** The arrangement of all the variables and objects in a game at a particular moment.

- **Collider:** A collider component defines the shape of an object for the purposes of physical collisions.

- **Voxel:** In 3D computer graphics, a voxel represents a value on a regular grid in three-dimensional space.

- **Spatialise:** To localize something in three dimensional space.

- **Electroacoustic music:** A genre of Western art music in which composers use technology to manipulate the timbres of acoustic sounds.

- **Realism:** Representing a person, thing, or situation accurately or in a way that is true to life.

- **Abstraction:** Dealing with ideas rather than events.

- **Soundscape:** A sound or combination of sounds that forms or arises from an immersive environment.

- **Re-spawn:** To be given another life after dying.

- **FPS:** First-Person Shooter – an action-based 3D game where the view of the game comes from the player's viewpoint. Thus they can see their arms and/or legs.

- **TBS:** Turn-Based Strategy – gameplay proceeds in a turn-based, non-real-time manner. Strategy is usually concerned with overarching elements from the position of a leader or general, involving resources, production, and other non-military concerns in addition to military-based ones.

- **MMO:** Massive Multiplayer Online.

- **RTS:** Real-Time Strategy: gameplay proceeds in a real-time manner. Strategy is usually concerned with overarching elements from the position of a leader or general, involving resources, production, and other non-military concerns in addition to military-based ones.

- **RPG:** Role-Playing Game. Games that are based on pen, paper, and dice games like Dungeons And Dragons, where the player assumes the role

- **MMORPG:** Massive Multiplayer Online Role-Playing Game.

- **Sim:** Simulation Game. A game that simulates tasks in the real world, such as a flight simulator.

- **Platformer:** A subgenre of action games in which the core objective is to move the player character between points in an environment. Platform games are characterized by levels that consist of uneven terrain and suspended platforms of varying height that require jumping and climbing to traverse

- **Sandbox Game:** A style of game that provides players a great degree of creativity to interact with the environment, usually without any predetermined goal, or alternatively with a goal that the players set for themselves.

CHAPTER 7

Get in the Game: Applied Musical Concepts

Topic: Making the Leap into Game Space

- Learning Outcomes
- Game Engines
- Game Music Systems
- Game Music Analysis: *Persona 5*
- Game Music Analysis: *Tetris Effect*
- The Big Takeaway
- Discussion Questions
- Terms

Learning Outcomes

- Understanding game engines
- Differentiating between different types of game engines
- Understanding how music relates to game design
- Analyzing game music systems

DOI: 10.1201/9781003414728-9

DESIGNING MUSIC

As we start to focus more intently on the interactive aspect of gaming and how that affects music many questions of implementation and design start to arise. As composers, we should be aware of and have a basic understanding of the games we play and work on. Each one has its own specific way to handle music and sound. But beyond that, we need to start to think differently – we need to start thinking like game designers. But what exactly does that mean? How will understanding a game's design help me write music?

To answer this question, let's consider the very nature of games. Unlike film, there is a different sense of time in a game play session. There may be multiple ways that the same level can unfold and there can be multiple outcomes as well. Quite often in the real world of game development, producers will treat the production and integration of music just like they do in film for example – as a last-minute addition after editing has been completed. While this might work for linear media (although far from ideal), doing so in any kind of complex non-linear media can be immensely challenging and a recipe for disaster. Even a small game may contain multiple approaches and outcomes, and this will invariably create significant issues. The most likely result of this scenario is that the music requests and in-game usage will fall down to the lowest interactive model: static looping tracks that play without variation. We have all experienced games where the music becomes so repetitive that no matter how good it sounds initially, turning it off seems like a good idea. We have also all played games where the music simply cuts off abruptly in the middle of phrases, with no transition, as the game progresses from screen to screen.

These problems can be alleviated by including the music team, including composer/s at the start of production – this way music can be fundamentally integrated from story to interactive design. This also ensures that music will be part of the iteration and development process. The worst case scenario is the one in which audio teams are brought in and given a single week or other absurdly short time, to create and implement all of the music. In some cases, this may be music that was written much earlier in the development process, and is simply edited at the last minute to make it fit into the game. Unfortunately, this worst case scenario is actually very real and still happens all the time!

Let's examine the game *Uncharted 4: A Thief's End* from Naughty Dog Games, an action adventure title with a strong narrative and many challenges to overcome. In Chapter 10, there is a scene at an ancient ruined bridge that helps to elucidate just how vitally important pre-planning and implementation of the music and system are. During gameplay, there are just too many mercenaries to attack unless the player is either (A) a good combat fighter or (B) good at being stealthy, which means that there are two levels of music that must be available at all times. If you approach by stealth the music is quite spare and sparse, with only an occasional stinger at the point where you eliminate a sentry or lookout. However, once you decide to go all out, the music is right there with you, providing a propulsive rhythmic background as you enter into the fray. This kind of tight integration is triggered by player choice and must be taken into account during the design process in order to work. This is only possible if there is a music professional or musically inclined designer in the room during the development process.

Early in the development process as the GDD is being written, character descriptions, interactive flow charts, and gameplay loops and scenarios are being discussed and decided on. This may be everything from the reward system to specific locations and player interactions. In the case of a music game there may be style and instrumental choices that are involved as well. Composers should be able to read these documents and suggest creative ideas that will help to improve quality, simplify the development pipeline, and ingrain the music into the overall concept.

Here is an example of a typical game play loop and user flow diagram (Figure 7.1). Simply by looking at this the compositional wheel in your mind should already be spinning and questions should be popping up. Is there music on the preloader? Is that possible or necessary? Is the splash screen a title screen with a big melodic flourish or does the music here need to be subdued and pensive to get the player ready for the next stage? How will the music move from the splash screen to the story screen, and what kind of transitions are possible? What are simple stingers that fire off? How long should they be? Are they tempo aware? As you can see, these are all very important questions that will set the tone for the whole experience and require creative discussion. All of these questions once answered will significantly influence the music you write. From the start of the game design process, designers, programmers, animators, and other team members are plotting and planning. It may be cliche to say, but including music early on in the design process will make it possible to create transformative music that will deeply immerse the player in the game world.

Now let's get a bit more into the nuts and bolts and talk more about the particular tools that are used to build the games themselves, and that's a game engine.

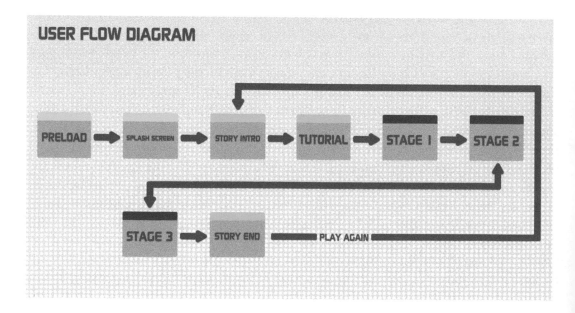

FIGURE 7.1 Flow chart/diagram.

GAME ENGINES

Game engines emerged once gaming platform hardware started to standardize, most prominently around the PC platform. Initially they were considered in-house, meaning proprietary and internal to each game developer or publisher, not commercially available for outside companies to license or use. In-house game engines are still in use at large companies like Electronic Arts, which use its own Frostbite engine, and Nintendo still uses its own game engine as well. These are just a couple of examples, and there are many others.

Starting in the 1990s however, some game developers realized that revenue could be made from licensing their game engine to other outside companies, starting with id Software's Doom engine, which debuted in 1995. This was followed by Epic Games, which released the Unreal Engine in 1998, many others followed after that. There are now dozens, if not hundreds, of game engines available, and many of them are completely free and open source, or if commercial, have very generous licenses that allow you to use them for free, provided your game's revenue doesn't exceed a certain amount.

A game engine is constructed around a code base and usually some kind of GUI (Graphic User Interface) that allows you to import assets, create specific assets, and then edit the characteristics of these in the engine. Depending on the engine, the ability to create some types of content may be limited. In most cases a game engine is a place to import content, especially binary content. This includes images, 3D models, animations, and yes, music and audio files fit into this category. Binary files cannot be edited, so music and audio are usually not editable inside most game engines, even if other types of media can be. There are however noteworthy exceptions to be discussed.

In general, the environment of a game engine is the place where the developer or programmer combines various assets and figures out how they relate to each other. This is done using some type of scripting or programming language, which can range from visual node-based dataflow-oriented environments that are connected by cords, on up to full-fledged low level C++ or C# code. Game engines, especially 3D-based ones, will often have very deep and involved ways to deal with lighting, shading, texture configuration, visual effects, physics interactions, animation, and rendering, which means controlling what's seen on screen and when. They may also have ways to deal with audio, from mixing, to 3D placement, to adding effects and automating them. Finally and most importantly, the game engine is where the game is built – i.e. where the code is compiled into a binary application that plays on whatever platform it's been configured to play on. A game at the end of the day is an application, and something has to make it into one, and that something is a game engine.

Let's look at a few game engines available, bearing in mind that this is a very short list and there are a lot of engines out there to choose from, especially if you're making 2D games.

Unity 3D Overview

Unity Technologies was founded in 2004 by David Helgason, Nicholas Francis, and Joachim Ante in Copenhagen, Denmark after their first game, *GooBall*, failed to gain success. The three recognized the value in engine and tools development and set out to create an engine that any and all could use for an affordable price. Their stated goal has been, in their own words, "to democratize game development," in other words, to make powerful game development tools accessible for everyone. Unity is royalty-free, meaning that you completely own what you make with it and that you don't need to pay any additional fees to them, even if your game is earning money. There is a free version as well as Pro and Plus versions that offer more functionality (mainly through services) and do cost money. Successive versions have offered more features as they have been released. Interestingly, the first version of Unity was actually written as a Mac OS X application! Unity 1.0 debuted at the Apple Worldwide Developers Conference in 2005. As of July 2021 Unity boasted over 2 million developers, and is responsible for roughly half of mobile game titles and slightly more than half of AR and VR titles, though as always, these figures may change over time with competition from other engines.

Unity is functionally similar to other game engines in the way it handles music and sound. It can support multiple formats, 3d sound, and spatial and ambisonic audio, and importing audio is fairly easy and hassle free. Once inside the engine, audio can also be easily previewed and tested, but not edited. Unity also provides a basic mixer that is fairly easy to use and understand as it looks like a typical sound board. With it you can set up multiple buses and even create snapshot mixes for each section or level of a game. Unity also comes with a suite of built in effects such as reverb, delay, and compression just to name a few. They are nothing to write home about and in most cases will not sound nearly as good as professional plugins that come with your digital audio workstation, but they do exist. The plugin interface varies from effect to effect and is not the most intuitive to work with, but can be decently effective in certain situations. Of course, using internal plugins always comes at a cost to the CPU and that must be kept in mind.

Unreal Engine

Unreal is the oldest game engine still actively in use after more than two decades! It is frequently updated and the Editor is now cross-platform, working on both Mac and PC with equal effectiveness. Furthermore, Unreal is completely free to use and open source. You can also distribute many commercial projects without paying any fees to Epic Games, including custom projects delivered to clients, linear content (such as films and television shows), and any product that earns no revenue or whose revenue falls below the royalty threshold, currently set at 5%.

Unreal offers a complete set of tools for creating a game, many of which are not available in other game engines, things such as visual scripting and mesh editing. Games like *Bioshock Infinite*, many versions of *Tom Clancy's Splinter Cell*, the *Borderlands* series, and *Batman: Arkham City* were developed in Unreal. Although Unreal was developed for use on PC and console games, it has recently made inroads into mobile and the web via WebGL. Still, generally, Unreal is considered a fairly high-end engine requiring a significant amount of graphics resources, especially to draw high quality imagery with its new rendering features like Nanite and Lumen. Due to its scalability and integration with other services, it is gradually becoming the tool of choice for AAA game developers as well as film studios and VFX houses going for maximum visual quality.

In terms of exciting developments for musicians and audio designers, the audio engine has received some special attention in the last few updates, thanks to their audio lead Aaron McLeran and his team at Epic pushing consistently for improving it. MetaSounds are essentially sound graphs that define the flow of audio. They can be created using a visual scripting language called Blueprint, which allows developers to create complex audio behaviors by connecting nodes that represent various sound sources, effects, and filters. MetaSounds can also be used to dynamically manipulate sound parameters, such as pitch and volume, in response to game events or player actions. By using procedural sound generation techniques, developers can create complex audio effects that take up less memory than traditional sound assets, allowing for more efficient use of system resources. You will find sample accurate timing, great for all of those rhythm-based shooter games, as well as full-fledged audio synthesis in the engine, which is a first one. For example, a developer could use MetaSounds to create a virtual synthesizer or sampler that generates music in real-time, based on player input or game events. Overall, it is worth checking it out. The system is fairly intuitive, not overly complex for composers to understand, and the commitment to continued development is refreshing.

CryENGINE

This is a powerful game engine developed by Crytek, a German video game company. It was first introduced in 2004 and was mainly bred for extremely high FPS gaming performance on PC and console platforms, though it does also support Android and iOS. The SDK and editor tools are free to download and use for non-commercial purposes, but the editor software is only for Windows. Crytek, the maker of the engine, also offers a monthly subscription that is royalty free. However, the source code is not fully open, and only available for full licensees of the product. All of the Crytek games like *Crysis*, *Far Cry*, and *Ryse: Son of Rome* are made using the engine and the company has continued to update and improve the offerings over the years.

As for music and sound, the engine does support multiple audio formats, and sound effects and music can be integrated without too much fuss. There is also support for features like spatial audio and 3D sound along with real-time mixing and processing of ambience and reverbs. You can define the acoustic properties of different locations, such as rooms or outdoor environments and by using what is called Audio Sandbox you can also preview audio effects and spatial audio settings, which helps in fine-tune assets. The Sandbox includes the Audio Controls Editor (ACE). This allows for flexible, drag and drop style creation, and connection of music through Events, Switches, States, and RTPCs. Additionally, the ACE includes a search and filtering component, making it fast and simple to find, view, or edit many audio events.

Godot Engine

An up and comer to the gaming engine world, Godot is now in the top 10 of gaming engines according to the Gamedesigning.org website, which is mainly geared towards indie developers. Although it started life as an in-house proprietary game engine, the developers later open sourced it under the very permissive MIT license, so it's entirely free to use and contribute to. Since being open sourced, it has gone through numerous updates which have added great features like visual scripting, and a flexible animation system suitable for 2D or 3D games. It's still not as commonly used as any of the top three mentioned but it definitely deserves to be in the running as a friendly game engine for newbies, indies, and hobbyists alike. One of the unique features of the Godot Engine is its support for collaborative development, with built-in tools for version control and asset management. The Godot Engine is also designed to be customizable, with a plugin system that allows developers to extend the functionality of the engine or create their own tools and features.

Much like the others, Godot supports a range of audio formats, and provides tools for importing and managing audio assets. It also includes support for spatial sound and reverb effects that run in real time. In terms of implementation, it is good to note that the engine includes an API for working with sound, as well as a visual editor for creating and editing audio. You can adjust volume levels, apply filters and effects, and add spatialization inside the framework. Similar to Unity, it features an audio mixer section called an audio bus (also referred to as an audio channel). Music and sound can be modified and re-routed through an audio bus and each bus features a volume meter as well as various effects that can be applied. Again, these are not going to be as high quality as you can get in your DAW, but they are available and like any engine will tax the CPU.

GAME MUSIC SYSTEMS

A typical game engine has an awful lot of things it has to do. In essence, it has to run an entire virtual world, complete with animations, shading and rendering, visual effects, sound effects, and of course, a lot of music as well. It must coordinate the overall interactive logic of a game. It needs to know both the location of all the rich media assets (including music, sound effects, and voice-over files) as well as when (and when not) to call them. Of course a game engine doesn't intrinsically "know" anything. It has to be programmed to do all of these tasks. But the engine is capable of doing them, given the right instructions.

Even in a small game, this can add up to a large amount of data that needs to be coordinated. In a large game the scope can be most impressive, verging into tens or hundreds of thousands of assets. In all cases, game engines are software packages that make games possible, and it takes a talented and dedicated group of designers to program the engine to do all this work efficiently. Now, in the case of music, it's covered under the category of audio files, and all game engines are not created equal—different game platforms have different capabilities in terms of how they play back audio, and how they manage it. Programmers will utilize the game engine's features and create systems to trigger audio efficiently and maximize the resources they will take up in the game.

As a subset of the main audio system, there is also usually some way to determine specifically how and when music gets handled, so we come to the topic of how a game's music system can be designed. These systems can be dynamically responsive to player actions, creating immersive and interactive experiences. Some game music systems even use procedural generation techniques to create music on the fly, without pre-composed tracks. These systems use algorithms to generate music that is responsive to the game state, creating a unique musical experience every time the game is played.

Game events and game states can be triggers for musical change. We can really see this in action by breaking down exactly how the music in a game is managed. By analyzing popular games with a specific interest and view into the music system, we can gain an even deeper understanding. Let's examine how this worked for the fifth in a series of well-known Japanese role-playing games called *Persona*.

Persona 5 is the most recent version of a very popular JRPG (*Japanese RPG*) game based on the Shin Megami Tensei franchise. Released in 2017 by Atlus and P-Studio, the overall look and feel of the game is a flashy, bold cartoon style, and the music soundtrack for it, created by Shoji Meguro, is more contemporary and modern than its predecessors. The soundtrack features a smaller band, not a large orchestra, with rhythm section, percussion, guitar, electric piano, and organ. Strings appear from time to time creating a fun retro disco feel. The style is more funky and hip, and many tracks feature a vocalist as well. Additionally, there are several alternate mixes that trigger depending on the situation.

The basic plot is that you're a high school student recently forced to move to a new area – you're working off probation from a recent incident in which you were unjustly framed, and meet student friends at the school, where you discover dirty and corrupt dealings among the faculty. But you also find out that you and your new buddies can go into an alternate reality (*called the Metaverse, ironically enough*) where you can change the hearts of these corrupt people by defeating enemies (*Shadows*) with a newfound spiritual power called a Persona – hence the name of the series. So all through the game there are two realities – that of the real world, and that of the Metaverse, and you are constantly popping in and out of locations in both of these realities.

Music Systems' Analysis: *Persona 5*

The best way to explain how the music works in this game is to understand that it functions as a relatively large system of comparatively simple interactions. In general, the music in the game is either changed by location or some other significant game event. All of the music tracks are looped, so they never really end, and instead simply fade out once the next action happens. Interestingly, there does not appear to be any use of cross fading between pieces of music. One music loop fades out on an action or event, and then the next track starts up. There are 113 music tracks that can play inside the game! But there's not a lot of programmed intelligence to the system. In most cases you will rarely be in a location for more than 2 minutes, so most tracks are not much longer than 3–4 minutes, and many are shorter.

Let's utilize a mixer channel analogy to explain the different categories, keeping in mind that we only ever hear one music track play at a time. What we hear will change depending on what we do, or the events that occur in the game's storyline. Using this channel analogy, here's how it basically breaks down:

Channel 1 - Open World *(Real)* - The actual world of 2016-era urban Tokyo gets several musical themes, which can be triggered by events or by entering specific locations.

- **Evening and Morning Theme** - This theme called "Beneath the Mask" is heard the most frequently when daily life is occurring and may or may not be affected by location in the real world. So going into the subway, or just arriving at school, or being in your apartment in the evening triggers the same music throughout. However, the theme appears in a few different versions. During the (*rather long*) prolog, the theme is played by a full band without the vocals but once you get past the prolog and into the early part of the game proper, the theme is reduced to a solo keyboard. This theme will return to the full instrumental mix at some point dependent on the player's story progress. Also this theme acts as a fallback in the evening or morning after any quests are finished and you're returning home, or traveling to school.

- **In Class Theme** - The game will put you in classrooms with different teachers each day, in order to give you an opportunity to level up your Knowledge stats.

- **Afternoon (After School) Theme** - This theme is more upbeat and funky, and takes place after school when the group meets on the rooftop of the school to determine plans.

- **Airsoft Shop and Doctor's Office** - These two locations deserve special mention as they are places to buy, sell and upgrade gear, and to purchase health potions, respectively.

- **Various Other Event or Location Themes** - This category can be quite large and is either dependent on a quest storyline or a location. So you might hear different music in the evening in your apartment if you're doing a special activity or you're on a quest. It also seems as if open world exploration can trigger different tracks and some locations have no music at all. Once you return to the streets, a different music track will trigger and the soundtrack will change once again.

- **Diegetic Music in Some Shops** - There are a couple of locations in Shibuya Central street map where you will hear "canned" music coming from the speakers in the ceiling. The music is actually mixed, filtered, and processed to sound as if it's coming from that location though it's not 3D.

Channel 2 - Alternate World (*aka Metaverse*) - The alternate world of *Persona 5* overlaps the real world, which you can travel to by warping or phasing out of the real world. This is where you will battle your enemies called Shadows, which you can do inside areas called Palaces or in the large procedural maze of subway tunnels called Mementos.

- **Exploration Loops** - When exploring Palaces or Mementos, you'll hear the exploration loop for that location a fair amount. These loops are groove based and can change depending on location, and the playlist for these seems limited.

- **Safe Room** - While exploring the indoor locations called Palaces, there are a few areas where enemies will never be present. Those are called Safe Rooms, and they have their own relaxed music. The soundtrack returns back to the Exploration loop once you depart.

- **Normal Combat Mode** - You can only enter combat mode while in the Metaverse if an enemy sees you or you decide to ambush them. Either way, it's a funky upbeat track with vocals and lyrics that gets you hyped up for a turn-based battle. Interestingly, most battles have the same music, so regardless of how powerful your enemies are, you get the same treatment. The exceptions are boss and sub-boss fights which do have different themes.

- **Victory** - Whenever you win a battle inside the Metaverse, the Combat music fades out, and a new music track starts up featuring electric piano and rhythm section. The game tallies your score, items, and any Level increases-this transition is the closest to an actual crossfade. Once finished, the music returns to the Exploration loop.

- **Game Management Screen Music** - The title screen has music, as does the title trailer in the game, these are encountered when you start the game and can be skipped if desired. Game management does not generally change the music that is playing. Compare this with Ori and Blind Forest where the soundtrack volume is considerably dimmed during user interface moments.

Channel 3 - Other Locations: These are places or even time periods that exist outside of either channel 1 or 2 and feature unique gameplay and musical qualities.

- **Velvet Room** - This one isn't the Metaverse, but it is a dream world of its own that is introduced in the storyline via cutscenes and eventually acts as a lab of sorts to help the player develop alternate Personas. It features a beautiful and romantic theme with piano and wordless singing.

- **Interrogation - Present Day** - In the game's "present" time, you're actually detained and being interrogated by the assistant DA about the doings of your "gang" called the Phantom Thieves. Most of the actions in the game happen as you are actually recalling past events of the last few months. However, the game will switch to the interrogation cinematic scene to highlight various plot points. This functions more like a "flash-forward" cutscene, since most of your activities with your friends actually take place beforehand. There's a suspenseful string orchestra music loop going playing as you are grilled concerning the group's activities. This music will fade out when the flash-forward ends and you return to normal game activity.

That's the rough high level description and basic layout of the music system for Persona 5. Notice that we did this analysis without getting into granular detail. Examining the way music is treated in a general overview like this can be very useful in helping any composer develop a syntax for how music systems function. Although the playback of tracks is not particularly complex in this example (*tracks start, loop, and fade out usually*) the decision on which track to play at what time and how they relate to specific story events can be more involved. This is a type of branching or horizontal sequencing structure that creates a large system of basically simple interactions.

Let's try another game music system – this time using a recent adaption of a well-known handheld arcade game.

Game Music Analysis: *Tetris Effect*

Tetris Effect is an update of the original block-dropping arcade game from 1984. Released in 2018 by Monstars and Resonair, the game gets its name from a phenomena of the same name, where intense players of the popular shifting puzzle game (*originally invented by*

Russian game designer and programmer Alexey Pajitnov) would see falling blocks even when away from the screen or when sleeping or dreaming. Co-producer Tetsuya Mizuguchi, already well-known for his earlier work on the rhythm-based rail shooter *Rez* had always wanted to create a unique rhythm-based version of *Tetris*, but was held back by the copyright ownership of the title by Electronic Arts. However once ownership of the *Tetris* copyright was sold to game designer Henk Rogers, Mizuguchi approached him with his unique idea and secured his permission to go ahead. The game was released on the PlayStation 4, and also supports VR mode on PC and Quest-based standalone headsets.

The soundtrack is mostly composed by Hydelic, a composing duo of Noboru Mutoh and Takako Ishida, who both worked previously on the remastered and extended version of *Rez, Rez Infinite*, but with a few other composers and collaborators occasionally guesting on vocals. The 40-track soundtrack spans over two and a half hours of music in a variety of styles and approaches, though mostly tending towards an electronic and sample driven palette.

The game features a myriad of levels, each with its own trippy visual effects, driven by and reacting to the music composed by Hydelic. Just like in normal Tetris, the iconic four blocks (called **tetrominoes**) appear and the object of the game is to move each piece and place it in a line in order to clear at least the required number of block lines without running out of space due to too many blocks falling down within the game space.

Music Systems Analysis: *Tetris Effect*

Let's get into how this game organizes the music.

The first thing to highlight is that in *Tetris Effect*, gameplay alone drives what tracks play. There's no story or cutscenes and the music only changes when a level is cleared. This is a completely abstract puzzle game that displays consistent internal logic from level to level. That being said however, there's a lot of musical depth and complexity at work.

1. **It's All about the Lines:** The main organizing principle is how many lines have been cleared, the player goal is listed on the left side of the playing area. The level starts with single musical samples which may or may not be pitched depending on the sound palette. If they are pitched, they will be within a specific mode or key center, and are layered on top of a largely static background, such as a single chord or loop. The individual notes and samples are different and tied to gameplay actions, such as moving or placing a block. They are programmed to be tempo aware and always in time with the backing track. The notes often have small rhythmic delays to add to the trippy and chill quality of the soundtrack. Once you clear the required amount of lines, the music will quickly transition you to the next, usually very different sounding level.

2. **Push a Button, Get a Sound:** You can move, rotate, and place a puzzle piece, and doing so will trigger a unique musical note or sound effect. These are based on a preset rhythmic grid, and usually set to faster rhythmic values, such as sixteenth or eighth notes. Additionally, your game progress will change the notes/sounds that are triggered once the required number of lines has been completed.

Here Are Typical Tetris Actions:

    a. Pieces can be rotated into the proper orientation

    b. Pieces can be moved around one block at a time in any direction

    c. Pieces can be "soft dropped" where they will accelerate downwards into position

    d. Pieces can also be "hard dropped" where they will instantly be in position

       In regard to the first two actions (rotation and position) these generate randomized sounds based on the repeated triggering of button or key and are quantized to the rhythmic grid. There's a tendency in the music system to treat each of these as a separate timbre. So, rotation gets one timbre and position gets another. Also, the sounds assigned to these actions may change even in the middle of a game level once it hits a certain threshold. Hard dropping will always get a sound while soft dropping almost always does not.

3. **Line Clearing:** Each time a line is cleared you'll get a stinger that plays in time, and this lasts a few seconds. As goals are reached and a certain number of lines are cleared, the orchestration expands and more parts are added. This is a perfect example of parameter driven vertical mixing.

    a. The number of levels varies, but when a level is achieved (usually around 30%–50% of the total required lines) a variety of things can happen – the mix might change fairly quickly to a thicker texture, with a more prominent beat. Muting and unmuting of musical layers change the orchestration virtually instantly. Alternatively, vocal parts may be added to the mix and in some cases the entire track will transition to another key or tempo.

    b. As the number of cleared lines increases, the tension builds. There are usually at least 3 stages of intensity, though there can be more.

    c. Once it reaches or surpasses the line requirement, the game will play a custom stinger to end the music for that level, and another more generic explosion stinger (and the particle effect) will introduce the next level. Once this fades out the new music for the next level begins to play.

    d. Interestingly, and it can only be speculated, but this generic explosion stinger/transition might be used in order to help with asset load management. It seems reasonable and likely that the sound files/banks from the previous level that just ended, need to be unloaded from memory and the next level's media and sound banks must be streamed in, cued up, and loaded to be ready once the stinger has finished and faded out. Thus the stinger covers the transitions between the end of one level and the beginning of another.

4. **Sound Palette:** There are a wide variety of musical and even non-musical styles covered in the game. Some levels have very accessible EDM music in various subgenres, while others sound like found samples with a rhythmic twist to them. The visuals also provide a lot of variety.

5. **Get Into The ZONE:** There is also another feature called the ZONE. Basically, it's a way to rearrange rows in order to clear more of them. You build up the meter by clearing rows in clever ways. Once the meter is filled you can activate the ZONE. When you instigate this action, ALL music tracks become altered with a low pass filter and added reverb. The ZONE timer will eventually run out and return you back to the regular unfiltered music mix.

6. **Music Progression = Get Good:** A really important observation here – the music is ENTIRELY driven by your progress in clearing lines, which is in turn based on your skill playing Tetris, that is, arranging and placing the pieces (called Tetrominoes) to fit correctly.

    a. In *Tetris Effect*, if you do this quickly enough, you will create smooth natural transitions to different musical states.

    b. If you are an inexperienced *Tetris* player, however (like your humble authors), the result will be a lot of looping music that doesn't seem to change very quickly at all.

    c. So in the game, the player's expertise and level progress directly drive the pace of musical transitions. No progress – no transitions.

Of course as all of this is going on, you get lots of trippy visuals that react to the music in time as well as the changes in tension level – this is a similar design feature of many other action games.

Remember, as always, the devil is in the details. Many of these levels can change key or mode which can create some significant hurdles even with fancy middleware options available. So in addition to the composer, the implementer and programmer had a fair amount to manage in order to keep everything in sync – as a rule, game engines do NOT normally have very precise musical timing, which is why rhythm-based games can present a huge challenge. To compare this with Persona's system, here you have a small system of complex interactions.

This is a fairly cursory overview of what's going on with the music system. In this case the music and the game go hand in hand. The music emulates the elegant yet simple game design in a very logical and immersive way.

The Big Takeaway: Everything we do when composing for a game must relate to the structure and function of the project. These words of wisdom from game audio veteran and adaptive music composer for games, Guy Whitmore, sum things up very well:

"The differences between interactive music and adaptive music have more to do with the design of the game experience and the users' perception during the game, than with the techniques used to integrate the music. Interactive music occurs when a player is making gameplay decisions based on what he/she consciously hears in the music, and thus is reacting directly to how the music is behaving. But with adaptive music, the interaction is between the player and other aspects of the game design such as visuals and game mechanics. In theory, that definition seems fairly black-and-white, but in practice there's a spectrum that spans interactive and adaptive music, wherein most scores land somewhere between each extreme. So the key for composers is to be aware of how their score will be consciously (or subconsciously) perceived by players, and to be intentional about their music design, i.e. asking the question: where along the adaptive–interactive spectrum will the score ideally sit, in order to best serve the overall game design?

We'll get to see more examples of Guy's adaptive music designs at work in the next chapter.

Discussion Questions: What are the basic functions of a game engine? Why is it important for composers to understand how game engines work? What are the basic functions of a music system? How does the music system in *Persona 5* Work? How does the game *Tetris Effect* trigger music? Does examining the music system for a game help you to think more creatively about how you might organize your music, if yes how if no why not? Does music in a game have to relate to the structure of how the game is built? Can you imagine a music game that has no visuals? How would that system work?

TERMS

Game Engine: A software framework primarily designed for the development of video games and generally includes relevant libraries and support programs.

Music System: A framework to create and manage audio within video games. This is achieved by integrating with the game engine software to make a cohesive system.

Gameplay Loop: Any repetitive gameplay cycle that is designed to keep the player engaged with the game. Players perform an action, are rewarded, another possibility opens, and the cycle repeats.

Codebase: The complete body of source code for a software program, component or system. It includes all the source files needed to compile the software into machine code, including configuration files.

GUI: Graphical User Interface.

Scripting Language: A programming language that employs a high-level construct to interpret and executes one command at a time. In general, scripting languages are easier to learn and faster to code in than more structured and compiled languages such as C and C++.

Compiled Language: A programming language that is generally compiled and not interpreted. It is one where the program, once compiled, is expressed in the instructions of the target machine; this machine code is undecipherable by humans. Types of compiled language – C, C++, C#, CLEO, and COBOL.

Binary Files: A file whose contents consist of a sequence of eight-bit length bytes, and the data are not human-readable. An interpreter program or processor reads the information and performs the instructions from the file.

CHAPTER 8

Middleware Music Concepts and the Technical Composer

Topic: Incorporating Middleware with the Game Engine

- More on Middleware
- History, iMUSE and *The Curse of Monkey Island*
- The Code
- The Process
- Scenarios and Common Methods: Intensity, Proximity, Parameters, and Raycasting
- System Breakdown, Guy Whitmore and *Peggle 2*
- The Big Takeaway
- Discussion Questions
- Terms

Learning Outcomes

- Understanding audio and music middleware
- Differentiating between different types of middleware
- Understanding how middleware relates to composition workflow
- Analyzing middleware function in games

DOI: 10.1201/9781003414728-10

MORE ON THE CONCEPTUALIZATION AND APPLICATION OF AUDIO MIDDLEWARE

The creative application of audio middleware has become a given in the game industry. Today, composers should have at least some level of experience with the concepts and practical application of these programs. Becoming familiar with middleware can often seem daunting. These are quite expansive tool sets, and are meant to work with game engines and thus understanding the specific context of what you are trying to achieve becomes very important. Without a game to work on or an understanding of the right questions to ask, it's easy to get lost in a fog of YouTube videos and new terminology. Successful use of these tool sets is all about comprehending the context, not just pushing buttons.

There are several reasons why composers may want to learn about audio middleware:

1. **Concept:** Middleware in relation to game design is used in support of interactive and adaptive scores. Understanding the concepts and working hands-on with these programs can help support dynamic new ways of thinking and composing.

2. **Workflow:** Middleware platforms offer interactive tools for creating and defining musical behaviors. They also feature built-in support for various file formats, compression schemes, and platforms. This helps composers streamline workflow and increase efficiency when working with game design and programming teams. By understanding the capabilities and limitations, you will make more complete and informed decisions concerning the composition, design, and implementation of your music.

3. **Control:** Middleware when used effectively puts the power back in the hands of the composer. Composers end up taking more ownership of their music and how it functions in game. By using a GUI, composers are able to do things that programmers would usually be responsible for. Remember, those programmers may have no understanding of beats and bars or anything musical at all. Translating complex musical concepts to a non-musician can be frustrating at best. Make no mistake; middleware is helpful in bridging that gap; however, it also makes a lot more work for you. But, we are not afraid of hard work, right?!

4. **Jobs:** Many game companies, studios, and design houses are using audio middleware these days, and it's just a fact of life. Understanding middleware can in many cases make you more competitive in the job market and increase your chances of getting hired.

HISTORY, *THE CURSE OF MONKEY ISLAND*

Audio middleware began as an in-house development tool. Composers and sound designers, working together with programmers at top game companies, began to design tools to both increase their productivity as well as to open new vistas of dynamic and adaptive music and sound control. One prominent system was developed by Michael Land, Peter McConnell, and others while working for LucasArts, the now-defunct game publisher of memorable point and click adventure games such as *Day of the Tentacle*, *The Curse of Monkey Island*, and our personal favorite, *Grim Fandango*. Called *iMUSE* (Interactive MUsic Streaming Engine), it was developed in the early 1990s out of frustration with the limitations of previous audio systems. iMUSE allowed an unprecedented level of control over what was then MIDI-based music triggering sound banks, as the systems could not yet handle full resolution digital audio playback.

The iMUSE System dealt with some of the basic problems that composers are still facing today. Chiefly one of these is how to move from section to section, and place to place in a musically coherent way. iMUSE was programmed to use what they called at the time, The Beat Synchronous Transition. In this case, the system simply waited until the next beat or musical appropriate place to move from track to track. Peter McConnell explains, "The metaphor we all understood was the pit orchestra, if you have ever been part of a musical theater piece you know that the conductor has to follow the actors and the timing of the action on stage. This requires slowing things down or speeding things up based on the actors. iMUSE used this as a metaphor, the system both composed and programmed by Micheal Land used what he called Jump Hooks. These were messages that the composers placed in the MIDI files to make sure that as the game moved from section to section, that much like a human conductor, the music would follow the action."

Even after third party commercial middleware debuted in the 1990s after being an in-house development tool, its usability often left a lot to be desired. Early audio middleware was proprietary, clunky, difficult both to use and understand, and frequently unstable. Over the years, however, the usability, stability, scalability, and power have all increased significantly, and today's middleware features interfaces that are more familiar to audio professionals, much more user friendly, and with a strong concentration on ease of use and simplified workflow. That is not to say that middleware is easy to use. Due to its power and flexibility, it will take you some time and effort to get a grasp of how it functions. To that end, let's set some basic definitions of what audio middleware is and how it can be used in games.

THE CODE

Audio middleware is an audio engine created from a codebase that can help to level the playing field and is another system that works along with the core game engine and sits in a sense in between the sound designer and the programmer. Its main job is to allow the designer, who may not be a programmer, to have more control over how, when and where their sounds are triggered in a game. Keep in mind that there are many different kinds of middleware in games, not just for audio. Anytime a process can be codified and pre-designed for less technical people to do their job in an easier manner; middleware makes sense; believe it or not, there are middleware tools that do nothing but build trees for use in games that need a lot of foliage!

Now, in the case of music, all game engines are not created equal – each platform has different capabilities. Some game engines, like the Unreal engine, have robust audio capabilities built in, and others can barely play two sounds at the same time. When audio folks get together and start to define what they want music and sound to do in a game, from simple things like starting and stopping a track to changing volume, to more complex behaviors like randomizing, pitch shifting, setting reverb zones, or applying real-time EQ for occlusion and obstruction in 3d environments, we are well on our way to defining a standard set of events that are common to all games. Products like Wwise and FMOD provide this kind of functionality in different ways. FMOD uses a more familiar DAW looking interface while Wwise has chosen a look and feel that is more common to the game engine itself. No matter the interface, all audio middleware programs are built upon this codebase and the understanding that a functional audio system can be authored once and then used in a multitude of game engines.

THE PROCESS

So how does it work? Well, back in the day, a composer made music and delivered the mastered mixes to a programmer in some file format or another, and that programmer put them in the game in some way or another, and then they both (if they liked each other) went out and had lunch. Since this was a one-to-one relationship, it was usually a pretty efficient, not to mention tasty, system. As games got more complex and people were not always close to each other, it became standard practice to make music and deliver tracks to a programmer, maybe over the Internet, along with a text document with file names and instructions about where these were supposed to go and what they were supposed to do. This process is still very much in use today. However, over time, middleware programs have emerged to help bridge the gap between the game engine, programmer, and composer.

Here's an example of the standard method of how you put music into a game. This process is usually known as **audio implementation** and occasionally **technical sound design**.

The Native method of audio implementation as shown in Figure 8.1 is still extremely common if the developer doesn't wish to use middleware or pay any extra money for technical sound design or implementation. This is often known inside the industry as "throwing it over the fence."

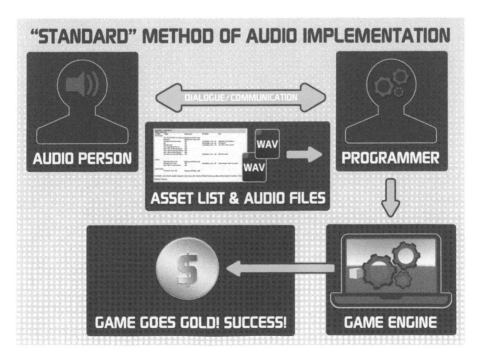

FIGURE 8.1 Native method of audio implementation. (Credit: Programmer Image from Corinne Yu (Flickr).)

1: The composer communicates with the programmer.

2: The composer sends the asset list plus the sound files.

3: The programmer puts these into the game and configures everything to trigger and sound correctly.

Steps 1,2,3 continue to loop as the game is developed and the sound approach is refined.

4: Upon success, the two can have lunch or not…

In this case, it will really help if the programmer and the composer can communicate well with each other in order to realize the composer's intention (Figure 8.2).

In Figure 8.2 we have the same situation, but this time using audio middleware the composer becomes an implementer with more control and responsibility over the audio behavior.

1: The composer/implementer communicates with the programmer regarding which parameters and/or actions or "hooks" to have in the game.

2: The composer/implementer uses the asset list and sound files and configures everything in the middleware tool.

3: They send the build file plus any bank files to the programmer.

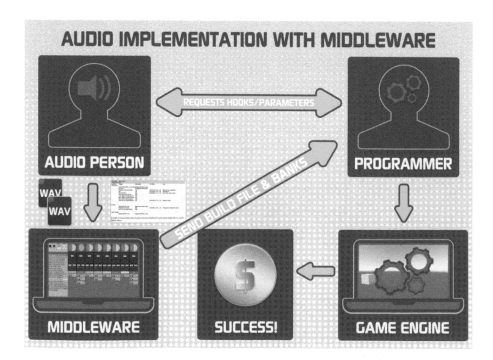

FIGURE 8.2 Middleware-based method of audio implementation. (Credit: Programmer Image from Corinne Yu (Flickr).)

4: The programmer puts these into the game and does not have to configure the sound to play – it just works! Yaaay!

Steps 1–4 continue to loop during development but the composer/implementer has as much control over how the sound is shaped as the programmer does.

5: Upon success, these two can have lunch or not.

There may be other custom arrangements different from the ones shown here, but these two cover most common use cases.

SCENARIOS AND COMMON METHODS

The use of music and music systems fall into large overarching categories that are somewhat standard in the industry. What do we mean by standard? Well, what it means is that these ideas are commonly referred to and you will most likely hear about them over and over again. By examining just a few of these structures we begin to understand the basic concepts behind their usage from project to project. Once digested, these concepts can be aid in developing the context needed to do this yourself and make middleware work for you. Middleware mastery comes in two parts. There is the understanding of general concepts in system design, and then there is the actual nuts and bolts implementation itself, hooking things up. Both have a ton of moving parts and will take time and experience to get right; they demand different skill sets, so give it time. And please keep in mind that the examples below only scratch the surface in terms of the multitude of variations and interactions you will find. They are included here to give you the perspective and tools to analyze and break down how some of these common methods apply.

SCENARIO 1 – TRAPPED IN THE MYSTERIOUS WAREHOUSE – INTENSITY PARAMETER AND GAME ACTIONS

The idea that music will follow the action and story in a game by increasing tension levels, or suspense, is a common theme. This can be done by tying any one of the basic building blocks of music to in-game events or parameters. Let's break down this idea even further by engaging in a thought experiment that shows how middleware works its magic.

Let's take a look at a game in which the player is trapped in a maze of rooms with doors that lead to copies of previous rooms, as we show in Figure 8.3. The player cannot escape the maze, so we want to have the music tension increase the longer we are trapped. If a

FIGURE 8.3 Mysterious warehouse game lesson example.

composer wants to try to solve this in a traditional manner they create a long music loop where each section increases in tension over time. However, if the player starts the game and doesn't open any of the doors, what happens to the music? If the music is unaware of what the player's actions are, it won't be able to match what's going on in the game, and will simply increase tension by itself, and after it finishes, it will suddenly lose tension as the loop repeats from the beginning. This is obviously not ideal, but in the past few decades, this situation of the music score being unaware of the action was just an accepted limitation that the developer had to live with.

Now, let's look at the same game situation, but this time we break up our loop's tension into different levels, and each level has more musical parts added. This is a classic vertical mixing example. How do we trigger those levels (notice we did NOT say "when")? In this case, we need a parameter – let's call it 'Intensity', and when that Intensity level is changed, the tension of the music changes as well. We now have a parameter driving the tension. Our next challenge is figuring what mechanic in the game can drive the intensity parameter. Remember, we can't use time because the player could stop at any point and the music would keep on going, changing tension by itself until it restarted the loop.

In this case we need to think like a game designer. What action is going on all the time in this specific game besides time? Some games have enemies that can serve as good ways to increase tension, but in this case there are no enemies – other than your frustration. What about the rooms? The game knows when a player goes through a door for sure, because it shuffles the room placements at that point. And if you think about it, the more doors you pass through, the more frustrated you'd be and the more trapped you'd feel.

So, tying the number of doors you pass through to the increase in tension seems like an ideal way to create more tension. More doors opened = More tension. Now, that part of attaching the action in the game code to increasing tension in the middleware may be given to the programmer or composer/implementer (depending on their code knowledge). But it's the thinking of what ACTION can happen in a game that can change the musical tension that creates the more accurate relationship of the music to the game's action. And middleware can help with that. Not only that, but if you wanted to create even more variety composing variations in your tension levels (like having three variations of each level for example) and randomize which variation would trigger, you could do it without even having to bother the programmer or change a single line of code – you could do it all in the middleware. That's some powerful stuff!

SCENARIO 2 – THIRD PERSON SHOOTER – INTENSITY PARAMETER VIA PROXIMITY, RAYCAST, AND HEALTH PARAMETERS

Let's consider another situation with enemies on the attack in a 3rd person shooter game. In this case, the desired behavior is for the music to play a low intensity loop of music, while the player is exploring. We want to increase that tension when the enemy engages the player and continue to increase the intensity as the fight progresses. Additionally, there may be multiple enemies to battle, so we will also want to increase tension when there's more than one enemy. When the enemy perishes or if the player runs away, we want the intensity to come down back to the lower explore level.

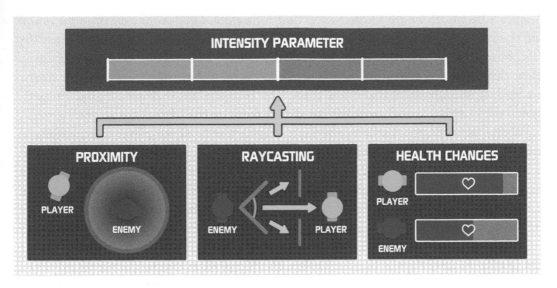

FIGURE 8.4 Intensity parameter changes via proximity, raycasts, and health changes. (Image: Austin Smith.)

This sounds like a pretty basic mechanic that you've probably encountered before in some games, but getting these music transitions to happen reliably can be a challenge. Let's just start with the enemy detection action shown on the leftmost image in Figure 8.4. Triggers can be used in multiple ways; they do not have to be static objects. For example, you can put a trigger on a moving object like the enemy and then by tracking a parameter value in a variable range enable that enemy to detect the player and move to attack. It sounds pretty basic, but remember the game's logic and context rules all. In a wide open world with enemies that are physically distant this method might work okay, but what happens when the setting changes to a sci-fi-based game in a medium sized space freighter with small rooms and enemies hidden behind doors, so you can't see them? If we use the trigger mechanic as described above, the triggers will overlap objects and will not care about walls or doors – so this means the music will increase in intensity whenever the player enters the trigger area, even if the player can't see the enemy directly. Additionally, keep in mind that in this scenario there are quite a few enemies patrolling around, so it's entirely conceivable that each time the player gets physically close (even on the other side of a wall or door), you'll get that increase in intensity, which to the player will feel strange since there is no apparent danger. The proximity effect is used all the time, but must be custom tailored to suit the needs of each gameplay environment.

Now let's introduce you to another game mechanic – the raycast shown in the center image of Figure 8.4. A raycast is a very common physics action that shoots an invisible line from one point to another. If we think about one way that damage works in games like this the line goes out from the gun barrel to the target and if the object that it encounters is identified as the enemy, they will then take damage when fired upon. So we decide to use this method and add it to the enemy, and as they get a clear line of sight to "see" you the intensity of the music increases. In this case raycasts are being used for player detection. The programmer hooks up music changes to any existing player detection code using a raycast function, which at that point seems like a simple and effective system.

Unfortunately, there are problems and decisions afoot. Let's say one enemy attacks you and then two more join in, which means they detect you as well. What happens then? By this point the fight is getting more intense, so we could have them increase the intensity when they arrive. A basic method would be to increase intensity every time an enemy is added. If we implement this in the game, and then the player dispatches one of them, should the intensity level then drop? How do we measure the intensity of a fight?

We do have some pretty reliable options to consider, because our player and the enemies will usually have health levels that are most likely being tracked in the game as shown in the rightmost image of Figure 8.4. With that in mind, we could have the programmer increase the intensity more if the enemies and/or the player are losing a certain amount of health. Additionally, if all of the enemies have been eliminated in your immediate area the music could return back to a lower exploration level of intensity. What if we run away though, if the fight is too intense? We could probably have the programmer make a timer that lowers the intensity after no further health drop or detection by the enemy is present and eventually we'll move back to our low level music. Lastly, we will of course have to make the music transition to our defeat stinger if the player is killed and the victory stinger if they win the game.

Does this solve all of our problems in this particular scenario? In reality, if you were the composer and implementer in a game like this (and involved from a relatively early stage in the game's development) you and the programmer would try these ideas in the test build of the game and refine and revise the approach multiple times both in the middleware and in the game code until you came up with a reliable method for the music transitions that satisfied the rest of the team. Maybe if there are a lot of objectives to meet and the player is getting close to finishing you might not want to drop the intensity back to the lowest level. Maybe you want to keep the intensity really high until they finish the game. The point being is that there can be as many ways to structure the music in a game as there are games to play.

DON'T GET CAUGHT UP IN THE TOOL AS A SOLUTION

These examples just scratch the surface as we start to employ design thinking and how middleware might help us achieve our artistic goals. Please do note that we did not mention anything pertaining to a single middleware tool or tool feature. Middleware is great for composers. You will see a lot of posts on social media about how such and such game's audio team used Brand X or Brand Y of middleware to achieve amazing game sound or music, and this is all well and good, but don't let yourself get caught up in using any one particular tool to solve all problems. You may transition from one company to another and they may not use that brand of middleware, or indeed any middleware at all. So it's really important that you are able to conceive of what kind of music behavior you want, what emotions you want the player to have, and how, in a basic way, you want the music to follow. At the same time, you must also keep in mind the kinds of game actions or conditions that will drive those changes. Games themselves are a relatively new medium, with sounds appearing only in the last 50 years. Middleware is even newer with third party products appearing roughly 25 years ago, and it's really only in the last 10 years that the tools have become widely available, usable, capable, and powerful.

A recent quote on LinkedIn by game audio pro Spencer Reidel (aka Spencer KR) really crystallizes the point. We'll paraphrase it to apply it to music:

> But ultimately, as a [music implementer/composer], it is important for the design to transcend the tools and become about human beings. When designing a building, an architect doesn't start by selecting what brand of crane will lift the girders. She starts with human behavior and how she wants to shape it. And that's what we must do also. Game audio tools are indispensable for helping you implement your solutions to these problems, but the solutions need to come from you. Agnosticism about tools isn't just about being versatile, it's about being able to design in a headspace without artificial limitations.

If you want to get a glimpse of just how deep this rabbit hole goes then you need look no further than the composer, audio director, and technical audio designer Guy Whitmore. Mr. Whitmore has much more than just a passing interest in interactive and adaptive music. With stops at Microsoft, PopCap, and Formosa Interactive, he's a leading figure and advocate for interactive and adaptive soundtracks.

Guy Whitmore. (Image: Used with permission)

Peggle 2 is a casual puzzle game developed by PopCap Games and published by Electronic Arts. It is the official sequel to *Peggle*. The analysis below gives us a first person, upfront, and personal view of how a composer might think about system design and how it is intimately tied to storytelling. Here in his own words, Guy breaks down his music and explains his thought process as he was working on the game:

- **Flexibility:** In order for a score to have flexibility, the musical elements needed to be kept in their elemental form within the audio engine. Again there's a spectrum here; for linear cutscenes a fully baked WAV file will work fine, but in order to match the nonlinear nature of gameplay, music must be broken into component parts. This is why *Peggle 2* used a live orchestra to record one orchestral section (violin 1, cello, clarinet etc.) at a time, and recorded individual phrases, sub-phrases, and even individual sample notes (for Peg Hits).

- **Audio Engine as DAW:** Once in Wwise, these pieces were reassembled in various music segments/tracks, phrase by phrase. While starting with the originally composed phrases, I often rearranged the elements to create variation, and extended phrases, as well as the 'Idle phrases' which occur if the user is inactive for more than 30 seconds.

- **Real-Time DSP:** Digital Signal processing, particularly music reverb, plays a few important roles. First, the reverb allows for smoother, more natural sounding transitions (baked in reverb and reverb tails can make transitions sound stilted, making the seams between them more obvious). Second, real-time reverb and mastering of the mix allows for the score to be mixed within the context of the game itself, rather than offline. Many game scores are mixed more for the soundtrack (higher compression, etc.) and that can make the music sound as if it's sitting on top of the mix, rather than being part of the overall sound mix. We were able to experiment with reverb settings and amount, as well as dynamics (and found we didn't want to over compress the music in-game) until it sat well with the rest of the sound elements.

- **Transitions:** In film, scene transitions are nuanced, and while they often change moods completely, it feels like the music is continuing, which helps the film's sense of continuity. The most common transition in games today is still sadly, the crossfade… And sometimes the muting/unmuting of music stems, still relatively basic by film scoring standards. (Of course there are a good many exceptions, but we're still at a place where these are exceptions rather than the norm.) The score for *Peggle 2* gameplay is broken up into 7 "phrases" or sections, plus the finale. These phrases follow the progress of gameplay, regardless of the length of a given game. To accommodate this, each phrase can go for an indeterminate amount of time (while not statically looping) then transitions on musically defined boundaries (usually two to four measures) to the next phrase in the progression. This approach allows for harmonic changes, tempo changes, thematic changes, and instrumental changes on each of these boundaries. Aesthetically the goal is to create an emotional "arc" to the gameplay, regardless of gameplay style/pace.

- **Peg-Hits Become Melody:** When the ball hits a peg in *Peggle 2*, it might be considered a sound effect, and it is. But it's also part of the music. We built the system so that peg-hits created an ascending diatonic scale which changes to match the harmony of the underlying "phrase" of music. This proved trickier than first conceived. Each of the 7 phrases is assigned a specific diatonic scale (26 notes up or 3 and 1/2 octaves) and that scale changes if the music progresses to the next phrase, i.e. phrase 1 may be linked to a G Major scale for peg-hits while phrase 2 is linked to an A Major scale.

- **Challenges:** If the music moved from phrase 1 to phrase 2 during a shot, the scale needs to change during the shot as well, while still continuing to ascend. To accomplish this, we tracked two RTPC (*Author Note: Real-Time Parameter Controls in Wwise*) values; peg-hit number from the start of a turn (so that it always ascends) and the current phrase (so that the correct scale plays). Yet when phrase 2 is called, it may take a few seconds for it to reach the transition boundary and begin playing phrase 2. Therefore, we needed a callback from the audio engine letting the game know when to really start the next peg-hit scale, therefore matching the start of its underlying phrase. All this points to the thorny challenges that harmony and harmonic changes present for adaptive techniques in general. But harmony must be dealt with head-on in game scoring if we are to break old patterns of monotony (there are many mono-harmonic scores out there that do so to avoid and work around these challenges).

- **The Road Ahead:** Over the past ten years or so, game music has made significant leaps. Live orchestra is no longer a novelty but common, often using the best for hire orchestras in the world. Surround is a given on console and is used to great effect in games. It's arguable that many game scores are reaching the caliber of film scores in sheer compositional prowess. What's left? Timing timing timing!!! Transitions, transitions, transitions!!! And the only way to get there is to expand and evolve our creative and technical tool-chest, with adaptability and flexibility at the forefront.

Now perhaps you can start to see how in-depth the use of middleware can get. Creating interactive and adaptive music can be super fun and quite complex. It is at the heart of what makes game music different from any other form of music composition.

THE BIG TAKEAWAY

What is music middleware? The simple answer is that it is a code base for an audio engine combined with a tool that allows composers to create complex events without having to be programmers. You will still need to work with the programming team, but there is much you can do on your own. Things like randomizing music tracks into a list so the player does not hear the same piece of music over and over again, or pitch shifting tracks and triggering stingers on specific beats to create perfectly timed endings – all of these are possible. Middleware puts more control in the hands of you as the composer/implementer, but it also makes more work for you because you are now taking over many (not all) of the duties of the programmer. This concept can be hard to get your mind around, but you can usually learn the tool for free. In fact, most middleware companies provide complete versions that are free to download and use. If you end up working on a game with a developer that wants to use middleware, and the budget is high enough to qualify, they will need to pay a license fee to the middleware company once the game is released. In all things, practice makes perfect, so watching tutorials and taking classes or certifications are highly recommended and will benefit composers as they build their resumes, demo reels, and careers. Keeping an open mind to new ways of working and new technologies is an essential part of game music. Since music in games can cover so many styles and forms and also touch on the cutting edge of science and technology, it is important to consider yourself not just a musician, but a technological evangelist as well. By keeping up on new systems, programs, and techniques, you will be able to better guide the composition of your music and communicate intelligently your needs with the game team.

Discussion Topics: What is audio middleware? Why use audio middleware? Are middleware programs like Wwise and FMOD the same as DAWs? What are some features common to all audio middleware? How does middleware change a composer's relationship to the game development pipeline? Do I need to use middleware for every game? Does middleware make more work for composers?

TERMS

- **Middleware**: A type of computer software that provides services to software applications beyond those available from the operating system.

- **MIDI:** Musical Instrument Digital Interface.

- **Sound Bank:** A collection of raw audio data of any kind at a specific format, bit depth, and sample rate, into a single large binary file, thus making it easier to manage, instead of having individual files.

- **Conductor**: A person who directs the performance of a musical group.

- **Codebase:** A codebase is the complete body of source code for a given software program, component, or application system.

- **Workflow:** A sequence of processes through which a piece of work passes from initiation to completion.

- **Occlusion:** The sensation of decreased or attenuated high frequencies when a sound wave is blocked and travels through another medium before reaching the ears.

- **Obstruction:** When a sound wave travels through a medium to another medium of greater density, such as an obstacle which is positioned directly in the path of the sound. This results in indirect reflections or delays of the original sound.

- **Reverb Zone:** In a Unity scene, these are spherical shaped areas that can be placed in the 3D space where the signal from 3D AudioSources passing through them can be routed to achieve reverberation effects. Used when you want to gradually change from a point where there is no ambient effect to a place where there is one, such as when the player is entering a cavern.

- **DSP:** Digital Signal processing is the use of computers or specialized devices, to perform a wide array of audio effects such as reverb, eq, and compression.

- **Diatonic Scale**: Any stepwise arrangement of the seven "natural" pitches (scale degrees) forming an octave – in particular, the major and natural minor scales.

- **RTPC:** Real-time Parameter Controls enable the control of specific properties of various Wwise objects (including sounds, containers, control busses, effects, and so on) in real time based on real-time parameter changes that occur within the game.

- **Callbacks:** In computer programming, a callback or callback function is any reference to executable code that is passed as an argument to another piece of code.

- **Raycasting:** The methodological basis for 3D CAD/CAM solid modeling and image rendering. It is essentially the same as ray tracing for computer graphics where virtual light rays are "cast" or "traced." It can also be used as a detection method when done in a simple manner in game physics engines.

CHAPTER 9

Advanced Approaches

Topic: Down the Rabbit Hole

- Learning Outcomes
- Introduction: The TDD
- Old and New: Rich Vreeland and Mini Metro
- Advanced Game Music Analysis
- Procedural Music: Daniel Brown and *Marvel's Avengers*
- Generative Music Using Pure Data (PD)
- Generative Music in VR
- The Big Takeaway
- Discussion Questions
- Terms

Learning Outcomes

- Analyzing advance approaches to music composition
- Understanding generative music
- Understanding the use of music in virtual and augmented reality

INTRODUCTION

Let's look at some more advanced usages of music in games by analyzing increasingly interactive and adaptive scores. These games allow for more adventurous creativity with their music soundtracks; indeed, some of them actually count more as musical experiences

DOI: 10.1201/9781003414728-11

than games per se. These games employ the use of interactive and adaptive procedural techniques. The term "procedural" implies utilizing some type of formula or algorithm for handling the music, and this can take multiple forms. Procedural techniques can be used to randomize the content of the music itself as well as the mix of tracks to create interesting organic musical variations.

It is customary to create a technical design document (TDD) that explains the use of music and sound in a game and breaks down how the music system will work. It also helps the developer understand how the composer is thinking about the technical aspects of the game design.

Technical Design: TAD (*Technical Audio Documentation*)

Basic Audio Requirements, these are the things that we might expect developers to be comfortable with

- **Music Triggers:** The proper starting and stopping as well as placement of all music events

- **Mixing:** The proper blending, volume balancing, and EQ'ing of all music elements

- **Looping:** The ability to trigger seamless music and ambient background tracks

- **Timing:** The proper timing and weighting of music in game

- **Transitions:** The proper triggering of transitions between menu screens and levels. Cross Fades, Stingers, and other technical means of blending seamlessly between screens and gameplay levels

- **Randomization**: The creation of pools of music and sound classes for randomized playback

- **Pitch Shifting of Music:** The use of pitch changing algorithms to speed up and slow down music tracks

- **3D Sound:** Distance attenuation as well as occlusion and obstruction algorithms for foreground and background music

- **Resource and Performance Management**: The ability to optimize the delivery of music during gameplay

- **Mixer Snapshots**: The ability to create separate mixes for game play levels and Menus

- **Parameter-Based Music Triggering**: The ability to program and implement parameter-based music, for creating interactive and adaptive scores

- **The Use of Third-Party Audio Middleware:** The capacity to use some available third-party audio engines and code bases to more completely integrate sound into the development pipeline or to create composer controlled parameter driven adaptive soundtracks

OLD AND NEW

Music by its very nature takes place in time and composers have been manipulating the concepts of structure, choice, and order in a myriad of ways. Arnold Schoenberg in the early part of the 20th century serialized pitch and changed the course of music by bringing formalized mathematical concepts into the art of composition. This method was used during the next 20 years almost exclusively by him and his most famous students of the Second Viennese School – Alban berg and Anton Webern. However, the influence of serialism was widely adopted and used by many composers, in the concert hall by Milton Babbitt, Igor Stravinsky, and others as well as in film by composers Leonard Rosenman, Jerry Goldsmith, and Hans Eisler to name just a few.

One of the most famous examples is Anton Webern's Symphony Op 21. Scored for clarinet, bass clarinet, two horns, harp, first and second violins, viola, and cello. Widely regarded as a masterpiece in miniature, Schoenberg himself was astounded and moved by the work's concision. Like most of Webern's 12-tone works, the Symphony is based on a single series or pitch set dominated by semitones. The work consists of two short movements. The first is in two parts – a statement and a development, and begins with a double canon in four parts; the second movement is a theme with seven variations and a coda, and also includes the use of canon.

Rich Vreeland (Disasterpeace). (Used with permission.)

While growing up in Staten Island, Game composer Rich Vreeland, better known as Disasterpeace was always into video games and surrounded by music, though not really delving into it until high school, and focused on graphic design as an early college career when he was firmly bitten by the music bug, dropped out of design school, and enrolled at the Berklee College of Music. While there, he got heavily interested in game music soundtracks and chiptune covers. After graduation from Berklee, he stayed in Boston, making connections with local chiptune music makers, participating in game jams, and working full time for a local game developer for a time designing robot sound effects. Since then he's done soundtracks for the games Mini Metro, the critically acclaimed adventure game Hyper Light Drifter, the card game Reigns, an episode of Adventure Time, and more films, and was the audio director for Solar Ash, the sequel to Hyper Light Drifter.

Influenced by ideas of serialism, Rich brought the concept into the game *Mini Metro* in a very unique and thoughtful way. *Mini Metro* is a puzzle strategy video game developed by the New Zealand-based indie development team called Dinosaur Polo Club. Players are tasked with constructing an efficient rail transit network for a rapidly growing city. Vreeland uses the idea of serialism to create a mathematical musical model. It's a beautiful score and at the same time a complex adaptive music system. Since the game is based around the idea of creating and maintaining a citywide transit system with lines, trains, passengers, and more, every element in the game makes its own musical gesture. Thus playing the game results in a near-infinite combination of harmonic elements that never repeat in quite the same way. The soundtrack is fully serialized and changes based on the parameters of gameplay.

Here Rich explains it in his own words,

> We combined data sonification and concepts taken from the musical approach of Serialism to build a soundscape for the game. In *Mini Metro* we apply this concept by using internal data from the game and externally authored data in tandem to generate music. The game has a clock and is broken up into time increments that represent hours, days, and weeks. The tempo of the music is derived from one in-game hour or 0.8 seconds where one pulse is equal to 72 beats per minute, also called the master pulse. As you draw and design metro lines in the game, you are also creating pitches and rhythms at the same time. Each metro line is represented by a unique musical sequence of pitches and rhythms and these change in real time along with changes in timbre.

PROCEDURAL MUSIC SYSTEMS IN ACTION

No Man's Sky – 2018 Hello Games

Procedural randomness was extensively employed by the developer Hello Games to create the music soundtrack for this popular and expensive title. *No Man's Sky*, an open-world space exploration game, is probably one of the most procedural games developed in the last few years. Every planet discovered has its own procedurally generated ecosystem, flora, fauna, and of course, sound and music. The music was recorded by the experimental rock band, 65daysofstatic, in the form of thousands of individual stems that were then randomly mixed in order to create unique custom soundtracks for each discovered system or planet.

It is important to mention here that the music itself is NOT procedurally generated, but the mix and selection of instruments and melodies and rhythms are procedural in which it is randomized based on a formula. The band improvised on the various musical elements found in the tracks for their album *Debutante* and recorded many variations of the melodies and textures, eventually ending up with two thousand five hundred or so individual stems. These were then organized and remixed by the game system based on random choice as well as the game's structure to provide unique soundtracks as the player explores a vast and ever changing open universe.

Wii Play Tanks! – 2007 Nintendo

Another example of inventive adaptive music mixing that is highly structured and based on a specific set of rules is the minigame *Tanks!* from the *Wii Play* series of minigames released with the console. In this case the rules are specifically based on which color enemy tanks appear in the game level and in what amount. Each colored tank results in a specific mix of the theme appearing; furthermore, some colors supersede others in controlling the content of the music mix. It's surprisingly complex for such a simple game.

The two examples above are relatively simple in nature in terms of the content they are playing but serve to create rich overall experiences that match the game play and serve the story as well as the emotional aspects of the game. Of course with such a vast number of individual stems the combinations and thus the exact mix can basically be infinite. There's another level of procedural music that is possible, where individual notes and instruments are triggered by the game engine itself. Let's take a look at a couple of examples.

Mario Galaxy – 2007 Nintendo

This Wii (and later Switch)-based title utilizes its music soundtrack in really creative ways, from triggering individual notes in dungeon scenes based on a grid, to Mario standing on top, rolling a ball, while you tilt the controller to move it. The ball's rotation then controls the tempo of the music in different ways. Sometimes it will change the playback speed of a digital audio file, which clearly affects the pitch, but other times it is playing back a sampled instrument via MIDI because the pitch does not fluctuate but the tempo does. There is also a small amount of elastic pitch modulation, but it's kept to a minimum, because the artifacts can be pretty noticeable.

This is an excellent and really creative example of a type of procedural music, or more accurately procedural tempo, maybe? But the effect is very obviously speeding up and slowing down the tempo of the soundtrack quite drastically, something that would be impossible to do with pitch shifting DSP without very obvious artifacts (plus a lot more CPU usage). Using MIDI triggering sample-based instruments is a very simple and effective method to get tempo changes from the music that would be nearly impossible otherwise. *Mario Galaxy* is filled with many other amazingly creative music implementations as well. Definitely worth checking out!

Ape Out – (Gabe Cuzillo, Bennett Foddy, and Matt Boch) – 2019 Devolver Digital

Here's another example of triggered samples in action. This crazy, violent, top down indie game uses homemade drum samples as the sole soundtrack to accompany your rampage as an escaped gorilla, hell bent on revenge against your captors and really anyone who gets in the way. It is also quite interesting visually as the camera's focal length is rather wildly exaggerated and the art style is both bold and abstract, based on outlines rather than having any detail.

Daniel Brown. (Used with permission.)

Daniel Brown is a composer and computer music researcher, and the owner of Intelligent Music Systems LLC. He received a Doctorate of Musical Arts in Composition from the University of California at Santa Cruz in 2012, where he studied under David Cope, and a Bachelor of Science in Discrete Mathematics from the Georgia Institute of Technology (USA). He also works as a composer, cellist, and educator. Along with his training in Western music in the USA, he has studied non-Western music in India, Korea, and Turkey. His compositions have been performed in the USA, Japan, Korea, India, and Central America.

Procedural Rhythm Systems for AAA

A fine example of procedural music in action in the AAA game world was developed by composer and audio programmer Daniel Brown. His system was first utilized in *Rise of the Tomb Raider* in 2015 and then later refined and expanded for use in the *Marvel's Avengers* game released in 2021 by Crystal Dynamics. Working closely with composer Bobby Tahouri, Dan developed a custom rhythm engine that intelligently recombines existing percussion parts. The engine interprets and extrapolates basic rhythmic structures in the music using MIDI data, and then a unique set of continuous variations is extrapolated and saved as presets. The system then generates sound by triggering various samples of drums and other percussion provided by the composer; these are the same samples that are used in the original tracks. These presets can be driven in a multitude of different ways, either by calling them directly or by crossfading between various parameters in the game to provide a significant variety of dynamic percussion that is intimately tied to game states (Figure 9.1).

Here is Dan in his own words describing his work on this project:

> The goal from the start was to develop a procedural system that could move seamlessly from one musical state or scheme to another as the mighty Avengers were busy saving the world from evil. The boundaries between these states work on a continuum utilizing Markov analysis or chains that make predictive choices based on probabilistic reasoning between the energy of the three states. Low being when you're walking around checking stuff out. Alert when you are in contact with the

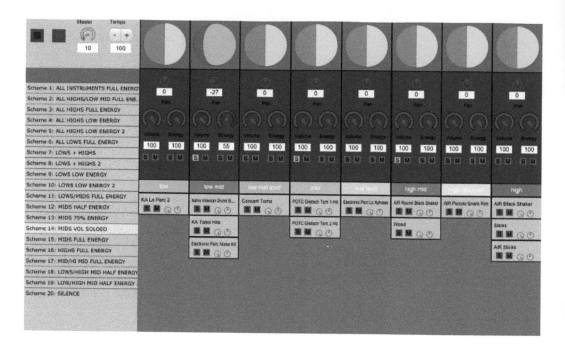

FIGURE 9.1   Daniel Brown's *Rise of the Tomb Raider* custom music system. (Used with permission.)

baddies, but you're not really fighting, and Combat when you're mixing it up. Each of these states sound different, but they are all set in the same tempo.

The interesting and tricky thing was defining how time and tempo would relate to energy. For example, the density or number of notes per measure is mathematically defined and controls the threshold in which these notes will play. In this way, as notes and phrases are pulled in and out, they continue to maintain the sound and feel of the basic rhythmic pattern. Sometimes many notes will play together, sometimes they play separately, other parameters such as volume and reverb effects are also layered in run time. In this way you get a sense of constant variation based on a predetermined piece of music. The game uses the tracking of these parameters to change between low and high energy schemes that are driven by the player. Distance, raytracing, and health were just some of the parameters that were used. One of our big unexpected challenges was memory management. Great sounding samples take up space. Downsampling percussion sounds and keeping them sounding good in relation to the audio budget of the entire game was a real challenge. In the end I was really proud of how it all came out.

Generative Music Scores with Pure Data

Okay let's up the ante again and take a look at generated music. So far we've mainly been looking at samples being triggered by the audio system, which is a very CPU "cheap" (meaning it doesn't use up much computing power) method. But other games actually generate the musical instruments as well as the notes in the game environment itself. Game engines don't actually do a very good job at this, as a rule, so developers have to rely on separate tools that can integrate with game engines, and that go beyond what a typical middleware application can handle. The benefit of using this method is that you're not usually using much memory (RAM) with this method, but that tradeoff comes at the expense of using more of the CPU to generate sound.

One of the more popular tools for music synthesis is Pure Data, which is similar to Max(Max/MSP/Jitter) in that it is a dataflow-oriented graphical patching environment. In the interface you hook objects up in a similar way as you would with a modular synthesizer. Pure Data, or PD for short, developed and maintained by Miller Puckette, is an open source music synthesis tool that allows you to run its patches in a game engine. In fact, in the early 2000s, PD was the engine used in the *Spore* video game to generate the procedural music soundtrack. At that time Maxis, the game company, had to pay for a proprietary version of PD that could be utilized in a commercial application. Since that time however, the PD developers have created an open licensed version of PD called libPD and this has enabled other developers to make games utilizing PD as the sound engine.

Here are a few examples of how PD can be utilized in a game.

FRACT OSC – 2014 Phosfiend Games

Probably one of the most interesting examples of PD in action *Fract OSC* is sort of a cross between *Myst*, *Rez*, and the movie *Tron*. It's a first person adventure game where you find yourself in a strange environment that contains the broken remains of a giant electronic music making machine. It's your job to figure out how to fix the system and bring it back to working order. The game features no voice over, text, or sampled sound effects, but the sound for the entire game is generated from one giant PD patch running in the application. Additionally, once you fix the system, you can then create your own music inside it as well, and the sound quality is quite impressive, going mainly for warm analog synth timbres with echo and reverb.

SimCell – 2013 Strange Loop Games

This educational game by Strange Loop Games has similarities to the opening section of the game Spore, where your created species tries to survive in a pool of other microorganisms, but whereas that game triggers samples from Brian Eno's synths with PD, *SimCell* instead uses PD to generate the audio itself. The result is quite similar but the sounds have a nice purity to them as a result of being generated instead of sampled. Audio designer/composer Leonard Paul was tasked with creating the generative music for the game as well as the sound effects.

Bad Hotel – 2012 Lucky Frame

Another indie developer using PD is Edinburgh-based Lucky Frame who does all of the sound in their games with it. The one we're going to mention here is the game *Bad Hotel*. This game is a tower defense game where you try to build your own hotel while at the same time enemies (usually birds) try to tear it down. Each section of the hotel is indicated by a musical pitch and as you add more sections, it adds more pitches to cycle through. It's not quite a 1:1 relationship, but an interesting experiment nonetheless.

EXPERIMENTAL MUSIC EXPERIENCES IN VR

Let's wind this section up by looking at applications and demonstrations of generative music systems that aren't really games but could more easily be classified as experiments or experiences involving music, and are played within a VR space.

SoundSelf: A Technodelic

Game designer sound designer and composer Robin Arnott is one of the more original voices to emerge in the indie scene and was an early convert to the recent incarnation of VR. He has been a prominent proponent of psychedelic therapies for personal enlightenment and spiritual evolution, and nowhere is this more true than in his project Sound Self, which is a meditative app/experience where singing produces changes in the visual output of the experience. This experience is capable of achieving measured states of altered consciousness and brain activity similar to taking psilocybin.

The application analyzes the pitch and timbre of the voice and adjusts the visual and audio output accordingly. Note that the audio output of the app doesn't contain the sound of the original voice, only the processed audio, and there appear to be some fairly sophisticated DSP processes happening; some appear to be involving manipulating samples as well as live processing, though this processing is very original and organic.

Constellation

This is a personal project of the composer and co-author of this very book Scott R. Looney. It is based on an $8 \times 8 \times 8$ cube, or really eight layers of 8×8 2D sequences all running in tandem. The cube can be rotated and individual layers soloed. Each layer can also be run with its own rhythmic relationship relative to other layers, and the length can be changed, and transposed in pitch as well. The sound engine and the sequencer is actually a recent version of Csound, which is a very old computer synthesis language from the 1980s, running inside Unity. The name is related to the fact that a star constellation's shape depends on the individual stars that are not only hundreds of light years distant from each other horizontally and vertically but also in terms of their actual distance from Earth. What if you could somehow rotate these shapes and view them from different angles? That's the idea at work here.

In this demonstration, notes are randomly distributed on all eight layers and then the cube of layers is rotated. Time always proceeds left to right and pitch is vertical. Using Csound, Scott managed to get much better musical timing than is normally possible in a game engine. The synth engine also consists of two sine synths, two sawtooth synths, and four sound font instruments. Two melodic ones and two drum/percussion oriented ones, and all instruments get a bit of reverb.

A BIT ON AI-BASED MUSIC

As we have been writing this book over the last months AI (Artificial Intelligence) has suddenly emerged into the world as a viable tool for text generation, visual design, and digital art, and is edging into animations and video. While the field has been developing for several years, the latter half of 2022 saw some significant advancements in the form of Stable Diffusion, a publicly released text to image models. While others were available for use a few years or months earlier like Midjourney and DALL-E, the openness of this tool's code spread AI usage like wildfire. But the seismic shift in public awareness came later in that year at the end of November with OpenAI's release of ChatGPT, a Large Language Model (LLM), trained on tremendous amounts of data, that users could interact with to generate any kind of text output. ChatGPT usage grew from 1 million users five days after public debut, to over 100 million users by January 2023, making it the fastest growing user base in memory. The public is now using ChatGPT and other AI tools at a furious pace, from anything from recipes to research papers. Co-author Scott Looney has even used it to generate Unity C# scripts that can mimic simple middleware behaviors and others have used it to code audio plugins.

This begs the question: what happens when an AI can compose really convincing music? In some respect, it's already happened. Earlier in May 2023 a user created a song using an AI generated voice mimicking Drake and the Weeknd and it became quite popular on streaming services until it was pulled for violation of copyright. It's not clear if the music itself was generated or composed, but it's clear that AI has arrived in a big way and the tools will only get better over time. Google has its own tool called MusicLM that can generate music with text descriptions, and there's another site that generates music by learning and generating spectrograms of styles that can be generated via text prompt. In the time this book itself will be published, and in the years afterward, AI-based music generation is sure to gain in sophistication and power, including very likely the ability to be utilized for or to be changed via interactive media. It is definitely a powerful tool, but like the saying in the "Spiderman" movies goes, "With great power comes great responsibility." AI has the potential to transform the whole of human society in radical ways, but it remains to be seen whether it will be a net positive move forward, or not.

All this being said, as game composers and tech evangelists, it is important to stay up on the latest tools that can make composition, editing, implementation, and integration into the game easier for our musical creations. We will see what the future holds here!

THE BIG TAKEAWAY

Keep in mind that these are just a few examples of composers in the field and the techniques they use, presented here to elucidate specific points. Writing music for games can be both a simple and complex task. The main thing to keep in mind is to stay creative, remain flexible, and work with the producer and implementer/ programmer to make sure that your music fits the requirements and flow of the game. Game composers have always had to be clever alchemists, part musicians, and part technologists. These days, a game composer can go from recording a heavy metal band one day to creating a fully synthesized orchestral score that includes no live instruments the next. Platforms are ever changing and being adapted and upgraded. Each change introduces new tools to master and new techniques to learn. There is room in the field for technical and non-technical composers alike. But in either case, a thorough understanding of the creative and technical challenges involved is essential. Being comfortable analyzing music and how it relates to game play is a very important skill. Games are changing all the time and composers need to be able to break down for themselves what is happening in various gameplay mechanics in order to make sure that the music creates the desired effect. Technology is also constantly in flux and new systems and ways of thinking are constantly cropping up. Composers working on games must to some extent be technological evangelists. It is not essential that you are a hard care gamer or that you know every game system in antiquity but, it is important that you understand the basic concepts and usages so that you can help to guide your team into choosing the most effective pipeline for the development of the music.

Discussion Questions: Do more advanced music systems make for better music? Why do we need advanced music systems in the first place? How does game music relate to the field of computer science? What are the benefits and drawbacks from having the game generate sound in real time? What is the difference between VR and AR? Where do you think music for games is headed in the next ten years? How will AI affect music creation in the near future?

TERMS

- **TDD:** A Technical Design Document is a method for a team of programmers to build and code the game's features. It allows the team's developers to specify the requirements, how they should be achieved, and the tools and technologies needed.

- **Serial Music:** A type of music composition that uses a series, or ordered set, of musical elements such as pitch, rhythm, and harmony. The elements are manipulated according to a set of rules or a system. Serial music is also known as 12-tone music, due to the use of a specific technique developed by Arnold Schoenberg and his students in the early 20th century.

- **Second Viennese School:** The group of composers that comprised Arnold Schoenberg and his pupils, particularly Alban Berg and Anton Webern, and close associates in early 20th-century Vienna.

- **Coda:** The concluding passage of a piece or movement.

- **Canon:** A contrapuntal compositional technique that employs a melody with one or more imitations of the melody played after a given duration.

- **CPU:** Central Processing Unit, also called a main processor, is the most important processor in a given computer. Its electronic circuitry executes instructions of a computer program, such as arithmetic, logic, controlling, and input/output operations.

- **Data Sonification:** The presentation of data as sound. It is the auditory equivalent of the more established practice of data visualization.

- **Gameplay Parameter:** A value in a game attached to some feature in a game's structure. For example, player health, or a character's experience level in RPGs.

- **Pure Data:** A visual dataflow programming language developed by Miller Puckette in the 1990s for creating interactive computer music and multimedia works. Pd is an open-source project with a large developer base

- **Max MSP:** Also known as Max/MSP/Jitter, is a visual dataflow programming language for music and multimedia developed and maintained by San Francisco-based software company Cycling '74.

- **Generative Music:** A term popularized by Brian Eno to describe music that is ever-different and changing, created by some type of system.

- **Procedural Music:** Composition that evolves in real time according to a specific set of rules or control logics.

- **Markov Analysis:** Involves defining the likelihood of a future action, given the current state of a variable. Once the probabilities of future actions at each state are determined, a decision tree can be drawn, and the likelihood of a result can be calculated.

- **Music Synthesis:** Creating music utilizing electronic synthesizer timbres.

- **Music Synthesizer:** An electronic musical instrument that generates audio signals. Synthesizers typically create sounds by generating waveforms through different synthesis methods including subtractive synthesis, additive synthesis, and frequency modulation synthesis.

- **Subtractive Synthesis:** A method of sound synthesis in which partials of an audio signal are attenuated by a filter to alter the timbre of the sound.

- **Additive Synthesis:** A sound synthesis technique that creates timbre by adding sine waves together. The timbre of musical instruments can be considered in the light of Fourier theory to consist of multiple harmonic or inharmonic partials or overtones.

- **Frequency Modulation Synthesis:** A synthesis method invented by John Chowning at Stanford, involving pairs of sine waves in a carrier/modulator configuration called an operator, and arrangement and modulations of these operators as algorithms to create timbral changes.

- **Fourier Transform:** In acoustics and DSP, the Fourier transform is a transform that converts a function into a form that describes the frequencies present in the original function represented as sine or cosine values. More commonly calculated as Fast Fourier Transform or **FFT**.

- **Pitch Modulation:** A sound recording technique in which the original pitch of a sound is raised or lowered. Effects units that raise or lower pitch by a pre-designated musical interval or transposition are called pitch shifters.

- **Elastic Pitch Modulation:** It is a real time pitch shifting solution for RTAS, VST, AU, and AAX. Powered by Zplane's 'élastiquePro' pitch shifting engine.

- **VR:** Virtual Reality is a simulated experience that employs pose tracking and 3D near-eye displays to give the user an immersive feel of a virtual world. Applications of virtual reality include entertainment, education, and business.

- **AR:** Augmented Reality is the integration of digital information with the user's environment in real time. Unlike virtual reality (VR), which creates a totally artificial environment, AR users experience a real-world environment with generated perceptual information overlaid on top of it.

- **XR:** Extended reality is a catch-all term to refer to augmented reality, virtual reality, and mixed reality. The technology is intended to combine or mirror the physical world with a "digital twin world" that is able to interact with each other.

CHAPTER 10

Lessons Earned

Topic: Final Thoughts and Summation

- Learning Outcomes
- Book Overview, Putting It All Together
- Where to Go from Here, Industry Thoughts and Resources
- Team Sport: Industry Roles
- Asset Management
- Where Do I Belong?
- Networking
- Community Organizations for Game Composers
- The Big Takeaway

Learning Outcomes

- Understanding the marketplace
- Building familiarity with professionals in the field
- Understanding the uses of networking
- Differentiating between various community organizations
- Understanding game jams

DOI: 10.1201/9781003414728-12

- Developing entrepreneurial spirit

- Building and maintaining a website and portfolio

- prepare students for careers in the game industry

- Help audio professionals advance their careers

- Prepare music educators of the future

- Prepare music researchers of the future

OVERVIEW

Congratulations on finishing this course of study!

The concepts, assignments, and lessons that you have been going through here are a guide and honestly, that guide will only take you so far. By applying yourself to the materials and concepts in this course, you now have the context and practical experience to ask all the right questions. Going forward you have to rely on your own creativity, curiosity, and ability to assess your work. In this way, you will move forward and develop a deeper understanding of composing for games. Remember, all of the tools that we have discussed here are potentially transitory. The concepts, however, will last and remain the fundamental conceptual building blocks of the art form. Programs themselves may disappear in short order or remain for many years. Use this course as a reference guide as you move boldly into the future at a rate of one second per second, and the rest is up to you.

WHERE DO I GO FROM HERE? INDUSTRY THOUGHTS AND RESOURCES

Team Sport: Game Design Roles

Game design is a team sport, and as such, it is of vital importance to understand the needs and concerns of the people you will be working with. In nearly all cases of game design, there are roles that are commonly encountered. In large AAA games for big companies and large franchises (like Assassins Creed, Mario Bros, Halo, and the Elder Scrolls), these roles are defined and assigned to different individuals. In small indie games, roles may devolve to just a few individuals or even just one!

Taking a 5,000-foot view, let's cover the major roles you will find in the field, keeping in mind of course that this is a general list of roles and functions that change over time. A game design team typically consists of several individuals with different roles and responsibilities. Some key members of a game design team include:

Note: The size of the game design team and the roles above may vary depending on the studio and the project.

- **Game Designer:** The overall creative leader of the game oversees the design of the game, including mechanics, systems, and player experience.

- **Level Designers:** Create and design levels, puzzles, and challenges within the game.

- **Systems Designers:** Design and balance the game's systems such as combat, economy, and progression.

- **Narrative Designer:** Responsible for creating and implementing the game's story and characters.

- **Graphic Artists:** Design and create the game's visual style and assets.

- **Programmers:** Write the code that makes the game run.

- **Quality Assurance Testers:** Test the game to ensure it is free of bugs and errors.

- **Producers:** Manage the game's development schedule and budget, and ensure that the team is on track to meet milestones and deadlines.

On the audio side of a game, the development team typically includes individuals with the following roles:

Note: The size of the audio team and the roles may change and vary depending on the studio and the game. Some studios may merge or split the roles or have a different name for the same function, and as we've mentioned before in small teams these roles will mean each member doing several jobs or even one person doing everything.

- **Audio Director:** The overall leader of the audio team, responsible for the vision and direction of all the game's audio.

- **Composer:** Writes and produces the game's music and score.

- **Technical Composer**: May write original music as well as implement tracks into the game engine itself or use third-party middleware.

- **Orchestrator:** Takes the composer's work and arranges it for DAW's (MIDI), or live instruments. Many composers do their own orchestrations as it is intimately tied to the composition itself.

- **Producer:** Is responsible for the sound of the recorded music; they also manage the budget.

- **Sound Designer:** Creates the game's sound effects and ambient audio.

- **Technical Sound Designer**: May create original sound designs as well as implement them into the game engine itself or use third-party middleware.

- **Voice Director:** Oversees the casting and recording of voice actors, and directs them during recording sessions.

- **Actors:** Bring the writers characters to life in the studio.

- **Dialog Editor:** Edits the game's spoken dialog.

- **Technical Dialog Editor:** Edits and also implements the game's spoken dialog.

- **Audio Programmer:** Writes code to implement the game's audio assets and ensure they function correctly in the game engine.

- **Audio Tester:** Tests the game's audio to ensure quality control and that everything is working properly, free of bugs and errors.

Advice on Interacting with Your Peers and Teams in the Industry

The information that follows will help you to understand some of the things that others on your team deal with on a regular basis. Understanding these common complaints ahead of time can help foster a better working relationship and ultimately lead to better games.

What Are Some of the Biggest Complaints from Game Designers about Dealing with Music and Sound?

Here are some of the most common ones:

1. **Limited technical understanding:** Game designers may feel that composers don't fully understand the technical limitations and requirements of the game engine and hardware. This can result in audio that doesn't integrate well with the rest of the game, or that can be too demanding on the hardware.

2. **Different priorities:** Audio professionals often prioritize different aspects of the experience. For example, audio designers may be focused on creating high quality music, while the game designer is more concerned with how the audio supports gameplay mechanics.

3. **Time constraints:** Music can be time-consuming to create and implement, which can cause issues when adhering to strict deadlines. This can lead to rushed or incomplete audio, which may not meet the designer's expectations.

4. **Cost:** Audio production can be expensive, especially for recording live players, studio, and editing time. This can cause tension for teams that are working with a limited budget.

What Are Some of the Biggest Complaints from Animators about Dealing with Music and Sound?

Here are some of the most common ones:

1. **Lack of synchronization:** Animators may feel that the music or sound is not synchronized properly with the animations, resulting in a lack of coherence between the two.

2. **Late delivery:** Frustration can develop when composers do not deliver the required audio assets on time, leading to delays in the development process. Animators often need the audio in order to complete their work.

3. **Limited variety:** The assets provided seem too limited in variety or not sufficient to cover all the animation in the game. This can lead to repetitive music or sound that doesn't match the diversity of the animations.

4. **Inappropriate music:** Animators may feel that the music provided doesn't somehow fit the tone or style of the game.

5. **Technical issues:** Technical issues with the music can impact the game. This may include music tracks that are too large or not optimized for the hardware, leading to slow load times or poor performance.

What Are Some of the Biggest Complaints from Programmers about Dealing with Music and Sound?

Here are some of the most common ones:

1. **Performance issues:** Programmers may feel that the asset or middleware implementation is causing performance issues in the game, such as excessive CPU or memory usage.

2. **Limited flexibility:** Oftentimes, music implementation feels inflexible during the development process. This can result in additional work for programmers when changes are required, or a lack of responsiveness in addressing bugs and issues.

3. **Lack of technical understanding:** In many cases, composers may not fully understand the technical requirements of the game engine and hardware, which can lead to audio that is not optimized for performance and doesn't integrate well with the rest of the game.

4. **Incomplete implementation:** Music implementation that is incomplete or missing important features, such as dynamic or positional sound can muck up the works and cause delays and headaches.

What Are Some of the Biggest Complaints from Producers about Dealing with Music and Sound?

Here are some of the most common ones:

1. **Lack of clarity in budget and timeline:** Producers may feel that the music team is not providing clear information on the project budget (not the audio budget) and timeline for audio development. This can make it difficult for producers to plan and manage the project effectively.

2. **Limited availability:** Frustration builds when the composer is not available when needed, or is not responsive to requests for information or updates, leading to delays and missed deadlines.

3. **Quality issues:** The quality of the music is not right or up to their standards, or doesn't meet the expectations of the target audience. This can be a tricky and sensitive subject filled with landmines.

4. **Technical issues:** Technical issues with the music implementation that impacts the quality of the game or causes delays in development. This can include issues with compatibility or integration with the game engine or problems with performance.

Now that you have some insight into the problems and concerns of your team members. Here are a few common themes that frequently come up for composers and other audio specialists.

1. **Lack of direction:** Composers may feel that game designers don't provide clear direction on what they want from the music, which can lead to ambiguity and confusion.

2. **Limited technical understanding:** Many times, team members may not fully understand the full impact of the myriad of technical and creative requirements involved with music creation and production.

3. **Changes to audio scope:** Composers often experience changes to the scope of the game late in development, which can be frustrating and disruptive. This can include changes to the music direction or style, or new assets that need to be created at the last minute.

4. **Unrealistic expectations:** Unrealistic expectations for the music, such as wanting live orchestral recordings on a limited budget or within an extremely tight timeframe can be hard to explain. This can often result in music that is rushed or of lower quality than the team envisioned.

Hopefully this has not stressed you out too much. The goal is to give you a little bit of a preview and an inside view of the team dynamics, phycology, and prevalent issues you might just encounter out in the field. We must highlight the fact that most of these complaints can be addressed and solved by regular and open communication. **Lack of communication is** one of the biggest complaints across all disciplines. Clear pathways of regular communication are vital and the absence of such can lead to many of the problems discussed creating misunderstandings, delays, and a lack of cohesion between music and the rest of the team.

ASSET MANAGEMENT

Make no mistake about it, game design is not only a team sport, but also a contact sport! Understanding what each of your team members does and learning to work with others in a creative setting has a learning curve. Sometimes, the things that should be on your radar are the farthest thing from music composition. Ultimately, the following subjects may not be the most creative use of your time, but they are very important to know about and understand.

Let's start out with two vital skills that are rarely if ever discussed!

Working with an Asset List

Games have a lot of moving parts, and as a result, we need to meticulously track things. Asset lists, either static or interactive, are an important part of keeping track of all the music that goes into a game. As you make creative choices, you'll also need to create a list of every track and its function. The document that contains this information is called the audio asset list. Usage of asset lists will vary from company to company and gig to gig. Not every project will use one and that is due to the rise of task tracking software like Jira, Asana, Trello, and Slack which replace a lot of the functionality. As long as there's a way to track the development of assets in a game project any of these methods can work, but relying on just your memory is definitely **not** a professional way to go.

These tracking methods are very important because they are your roadmap to keep you and the team on task during the development process. They are also an effective way of communicating your progress to the rest of the team. Sometimes the producers or developers will already have this information. Sometimes they will have it included in a game design document, or they may have nothing at all. It's up to you to ask about this list and if they don't have one yet and they don't have any asset tracking alternative, to go about creating it. Each item in an audio asset list should contain at least the following information:

- the name of the sound broken out by type (music, sound effect, or voice-over)

- a file name that follows a standardized file naming convention

- a description of the function of the sound (e.g., car sounds or dialog)

- an indication of whether the sound is looping or a one-shot (play once) trigger

As shown in Figure 10.1, the file name of the asset is listed in the fourth column. You can organize your list by whatever criteria you want. In this case, the creators of this game thought that game location was the most important category, followed by the trigger of the sound (a button, an object in game, and so forth), the description (or category) of the sound, the file name, and finally, a comment, which acts more like a description here.

The list in Figure 10.2 is created in Google Docs, and uses multiple color fields to delineate what stage in the development cycle each sound is in.

We can't stress enough the importance of a well-thought-out asset list and file naming convention in game audio design. Without it, hundreds or thousands of assets (or more) will have no description as to their function within the game.

Let's look at a few commonalities:

- **No Spaces** – use underscore or dash instead. Probably the most common characteristic of a file naming convention is that it has no spaces, using either the understroke character like_this or a dash like-this. The reason for this is that many systems will regard the space as a separator and consider your filename as two objects.

KinderBach - Audio Matrix
Zephyr Games Inc.

Location	Trigger	Description	File Name	Line
Title Screen				
	End of Music Start or Continue	Background Music Loop		
	Entrance	Background Music Start		
	Entrance from Game Start	VO	KinderBack_Line__01	Welcome to KinderBach!
	ALT	VO	KinderBack_Line__02	KinderBach!
	Idle Reminder	VO	KinderBack_Line__03	Let's learn about music!
	User Taps Upsell Button	SFX		
	User Taps on Games Button	SFX		
	User Taps on Lessons Button	SFX		
	User Taps on Store Button	SFX		
	User Returns from Sub-Menu	VO	KinderBack_Line__04	Welcome back!
Credits				
	Continued from Title	Background Music Loop		
	Entrance from Title	VO	KinderBack_Line__05	These people made this game!
	User Taps on Back Button	SFX		
Upsell Screen				
	Continued from Title	Background Music Loop		

Example of a basic Audio Assets List from the Game Kinderbach, produced by Zephyr Games. Credit: Zephyr Games

FIGURE 10.1 Audio asset list example.

A	B	C	D	E	F	G
			STATUS/ Key			
Game Engine:						
Platform:						
File Format:						
DELIVERY DATE MUSIC	Developer Please Fill In Required Delivery Dates Here			Needs to be made		
DELIVERY DATE SFX	Fill In Delivery Date Here			Made/delivered waiting to be put in game		
DELIVERY DATE VO	Fill In Delivery Date Here			In game awaiting Approval		
				Approved		
				In game needs to be removed and updated		
Sound ID/File Name	Description	LOCATION	Audio Status	Licenced Sounds (Music SFX)	NOTES	
Game Play SFX (File name here)	Type of sound/function of sound	Where in the game?	See key Above	If used, Library info here		
Example: gameabreviation_soundname_sfx_01.wav						
UI/Interface SFX						
Example: gameabreviation_soundname_ui_01.wav						
MUSIC						
Example: gameabreviation_trackname_music_01.wav						

FIGURE 10.2 Audio asset organization by color.

- **Type Prefix** – Breaking sound filenames out by type is another pretty common approach. So if you have a piece of music for a specific section, rather than just using "*music.wav*" or something similar, you extend it with a prefix like MUS_ in front of it. So now it's "*MUS_music.wav*".

- **Get More Descriptive** – You know it's music, but where is it used? Now we can extend to "*MUS_opening-screen.wav*" instead. This way the description is helpful even without having the asset list handy to translate.

- **Variation Numbering** – Let's say you've got a bunch of variations of the music. Now you need to include the number of the variation. We now have "*MUS_opening-screen_01.wav*". The use of the leading zero has to do with alphabetical sorting. Doing it this way means that the variations will come in order. If you instead use a single digit like "1" and you have less than 10 variations you'll be fine, but if you get more than 10 the result when sorted will be "1" followed by "10,11,12,13", etc. on up to 19 and then you'll get "2". So putting a 0 in front ensures the sorting will work, up to 100 variations anyway.

- **String Matching** – This is sort of at the heart of how programmers can efficiently deal with integrating audio assets into the game. If we have a consistent naming convention, a programmer can match certain characters in the file (the whole name is called a string and the smaller part a substring) to get access to it. For example, if the name contains "MUS" at the front of all music in the game, then running a match for "mus" will get us all the music. But let's say we want to divide it up differently. Let's say we have a game and our first environment is a warehouse. So, we'll use a two-character extension "WH" to designate any asset belonging to the Warehouse. This means if the programmer matches for "Music_WH" that means they will access all the music for that particular level.

This is obviously just scratching the surface. But as you can see, getting together with the producer and programmer ahead of time and settling on a coherent file naming convention and asset tracking system in advance is something you will encounter frequently.

Source Control

Imagine you are working on a game that is being developed by a company with 100 employees. How can everyone's work, changes and alterations that are happening simultaneously, be tracked and saved? Welcome to source control, also known as version tracking. This is a system that tracks changes to the source code and other assets of a game project over time. It allows game developers to work collaboratively on a project, making changes to the code, art assets, music, and other components without overwriting each other's work or losing any previous changes. Source control systems typically use a central repository where various team members create and save different versions of the game as they work on it, and the system keeps track of all those changes. Some systems like Git allow several individuals to work on code at one time while others like Perforce are more like centralized libraries that can only allow "loaning" of an asset to one person at a time. These tools may also provide features such as branching and merging, which allow developers to work on different parts of the game simultaneously without conflicts.

These tools are usually free to use and learn from. Version tracking is one of the lesser known and desired skills for game audio and music professionals that is consistently overlooked by most game audio education programs, so experience with this will certainly help out when looking for work in the industry.

WHERE DO I BELONG, FREELANCE OR IN-HOUSE?

There are two main categories of positions when looking for composing work in the industry:

In-House Composer – This would be a full-time salaried position at a game company. Pros:

- You get a full time salary with benefits, possible stock options, and more.

- You may get a lot of opportunities to broaden your skills or wear a lot of hats or have a lot of responsibilities (in small to medium size developers).

- You will likely work closely with a team for an extended time, which will create good networking connections for future growth.

- You may get recognition for outstanding music work for large game companies, which will help your game composing career if you decide to go freelance later.

Cons:

- You may have to do a lot of sound design work as well as composing (especially true in small to medium size developers).

- You may have to work long hours, especially during crunch time before the game releases.

- You might still get laid off, especially after a project's completion or if a bigger company merges with your company.

- In large companies, you might not have as much room for advancement.

In general, the basic rule of thumb is the smaller the company, the more likely it is that you'll be handling all of the sounds as well as the music, and the team won't have much in the way of other composers/sound designers to connect with. However, you will likely work with a development team of other specialists – programmers, artists, and animators, which helps you get familiar with how the development process works in general. Some companies will just hire you as an in house composer, but these opportunities are becoming increasingly rare. In this case, you will focus on your compositions and may not have as many opportunities to advance or explore other roles.

Freelance Composer – This is a part time position with a contract.
Pros:

- You will get to work with a lot of different developers and companies.

- You will likely get to work with game audio pros, and audio directors.

- You can mainly concentrate on composing and mixing the music though you might have to implement the music in middleware like Wwise or FMOD.

- Leaves time free for composing for film, video, or other projects.

Cons:

- No salary with benefits and no stock options. Taxes are not likely to be withheld.

- It's often too many projects at one time or not many projects (aka "feast or famine").

- Time management has to be important. If you offer a flat fee for music composition, you may spend too many hours, and thus make little money.

- Establishing continuing working relationships with producers or developers can be difficult.

- You may be brought in at the last minute to add music and thus be limited by what's already set up by the audio team.

Again, the same caveats apply to being a freelancer, meaning you might be brought in much earlier in the project and have a much larger say in how the music is organized or what tools to use. In really small indie companies, they might hire you as the audio director and you get to handle everything-music, sound effects, and VO. In general, though, in a freelance scenario you will usually be the one working in an existing framework established by the audio team (if there is one).

NETWORKING

So if you're going out there in the world seeking opportunities to compose music for games, you will definitely be required to have this skill. There are absolutely reams of information about this topic, and in this dynamic and frankly, volatile world where jobs may be plentiful, but careers at one place are often not, establishing connections becomes absolutely vital for your survival. It is depressingly commonplace for well-established game companies to lay off whole sections after a big title release or go out of business due to any number of factors, and when that happens your networks are just as valuable as they would be in getting the work in the first place.

So, you might think that networking is meeting people in the game industry and selling who you are and pitching them for job openings. It can very occasionally be that this works out for you to land a job this way. However, most of the time this is exactly the WORST way to go about networking. It's definitely about meeting and connecting with folks, both your peers in the game-audio world as well as the other areas like art, animation, programming, producing, etc. But doing so with the focus primarily being on your needs is a limited way to go about doing it. Networking is a long game, and to benefit from it, you need to help others first. It may seem a bit strange to say this, but it's totally true and those are the types of connections that can help you in the future.

Here's a scenario: Let's say you meet an artist who's really amazing and you connect with them. Then some months later you happen to meet and connect with a game designer, who just happens to be looking for a great artist for their game and you suggest that person to them. Then that artist gets the gig doing art and then maybe goes on to do another gig with a different company and that company is looking for some music and sound design, and the artist remembers you and recommends you for the job. That's a relatively simple example; in some cases, it may take a while to get any benefit out of a connection, and sometimes nothing happens at all. There is also the situation where you have to really trust your recommendations, which in this case means really knowing what great game art looks like. It also means you don't recommend somebody solely on them being a friend of yours or just a connection.

Primarily you have to get out there and meet and interact with people, online and in person. When you're passionate about games or even certain genres like JRPGs or *Call of Duty*, or 16-bit games, you can make solid connections with other fans who are working in the industry, and it's those connections that will likely pay more dividends than sending résumés out or pestering connections for work.

You definitely want to make connections with other game audio/music professionals as well, but don't expect them to immediately recommend you for work. If they do, that means they trust you with their reputation to deliver at a level equivalent to themselves, and you don't achieve that level of trust overnight. Basically, the idea is to connect with others, and share your love of games and ideas about games first, recommend those who you think are awesome to others, and occasionally benefit down the road.

Also, you can potentially get work opportunities as a result of great connections and meetings, but your best approach is to fully understand your client's needs and offer yourself and your skills as a solution to those needs, rather than looking for any kind of job.

COMMUNITY ORGANIZATIONS FOR GAME COMPOSERS, AKA ENLIGHTENED SELF-INTEREST

Interactive Audio Special Interest Group (IASIG) https://www.iasig.org/

The IASIG is an independent entity with a huge emphasis on video games and interactive audio of all kinds. This organization tends to focus a lot of its work on creating standards that developers and hardware makers can adhere to, in order to make life easier for musicians working in interactive music. Part of our curriculum structure is inspired by work done at the IASIG to develop a thorough grounding in game audio, and recently the IASIG has become part of the International Game Developers Association (IGDA), so an IGDA membership automatically gets you membership in the IASIG. Read below for more info on the IGDA.

International Game Developers Association (IGDA) https://igda.org/

IGDA is one of the premier organizations promoting game developers and game development in general. There are several dozen chapters spread out all over the world and events of different kinds are always happening. It's a great organization to connect with because as an audio professional you need to know more game designers and developers to add to your contacts. The group has various committees and subcommittees that allow opportunities to work for the greater good of sound standards for the game audio industry. It also has a significant presence and usually assembles for a social mixer in March during the GDC (Game Developers Conference). At this mixer, you can meet and greet lots of folks who are in the industry or are looking to get in.

Game Audio Network Guild (GANG) https://www.audiogang.org/

This organization features a range of members, from newbies to grizzled veterans, all working together to raise the profile of game audio to the wider world of entertainment. They have a lot of resources for helping new composers and sound designers, including mentorships, software giveaways, and more. Its awards ceremony for game audio and music (given during the GDC) is the closest thing the game-audio world has to the Oscars (i.e., it offers recognition from peers and colleagues for high-quality work in design or originality in creating sound or music for games).

Facebook Groups

These groups are good resources to get advice from as well as potential feedback on your portfolio items. Be aware of their policies though; some groups are strictly against self-promotion in any form.

- **Game Audio Denizens**
  This is one of the oldest groups covering game audio and it has veterans, pros, and newbies. Do NOT ask for portfolio review or do excessive self-promotion. However, it's a great place to ask for DAW advice, sound design tips, how to learn more about game audio, etc.

- **Wwise Wwizards and Wwitches**
  This is a lovely group of folks dedicated to all things Wwise related. There is lots of technical talk here, but the forum is useful when you start working with it and run into issues.

- **FMOD Community**
  Just like it says, this is a community of Facebook friends posting about issues and solutions related to FMOD Studio. There is a lot of technical talk involving FMOD software, plugins, and integrations in game engines.

LinkedIn Groups

There are many groups on LinkedIn that can be good forums for discussions about game audio and game development in general. Here are some to mention: Game Audio Professionals, Game Audio, Game Developers, and Careers in Games. There are many more so this is barely scratching the issue. Search on your own and see what can be found!

And finally, **Game Audio Jobs** is a great place to see what employers are looking for if you want to do full-time work as a game audio pro!

GAME JAMS

One last thing to mention is a phenomenon known as a game jam, occasionally known as a hackathon as well (Figure 10.3). Game jams happen frequently throughout the year where developers have a certain amount of time to assemble a team and create a game. Usually that time is limited. Most frequently it's 48 hours, but it can be 72 hours, 24 hours, a week, or even as little as an hour. Game jams can happen onsite physically or online, but in either case they are prime opportunities for networking with other developers and for practicing your craft under a tight deadline – both very important parts of your career. Although there are frequently several jams each year, they do not keep regular, recurring schedules. They will often run for a few years and then stop, or simply happen one time only. Or they might be somewhere in between. Here are a couple of the game jams that occur regularly every year:

Global Game Jam (late January): https://globalgamejam.org/

FIGURE 10.3   Game Jam by Jason Krüger. (CC BY-SA 4.0.)

This is the granddaddy of them all. There is huge participation in this one. In 2012, onsite and online participants in 242 locations across 47 countries created over 2,000 games in one weekend. It's probably the one event you don't want to miss, but be prepared to do a lot of work for multiple teams.

Ludum Dare (three times per year): https://ldjam.com/

Probably the most well known of the online-based competitions/game jams, Ludum Dare has offered two options for participating since 2010. The first is a stricter competition, but the other is a more open and team-friendly jam. Everything is online, although some onsite locations occasionally host the jam.

Here are a couple of pointers about participating in a game jam:

Be there on the initial day of the jam. The first day of a game jam is by far the most important – this is when they socialize, form teams, and devise the ideas for games. If you can't make the first day of the jam and you don't know anyone attending (if the jam is onsite), you likely won't get to have any part in designing the game at a minimum, and you may not end up with anyone to work with.

You don't have to be onsite the whole time (onsite jams only). This might sound contradictory since we just discussed how important it is to be there on the first day. However, after that, it may be better for you to work from home. An onsite game jam can be a chaotic affair – lots of teams talking, being excited about their various games, even test-playing them. All of this can be a distracting experience for a sound person. Thus, you have the option of working from home and supplying your assets remotely via Dropbox, email, or some other service. If you do decide to work onsite (which can have its benefits in terms of getting on multiple teams), make sure you have a good-quality, sealed-ear headphone and be prepared to move to the quietest area in the jam space to do it.

Be prepared for any outcome. It must be said that your team may not end up finishing the game or you might not be able to make the assets required. The team's internal dynamic might implode halfway through, or you might have a wonderful experience. This takes a while to get used to. After all, you're there to make music for a game and get your sounds out there in front of everyone else.

However, if you think of the experience as simply being exposed to a game-making environment – getting to know a bunch of games and game developers, and networking with them – you'll more than likely have a great time, regardless of how your team's game turns out.

GAME ORIENTED EVENTS

Game Developers Conference (GDC) https://gdconf.com/

This is the mother of all game conferences, and it's usually the largest in terms of attendance. It is held every year in San Francisco at Moscone Center and is a huge opportunity to meet and connect with folks from all over the world covering every aspect of the game industry. There is of course a healthy amount of game audio talks happening and even if you can only manage the expo pass, there are usually a lot of events that happen around this time that are generally open to anyone who attends. Various procedures and passes are available and change year to year.

GameSoundCon https://www.gamesoundcon.com/

Originally started as a one-day conference, it has now expanded to three days and has a very big attendance from game audio folks of all stripes and types. If you want to learn about the state of game audio and connect with your peers in the field, this is definitely the convention to attend. It's usually held in Los Angeles in fall. Attendance costs are a bit higher than the expo prices of the GDC, but far cheaper than the Audio pass.

PRACTICAL MATTERS

It is a big world out there and the good news is that there is a lot of opportunity in games for composers these days. However, the competition is fierce, so you have to think entrepreneurially. Remember, there is a lot of creativity that can be applied to the business of composing. While you think about that, here are some steps you can take to get work and stay active.

1. **Build your portfolio:** Create a strong portfolio of your work by composing music for games, whether it's for your own projects or for others. This will demonstrate your skills and allow potential employers to see what you are capable of. Use the Game Lessons in the course or anything else you find to demonstrate that by putting your music into a real working game, and you understand how game music and sound are different from other music fields.

2. **Get education and training:** Consider getting a degree or certificate in music composition or a related field. There are also many online courses and workshops available that can help you learn the skills you need to succeed in the field. More education is never a bad thing. And the more you understand about other aspects of the industry more opportunities might crop up.

3. **Network with industry professionals:** Attend game industry events and conferences, join online communities and forums, and make connections with people working in the game music field. This can help you learn about job openings and get your foot in the door.

4. **Look for job openings:** Keep an eye out for job openings at game studios and other companies that produce games. Many studios have dedicated audio teams, and some also hire freelance audio professionals for specific projects.

5. **Consider starting your own business:** If you have the skills and experience, you could consider starting your own game music business. This can allow you to work on your own terms and create your own opportunities.

THE BIG TAKEAWAY

It takes hard work, dedication, and persistence to succeed in the game music field. But with the right skills, education, and connections, you can find rewarding and exciting work. Composing music for a visual medium like games is an applied art form. It's also an industry that involves a lot of technology. But we must never forget that the most important thing is imagination. Your creativity, the spirit, and the passion that you bring to each project that you work on are paramount. Programs will come and go, technology will change over time, but the overarching concepts and commitment to the process of doing good work for its own sake will always be the catalyst that launches a rich and fulfilling life. If your goal is to have a career in games, concentrate on your art and craft. I am certain that if you apply yourself to the process, good things will follow.

Section-02 Assignments

Assignment 01

Composer Report

RECOMMENDATION: CHAPTER 1 OR 2

Context: In the early days of gaming, composers and sound artists were not credited for their work. Believe it or not, this practice still goes on today in many companies. This assignment is very important, because it gives credit where credit is due to the creative artists that pour their heart and soul into creating beautiful music for us all to enjoy. For teachers, this can also serve as a database of composers to share from semester to semester.

For this assignment find a game composer you like and produce a short report detailing their life and career in at least 500 words.

It should cover the following:

- Biography

- Musical influences

- Games they have worked on

- Musical examples

- Gameplay examples with music

DOI: 10.1201/9781003414728-14

Assignment 02

Create the Music Section of a GDD (Game Design Document)

RECOMMENDATION: CHAPTER 2

Context: This thought experiment will help you to understand many of the elements that go into composing music and designing a music system for a game. It will also give you practical experience in creating the music section for a GDD so you will already be familiar when tasked to do so in the real world. Being able to communicate clearly effectively when describing music for and function is a very important and needed skill in the industry.

Assignment: In this assignment, you will be tasked with creating an imaginary game and then coming up with a coherent description of all aspects of the music and music system. Include answers to all the questions and sections below.

GENERAL INFORMATION

- **Team/Game:** (*List the name of the game team and project here*)

- **Style and form of the game:** (*A short description of the look and feel of the game, include scenarios, narrative, and characters*)

- **Gameplay mechanic:** (*A short description of how the game works, including game loop, screenflow, and transitions*)

- **Schedule:** (*List the music development timeline including delivery dates*)

- **Game Engine Information:** (*List what game engine will be used*)

- **Audio Delivery Quality and Format:** (*List bit rate, sample rate, and file type here*)

- **Target file size for all the music in the game:** (*List how much space will be allotted for music in the game*)

DOI: 10.1201/9781003414728-15

OUTLINE/OBJECTIVES: (*This is your overview. It should contain a statement or two describing the goals, purpose, and style of the complete music design for the game. Use word and flow charts and graphs*)

- **MUSIC:** (*Make a brief statement about how the music will work, outlined in very simple terms with descriptions of transition types, flow, and function*)

- **RESEARCH:** (*List any games that are similar, what styles, and include any references here*)

- **IMPLEMENTATION:** (*Define a set of rules: permutations and boundaries (limits) as to how the music works on a more detailed level. This section should be more technical. The goal here is to clearly describe how our music world is defined*)

- **Testing:** (*List the main areas of the music design that will need to be included in testing*)

- **Relevancy:** (*List and rank what part of the music design should be considered higher priority than others*)

- **Middleware Information:** (*List the name of the music middleware to be used here if any*)

Reminder: Don't forget to add this to your portfolio!

Assignment 03

Setting Up Your Work Space

RECOMMENDATION: CHAPTER 3

Context: Setting up your tools and making a place to do your work that is comfortable and familiar are very important. Morton Feldman, a prominent American composer of the 20th century, placed great importance on his composing space and the environment in which he worked. He believed that his workspace was essential to his creative process and that the right atmosphere was necessary to cultivate his ideas. Feldman said, "My work environment is of great importance to me. I like a kind of darkness around me, and I need silence. I'm very sensitive to the environment in which I work, and it has a direct impact on my music." In addition, Feldman believed that his workspace should be free of distractions, such as phone calls and visitors, so that he could fully focus on his work. He once said, "I don't like the telephone to ring when I'm working. It's like a thief. It takes away your thoughts, and you have to start all over again." Composers have varying opinions about setting up their workspace, but many emphasize the importance of creating an environment that is conducive to their creative process.

If you are already working in a professional recording studio, bravo! If not and for many readers, you will be setting up a home recording studio and this can be a complex process, but there are some basic steps that can help ensure that you create a space that is functional, efficient, and capable of producing high-quality recordings. Here are some key tips for setting up a home recording studio:

1. **Choose a suitable room:** It's important to choose a room that is suitable for recording and mixing. Look for a space that is quiet, with minimal outside noise and minimal echo or reverb. Ideally, the room should be large enough to accommodate your recording equipment and any additional furniture or instruments you may need.

2. **Acoustically treat the room:** Once you've selected a suitable room, it's important to acoustically treat the space to optimize the sound quality. This can include adding acoustic panels to absorb sound reflections, installing bass traps to control

DOI: 10.1201/9781003414728-16

low-frequency resonances, and using diffusers to scatter sound reflections. You can also use furniture, rugs, and curtains to help dampen sound reflections.

3. **Choose your equipment:** Select the appropriate recording equipment based on your recording needs and budget. This can include a computer or laptop, audio interface, microphones, headphones, and monitors. Invest in high-quality gear that can produce the best results within your budget.

4. **Set up your equipment:** Once you have your equipment, set it up in a way that is ergonomic and functional. Make sure that all cables are neatly organized and properly connected, and that your equipment is easily accessible.

5. **Install software:** Install software that is compatible with your operating system and audio interface. Familiarize yourself with the software and learn how to use it effectively.

6. **Test your setup:** Before you start working, test your setup to make sure everything is working properly. Check for any background noise or unwanted sound, and adjust your equipment and settings as necessary.

7. **Continuously improve your setup:** Finally, keep in mind that a studio is an ongoing project. Continuously work on improving your setup and upgrading your equipment as your needs and budget allow.

ASSIGNMENT

- Setup your work desk
- Setup your speakers
- Setup your computer and audio interface
- Install your DAW
- Install your Notation Program
- Install the Unity game engine
- Install FMOD
- Install any other programs you use

For more information, this is a great reference book about digital recording and studio setup
Modern Recording Techniques (Audio Engineering Society Presents) 9th Edition
by David Miles Huber (Author) and Robert Runstein (Author).

Assignment 04

Welcome to the Screen Shot Challenge

RECOMMENDATION: CHAPTER 4 OR 5

Context: In this exercise, we start from a single static image. Nothing is moving yet, but the process of composing a short piece of music even for a non-moving screen can be very illuminating. You may be surprised by how much information can be translated to the viewer by a short piece of music, composed for a single image. The goal is to build a step by step vocabulary to help understand the power and effect music has on visual imagery in the broadest sense. It also provides a constant reminder that the principles of composition relate to games by providing information to the experience. This information affects a game's pace, emotion, and immersive quality.

For example, melody can be tied to character animation in games by matching the line to an animation's look, feel, or actions. Check out our little ant character, wearing sunglasses (Figure A4.1); imagine them running around really fast. The composer in me might reach for fast high-pitched melodic minor melodies that use octave jumps and skips played on xylophones to create a satisfying scurrying feeling and then I might just add a funky groove to give our character a hip adult attitude. However, if I went another direction and instead employed stepwise major scale melodies that move up and down along with a rolling polka in the bass, we might think of this character as more childlike or silly.

Assignment: In this assignment, you will be asked to take a look at the screenshot provided on this page and then compose a single 30-second piece of Looping music based on that image. The idea is to analyze the image and then let your eye and ear take over. Compose what you feel the image needs.

- Export and deliver as a 16bit 44.1k .wav LOOPING Stereo file (*this loop must be seamless, no slips or pops*)

- Use the following naming convention when you deliver; **yourname_music_nameofpiece_01.wav**

DOI: 10.1201/9781003414728-17

FIGURE A4.1   (Image: Austin Smith/GAI)

Once delivered, listen to your piece along with the entire class as everyone looks at the image up on screen. Let it loop around a couple of times and then drop the volume and let it play in the background while you have a short class discussion.

HERE ARE SOME QUESTIONS FOR EVERYONE TO CONSIDER

- **Discussion Questions:** Is the image a natural one? Does the music match or contrast the image? Does the orchestration match the image, if not why? How does the music make you feel about this picture? How do we go about matching music and images?

- **Melody:** Is there a strong melody in the music? If so, what effect does melody have on the viewer's perception? If not, what effect does that have on our perception?

- **Harmony:** Is there a strong harmonic element to the piece? If so, what effect does harmony have on the viewer's perception? If not, what effect does lack of harmony have on the viewer's perception?

- **Rhythm:** Is the rhythm of this piece regular or disjoined? What can you tell about the rhythmic aspects of this piece and what effect does the rhythm have on the image?

- **Visual Cueing:** What visual elements, if any, does the music bring out in this image?

- **Function:** What would you say is the function of the music for this image? Does the music suggest any function if it were to be used in game play? Would it be a title screen for example or function better in another part of the game and if so, why?

- **Mix Quality:** What about the mix and the production of the track, is it well balanced, and does it serve the image well?

- **Repeatability:** The music has been on for a while in the background, are we tired of listening to it, if yes why, if not why?

SOME GENTLE RULES FOR IN CLASS CRITIQUE AND RESPECTING THE CREATIVE PROCESS

As we enter into group discussions, the goal is to have everyone express their point of view so that it might help to illuminate to the composer/artist the effect of their work on others.

- **Begin:** With something you like or enjoy about the work (*Compliments*)

- **Notice:** Simply notice something about the work (*Observation*)

- **Wonder:** Inquire about anything in the work that caught your attention; this is the time to give constructive feedback to the composer

- **End:** With something you like or enjoy about the work (***More Compliments***)

After all of this discussion and investigation and after the composer of the piece absorbs the feedback, invite them to speak about what they were trying to accomplish and if the comments were helpful.

Reminder: Don't forget to add this to your portfolio!

Assignment 05

Notation Exploration

RECOMMENDATION: CHAPTER 4

Context: This exercise is designed to increase your awareness of how written music, scores, and parts are developed and constructed. By examining many types of scores from all different time periods as well as varying ensembles, we start to become aware of the many conventions that are used. By hand copying some of your favorite music, you will also slow down the process of composition and arranging, giving yourself the opportunity to absorb the work of master composers throughout history. This is a chance to match eye and ear and make the process of dealing with written music both more comfortable and enjoyable.

Assignment part 1: Go out and find a complete score and set of parts to a string quartet, a woodwind quintet, a Beethoven symphony, a big band piece, and any others that you might find interesting. As a group or on your own, examine all of this material, discussing and comparing the details of the preparation.

- Produce a short report detailing your findings in at least 500 words

Assignment part 2: Take one of the scores that you like the most from the above and either hand copy or enter the first 12 bars onto sheet music paper or into your notation program of choice.

- Export or scan in PDF format

Discussion Questions: Is the format clear? How clear are the passages? Is there enough detail for the players (*articulations, cues, and phrase markings*)? Is the music well orchestrated? Could you suggest ways of improving the score or parts?

DOI: 10.1201/9781003414728-18

Assignment 06

Classic to Modernity, the Art of Translation

RECOMMENDATION: CHAPTER 4

Context: What is music? What is game music? This exercise is designed to start a dialog through music. By expressing our individual ideas and composing and listening to the music thoughts of others. Perhaps this way, we can begin to discover some common threads that help answer these questions!

Assignment: Go out and choose any piece of music from any culture that is **AT LEAST** 100 years old and then re-orchestrate it to go in an imaginary game. It's very common in games for composers to have to work with music that already exists in one form or another and re-orchestrate and translate that music into the game world. This may be branded music that serves a specific style from a franchise, or a style of music from antiquity that is referenced. Here we are using older tracks in order to explore the question of what is game music and further develop our sense of how music affects perception.

This assignment will help to develop your skills in transcription, orchestration, and culture by helping to better understand the music of the past and how it relates to the present day.

- Export and deliver as a 16bit 44.1k .wav LOOPING Stereo file

- Use the following naming convention when you deliver; **yourname_music_nameofpiece_01.wav**

Discussion Questions: Why did you choose your piece? What is the historic and cultural significance of the music and composer? What is or is not game music and why? What makes this music game music? What is gamification and what does gamify mean? How and why do we need to translate music from the past into the world of games? What specific instruments and techniques did you use to create this work? Did you increase or decrease the tempo of the music, if so why if not why? What function does the music suggest, where do you think it might be used in a game, and why?

DOI: 10.1201/9781003414728-19

Some Gentle Rules for in Class Critique and Respecting the Creative Process

As we enter into group discussions, the goal is to have everyone express their point of view so that it might help to illuminate to the composer/artist the effect of their work on others.

- **Begin:** With something you like or enjoy about the work (*Compliments*)

- **Notice:** Simply notice something about the work (*Observation*)

- **Wonder:** Inquire about anything in the work that caught your attention, this is the time to give constructive feedback to the composer

- **End:** With something you like or enjoy about the work (***More Compliments***)

After all of this discussion and investigation and after the composer of the piece absorbs the feedback, invite them to speak about what they were trying to accomplish and if the comments were helpful.

Reminder: Don't forget to add this to your portfolio!

Assignment 07

Composing for Cinematics

RECOMMENDATION: CHAPTER 5

Context: The process of composing music for moving images is very similar to static imagery, but now we add the dimension of time into the equation. We need to consider when music should start and stop and what does and does not need underscore. Things are still not interactive but much can be learned as we deal with story arcs and timing. We also need to be thinking about the music in the rest of the game and how it does or does not reference our cinematic. This is quite an important point and part of creating a cohesive whole so that the music of the game develops in a cohesive manner.

Early games told a story mainly through gameplay. As platforms became more sophisticated and file sizes increased, the idea of telling more of a story using video became popular. As the 1980s use of generated music and sounds from consoles like the NES gradually gave way to the use of MIDI-triggered music and compact sample banks, the next decade ushered in the advent of the CD-ROM and a corresponding huge increase in storage capacity. This innovative leap opened up the doors for composers to move away from MIDI, and for the first time start to use live digitally recorded instrumental music, from rock bands, on up to full orchestras.

Cinematic music for games accompanies various video clips – depending on the focus and placement in the structure, these clips can be called cutscenes, introductions, endings, or story transitions. They are linear pieces of media that help propel the storyline forward. Writing music for these is much like scoring for other linear mediums like film, cartoons, and TV.

ASSIGNMENT: FIND A GAME PLAY CUTSCENE ON AND CREATE AN ORIGINAL SCORE

- Go to YouTube, **search for games, and cutscenes and pick your favorite.** (Not too long one to three minutes, also the clip should not have music in it already, just SFX and VO, it can also be completely silent, or you can remove the existing soundtrack all together. The point is there must be no music, you will be writing that!)

DOI: 10.1201/9781003414728-20

- Using a converter tool, **export the video as a .mp4 file** (*Converter tools are common and can be found free online*)

- Once converted, **import** the cutscene video into your DAW

- **Create** your own original soundtrack to the video

- When finished, **export from your DAW as an Mp4 file**

- Deliver use this naming convention: **yourname_music_nameofpiece_01.wav**

Once delivered, listen to the piece along with the entire class as everyone looks at the video on screen, and then have a class discussion.

HERE ARE SOME QUESTIONS FOR EVERYONE TO CONSIDER

Discussion Questions: Does the music match or contrast the video? How does one decide when music is needed and where, explain? Do you think the music was successful in supporting the story and characters if yes why, if no why not? Does the music match the timing in the clip, if not why? Does the orchestration of music support the look and feel? Are there moments in the clip that you wish had been punctuated by music, explain?

Reminder: Don't forget to add this to your portfolio!

Some Gentle Rules for in Class Critique and Respecting the Creative Process

As we enter into group discussions, the goal is to have everyone express their point of view so that it might help to illuminate to the composer/artist the effect of their work on others.

- **Begin:** With something you like or enjoy about the work (*Compliments*)

- **Notice:** Simply notice something about the work (*Observation*)

- **Wonder:** Inquire about anything in the work that caught your attention; this is the time to give constructive feedback to the composer

- **End:** With something you like or enjoy about the work (***More Compliments***)

After all of this discussion and investigation and after the composer of the piece absorbs the feedback, invite them to speak about what they were trying to accomplish and if the comments were helpful.

Assignment 08

Defining Form

RECOMMENDATION: CHAPTER 6

Context: Below are just some of the important questions to ask as you start any project. If you talk to professionals in the field (which you absolutely should), they will probably have more questions and ideas to add to this list. Many times we are asked to start composing too soon in the process. If we don't understand the process and how the entire game and music system works, this is a recipe for disaster, wasted time, incrimination, and multiple rewrites. All of the questions below and more will come into sharper focus once you have had a chance to experience gameplay in real time. Additionally, if there is any kind of a build of the game available, you should request to play it, even in the most nascent stages of development. For the purposes of this assignment, we will ask you to use an existing game. Don't ever be afraid to ask questions like these – in game development, knowledge is king!

Assignment: Find a game you like and answer these questions in writing to the best of your ability. Use a video playthrough or better yet play the game itself in real time! **Deliver as a PDF.**

- **What Kind of Game Is This?** Is it a side-scrolling kids' game with goofy cartoon graphics, or is it a big budget console game with super life-like animations?

- **What Is the Target Audience for This Game?** Is the game for adults, or is it for small children? Is the game aimed at boys or girls? Some sounds are more appropriate for certain audiences than others.

- **What Is the Pace of the Game?** Is the game fast or slow? Is it supposed to feel frenetic or mellow? These considerations affect sound choices. A puzzle game will likely have more relaxed sounds, while a fast-paced action title will result in a more frenetic palette.

- **What Platform Is the Game Developed For?** The platform determines how we prepare the music for final delivery. You can generally expect different workflows for different platforms. Also, the more you know about each system, the more optimized your design can be.

DOI: 10.1201/9781003414728-21

- **What Is the Audio Budget for the Game, How Big Can the Files Be?** Impossible to know, but based on your detailed analysis make your best guess!! It is important to know what you are up against, before you get too far down any road. Nothing is worse than spending considerable time creating awesome sounds only to find out there is no room for them in the game. You may also have a processor limitation in addition to the audio budget. For this one you will have to make your best educated guess based on your play thru and knowledge of the title you have chosen.

- **What Is the Hardware Space Budget of this Game?** Even if you have the audio budget allotted to you by the producer, you may not have the actual physical memory or storage space to apply them. This is especially true for portable and mobile games. In many cases, the game designer or producer will have the answer to these questions. In other cases, you may need to speak with the programmer or integrator to get the correct information. You need to know a device's hardware limitations relative to the budget you're given. For this one you will have to make your best educated guess based on your play thru and knowledge of the title you have chosen.

Assignment 09

Welcome to the Limbo Challenge

RECOMMENDATION: CHAPTER 6

Context: Now that we have covered some of the basics and how they relate to the form and structure of music. Let's break down a specific project and look at how the music was consciously designed, and made to work for an original, and award winning game, involving a music soundtrack with a very unique approach combining sound design and music.

Assignment: Compose an interactive score for Limbo

Get a working copy of the game Limbo or grab a YouTube video clip (*no commentary*) and compose your own soundtrack using the asset requested below. Do yourself a favor, and get a screenshot video or rip a video of Limbo game play from the web and score that inside your DAW for inspiration. You need to keep in mind that this is a non-linear assignment. Use the video as a guide for pacing and tempo and feel, then you will break all the music into individual files. In class, play the game or show the video of Limbo and trigger the music and stingers in real time. One computer can be used for video, and the other for triggering the music tracks using a DAW or program like VLC. The idea is to slow the process of syncing music triggers down, so that everyone can see in real time how the process works. Include a class discussion of what style of game this is and what is most likely happening behind the scenes with the game's coding and design.

LEARNING OUTCOMES

- Create music for Limbo
- Prepare and edit your music for the game via your DAW of choice
- Get a gameplay video with no commentary from YouTube or play the game on your platform of choice
- Export and deliver all your music as 16bit 44.1k .wav, stereo files
- Use this naming convention: yourname_music_nameofpiece_01.wav
- Deliver your music tracks compressed into one ZIP file

DOI: 10.1201/9781003414728-22

Asset List

- Title/Menu Screen Loop 20–30 seconds

- Title Singer/Transition 5–10 seconds (one Shot)

- Gameplay Music Loop 60–90 seconds

- Death Stinger 5–10 seconds (one Shot)

Discussion Questions: Did your music transition work in real time? How did your music affect the emotional content of the game play? How does game play in real time change or not change the way your music is perceived in the game, please explain? Why is the idea of iteration so important in game music? How did the process of prototyping help or hurt your workflow? Is your score a complete whole, and do all the musical parts fit together including the stingers? If yes why, if no why not?

Some Gentle Rules for in Class Critique and Respecting the Creative Process

As we enter into group discussions, the goal is to have everyone express their point of view so that it might help to illuminate to the composer/artist the effect of their work on others.

- **Begin:** With something you like or enjoy about the work (*Compliments*)

- **Notice:** Simply notice something about the work (*Observation*)

- **Wonder:** Inquire about anything in the work that caught your attention; this is the time to give constructive feedback to the composer

- **End:** With something you like or enjoy about the work (***More Compliments***)

After all of this discussion and investigation and after the composer of the piece absorbs the feedback, invite them to speak about what they were trying to accomplish and if the comments were helpful.

Reminder: Don't forget to add this to your portfolio!

More Context: *Limbo* is a puzzle-platform game developed by the independent game developer Playdead. The game's visual style is stark, with a monochromatic black-and-white color scheme and minimalistic design. The main protagonist is a nameless boy who wakes up in a forest on the edge of hell and must navigate through various puzzles and obstacles to find his sister. As the player progresses through the game, the challenges become increasingly difficult, and the environment becomes more surreal and unsettling. The game's mechanics include jumping, climbing, and interacting with various objects in the environment. The game's narrative is minimalistic, with no dialogue or text, and the story is left open to interpretation. The game has been praised for its haunting atmosphere, innovative gameplay mechanics, and minimalist storytelling. It has won multiple awards, including the BAFTA Games Award for Best Indie Game and the DICE Award for Outstanding Achievement in Art Direction.

FIGURE A9.1   Martin Stig Andersen. (Used with permission.)

Danish composer Martin Stig Andersen (Figure A9.1) is perhaps best known for his work on *Limbo* and another Playdead title *Inside*. He has also made sonic contributions to *Wolfenstein II: The New Colossus*. Andersen studied orchestral composition at The Royal Academy of Music in Aarhus, Denmark. After graduating in 2003, he went on to study electro-acoustic composition at City University in London and cites the spectral school of composers as inspiration.

The soundtrack for *Limbo* was composed in 2009–2010. In this case, the use of the word "Soundtrack" is meant in the broadest sense of the word. Mr. Anderson's work is exceedingly creative, a haunting mix of music and ambient design. The result is riveting and matches the game's form and structure perfectly. To properly understand the detailed, careful thought and methodology that went into the music for *Limbo*, perhaps it is best to get the news straight from the composer's mouth. We have chosen the composer's own words as an excerpt from an interview with Damian Kastbauer on the Designingsound.org website to represent his work and thoughts:

> As a game composer, I think it's important to embrace the nonlinear nature of games. I have always been interested in musical properties beyond melody and harmony, beyond the time and pitch grid of the score. Working with scores, I was inspired by spectral composers such as Tristan Murail and the idea of translating recorded sound into musical performances.
>
> I learned some interesting things. Trying to make *Limbo* sound like an old film, I put everything into mono but discovered I couldn't engage with that sound. It just wasn't immersive enough. I saw *Limbo* as such a tiny world, so I was trying to reduce all the sounds to something very simple and thin sounding. I distorted sounds, then afterwards I expanded them again to really spatialise them; almost anti-phase. I ventured into using antique audio devices; wire recorders, spring reverbs and tape recorders. In linear media you can make your mix from moment

to moment, whereas in a game the sounds might be mixed differently every time you play. I discovered that using old machines created a homogenized sound. Running all of my sounds through an old tape recorder made them sit very well together in the mix. I was trying to achieve the creation of a world structure with the audio going from the quasi-realistic, naturalistic sound you hear in the forest to becoming more abstract and almost transcendent as the boy progresses through the world. You have the most horribly traumatic moments and the sound suddenly turns into something melancholic, contrasting with what you see. I wanted to make it feel like the boy got habituated to the violence rather than the player, leaving the player to wonder how they should feel. Sometimes the music would almost represent forgiveness.

On a global level, a lot went into implementing custom sound transitions between death and re-spawn in order to maintain immersion through the unloading/reloading process. That attention to the overall experience by embracing death/re-spawn is something I often miss in games. There's an intangible dynamic between real-world and game-world time there. Even though my character dies and I go back in game-world time, real-world time still frames my experience, and I easily get annoyed hearing the same line or music cue over again as I die and re-spawn. However, if I quit the game and get back to it after a few days I probably do want to hear those sounds again."

My compositional studies at conservatory and university were very much biased towards the artistic side. At City University in London where I studied electroacoustic composition the general agenda was to discuss "whys" rather than "hows," for example why a specific sound or sound structure evokes certain associations rather than how it was created. So, as far as technology is concerned I'm pretty much self-taught. On the aesthetic side, at university we dealt with all kinds of electroacoustic music, including interactive music, combining live performance (voice or instrument) and electronics. However unlike games in which interaction happens directly between the player and the game, in interactive concert music the interaction is something happening between the performer(s) on stage and an interactive playback system. In such situation the listener may not at all grasp the interactivity of a composition, which of course posed a lot of questions, like whether or not it's important for the audience to actually experience such interactivity.

In regards to interactive media I guess the most important skill I took with me from university is what you could call temporal awareness. By studying the perception of form and structure in music and audiovisuals I acquired an understanding of the various temporalities inhabiting not only sound but also visuals, and learned how to match and contrast such temporalities creatively in order to make sound contribute to the overall flow or even structure of an audiovisual experience.

What I found interesting in relation to audiovisual media was that soundscape and acousmatic music together embraces the entire continuum between representational and abstract sound, in this way dismissing the traditional dividing line between sound design and music. By deploying such approaches in audiovisual work you can make seamless transitions between realism and abstraction, and make sound travel smoothly between the diegetic and non-diegetic space of a represented world. For me it has a much bigger psychological impact when you turn a naturalistic soundscape into abstraction by making your sound effects play as "music" rather than adding some traditional background music. Moreover, making your "music" emerge from the environment is likely to make the audience more forgiving towards it since they'll accept it as stemming, however abstractly, from the environment. This feature attains special relevance in video games where the player may get stuck from time to time and the audio elements need to be flexible in terms of duration. It's important to note that although acousmatic composition does have certain potentials in relation to audiovisual work it doesn't really make sense to use the term "acousmatic" in this context. Not at least because in the context of film the term has merely come to denote diegetic sounds that are off screen.

Limbo was my first game, although I consider it more as an artistic venture.

– MARTIN STIG ANDERSEN

Assignment 10

Gameplay Music Analysis

Context: Analyzing the music and form in video games is not only fun but also essential to developing a feel for the syntax of what makes music for games so special. In-depth analysis helps us gain insight into the artistic choices made by composers, programmers, and designers, and it also helps to hone our understanding of how games are built and subsequently how music fits into the overall structure. By examining the flow and form of a game, we are able to identify specific techniques such as leitmotifs, thematic development, or harmonic progression and how all these elements work when tied to the programming of interactive and adaptive behaviors. Each time we break down a game and truly understand how the music works, we are preparing ourselves to work on original games in the industry.

Assignment: Play through one of your favorite games and analyze it in detail. This can be done using a YouTube Clip or a play thru on the platform with no commentary and prominent music.

Submit the analysis in at least 500 words.

Include the following:

- **A description of game,** including developer plot and basic game mechanics.

- **A description of the Music System**, what are the organizing principles – what mostly drives music changes in the game?

- **A description** of the music, including style form, melodic and harmonic structures, rhythm, tempo, and orchestration.

DOI: 10.1201/9781003414728-23

Assignment 11

Breakout!

RECOMMENDATION: CHAPTER 7

Grab the Breakout Game Lesson from the Game Audio Institute here:

https://www.gameaudioinstitute.com/crc

Context: Although this is a relatively small game lesson, it's a great first step for composers to practice the use and understanding of individual triggers. It is also a great way to practice solving problems compositionally. Since the transitions between screens are not tempo aware in this game, composers must use their interactive musical muscles to write music that, when implemented, will create smooth transitions. This exercise is a fun musical puzzle, where all the elements must fit together and play at any time while being musical, technically correct, and aesthetically pleasing. Also, it is such a fun classic game!

This is also an effective Game Lesson for teaching composers how to develop continuity in their scores. From the opening screen, transitions, gameplay, side bumpers, and paddle to the winner and the loser stinger, the music can sew a continuous thread. How does the opening screen music relate to the gameplay screen? Did the composer forget about the stingers? In many cases, students take the stingers for granted or simply grab something that's not related to the music track for comedy effect. Classroom settings have shown that the most effective and compelling musical compositions for this Game Lesson develop the stingers as an extension of the gameplay track, so that from beginning to end you hear an integrated composition. **For example,** choosing to place the background track in the key of A minor while setting all the paddle, bumper, and side wall hits in the A harmonic minor scale creates such an effect. Maybe the backing track is just drums and bass and each time the side bumpers are hit you get a horn stab or fall, all in key with each other. In this way, you will hear a cohesive interactive soundtrack that changes each time we play the game. This kind of composition puts us squarely in the realm of game music and develops our sense of what makes game scores unique.

Assignment: Compose and implement an interactive score for Breakout! Read the Step by Step Guide and watch the video tutorial (*provided in the same .ZIP file as your Breakout Game Level*).

202   DOI: 10.1201/9781003414728-24

LEARNING OUTCOMES

- Create music for the breakout game
- Prepare and edit your music for the game via your DAW of choice
- Implementation of music into The Breakout Game Lesson via Step-by-Step directions
- Play the game and if changes are needed, iterate by going back and re-exporting your music to adjust
- Create and submit a playable Mac/PC Build

Asset List

- Title/menu screen loop 20–30 seconds
- Gameplay music loop 60–90 seconds
- Winner stinger 3–5 seconds (one shot)
- Loser stinger 3–5 seconds (one shot)
- Paddle 1–2 seconds (one shot)
- Bumpers 1–2 seconds (one shot)

Discussion Questions: How does game play in real time change or not change the way your music is perceived in the game, please explain? Why is the idea of iteration so important in game music? Is your score a complete whole? Do all the musical parts fit together including the stingers? Was your music mixed and mastered well, if yes why, if no why not? How was your experience working in the Unity game engine?

Some Gentle Rules for in Class Critique and Respecting the Creative Process

As we enter into group discussions, the goal is to have everyone express their point of view so that it might help to illuminate to the composer/artist the effect of their work on others.

- **Begin:** With something you like or enjoy about the work (*Compliments*)
- **Notice:** Simply notice something about the work (*Observation*)
- **Wonder:** Inquire about anything in the work that caught your attention; this is the time to give constructive feedback to the composer
- **End:** With something you like or enjoy about the work (*More Compliments*)

After all of this discussion and investigation and after the composer of the piece absorbs the feedback, invite them to speak about what they were trying to accomplish and if the comments were helpful.

Reminder: Don't forget to add this to your portfolio!

TABLE A11.1   Grading Rubric for Breakout

Criteria	Best Score	Better Score	Good Score	Points
Technical Mastery Music transitions, Intensity levels, Clean looping	**40 to >35.0 pts** Transitions are clean and smooth from start to loop to end. Music intensity levels are clear and effective, and looping is musically accurate.	**35 to >30.0 pts** Transitions are mostly clean and smooth from start to loop to end. Music intensity levels are generally clear and effective. Looping is musically accurate.	**30 to >0 pts** Transitions are not clean and/or smooth from start to loop to end. Music intensity levels may be unclear or not present. looping may not be accurate.	40 pts
Audio Balance Mix Balance, Quality of Audio, No Distortion	**30 to >25.0 pts** Mix Balance Instruments all clearly heard. Quality Excellent, with No Distortion.	**25 to >20.0 pts** Mix Balance Instruments mostly heard well though some may not be. Quality Excellent, with Occasional Distortion.	**20 to >0 pts** Mix Balance Instruments frequently unheard. Quality Acceptable but may have More Distortion.	30 pts
Artistic Approach Orchestration is clear, Coherent music approach.	**30 to >25.0 pts** Very clear orchestration, Very coherent musical approach.	**25 to >20.0 pts** Orchestration is mostly clear. Musical approach is largely coherent.	**20 to >0 pts** Orchestration is less clear. Music approach lacks coherence overall.	30 pts

Permissions: GAI.

Assignment 12

The Music Maze

RECOMMENDATION: CHAPTERS 7, 8, AND 9

Get the Music Maze Game Lesson Here: https://www.gameaudioinstitute.com/crc

Context: The Music Maze is a wonderful tool for exploring interactive music design along with branching and looping structures, while lost in a hedgerow maze with only the music to tell you how to escape. Based on a series of music loops and transitions, this lesson uses the native Unity game engine's own audio system. It gives the student a chance to compose a fair amount of music while thinking creatively about music as information. If you tell the player too soon that you're going in the wrong direction, perhaps by creating a very dissonant track you may be giving too much away too soon. However, if you don't provide enough information, the player may get lost for a long time, maybe that is the desired effect. The only way to really know is to compose the music, put it in the game, play test, and see if the result is satisfactory, if not, back to the drawing board. The design of the game controls the way the game unfolds. The way the player will experience the game is all controlled by the music.

The Music Maze comes with a complete Game Lesson and step by step guide, along with a video tutorial for developing music tracks that change as the player moves through the maze. The complete package comes with a Unity level, step-by-step instructions on how to implement music and more. This is the perfect level for teaching the basic concepts of interactive scoring.

Assignment: In this assignment, you will compose an interactive score that must lead the player out of the maze to complete the game.

Read the Step by Step Guide and watch the video tutorial (*provided in the same .ZIP file as your Breakout Game Level*).

LEARNING OUTCOMES

- Read the Step by Step Guide (provided in the same .ZIP file as your Music Maze Level)

- Create music for the Music Maze (*See the asset list in step-by-step guide and as discussed in class*)

DOI: 10.1201/9781003414728-25

- Prepare and edit your music for the game via your DAW of choice

- Implementation of music into the Music MazeLesson via Step-by-Step directions and video tutorials

- Play the game and if changes are needed, iterate by going back and re-export your music to adjust

- Create and submit a playable Mac/PC Build

Asset List

Compose three positive *(left side of the Maze)* and three negative pieces *(right side of the Maze)* of music displaying increasing intensities:

- Low(01)

- Medium(02)

- High(03)

Each Loop Must Have the Following Characteristics

- All Loops must be the same length and tempo. Any difference in length will cause significant problems. *(30 seconds to 1 minute loops are a good length for this game)*

- The Music Loops should be bounced out and delivered as 16bit 44.1k stereo .wav files

- The Music Loops must be imported and configured into Unity as a 2D AudioClip*** and set it to Streaming or Stream From Disk.

Stingers: This is a musical sound effect that can serve either as a transition or as a feedback and does not loop. It plays once per trigger; this is also called a one shot. You will need to deliver three positive and three negative versions of these.

- All stingers should be between 3 and 5 seconds in length

- The stingers should be bounced out and delivered at 16bit 44.1k stereo .wav files

- The stingers must be imported and configured into Unity as a 2D AudioClip***

Pipeline/Process (In The Box, No Live Players)

- Play thru the game; discuss ideas and strategy

- Compose the positive and negative sides of the maze

- Work in your DAW to compose, mix and master the final music tracks, and export your music as 24bit, 44.1 Stereo .wav files into a single folder on your hard drive (now you are ready to start implementing in Unity *(see the step-by-step guide)*)

- Open up the Music Maze Game from GAI and implement using Step by Step Guide and video tutorials

- Play the game and if changes are needed, iterate by going back and re-exporting your music to adjust

- Have some besides yourself play test the game

- Create and submit a playable Mac/PC Build

Additionally, if you choose to do so, you can use live instruments in this assignment. If you do, you will also have the opportunity to prepare a full score and set of parts as well as a DAW session for comment and feedback.

Pipeline/Process (With Live Players)

- Play thru the game; discuss ideas and strategy

- Compose the positive and negative sides of the maze

- Create a master session for the recording (*Your DAW session and Score need to match and don't forget the count in*)

- Prepare score and parts for the recording session for the players

- Record live instruments in studio

- Work in your DAW to mix and master the final live music tracks along with your MIDI and export your music as 24bit 44.1 Stereo .wav files into a single folder on your hard drive (now you are ready to start implementing in Unity (*see the step-by-step guide*))

- Open up the Music Maze Game from GAI and implement using Step-by-Step Guide and video tutorials

- Play the game and if changes are needed, iterate by going back and re-exporting your music to adjust

- Have some besides yourself play test the game

- Create and submit a playable Mac/PC Build

Study Questions: What was your initial musical concept for the maze? Did your original idea change over the course of working on this Game Lesson? Was your music successful in leading the player out of the maze? What were your biggest challenges and problems while working on this lesson? What were your biggest successes? Why is the idea of iteration so important in game music? Is your score a complete whole? Do all the musical parts fit together including the stingers and if not why? Was your music mixed and mastered well, If yes why, if no why not? How was your experience working in the Unity game engine? If you used them, how did working with live instruments change your compositional process?

Some Gentle Rules for in Class Critique and Respecting the Creative Process

As we enter into group discussions, the goal is to have everyone express their point of view so that it might help to illuminate to the composer/artist the effect of their work on others.

- **Begin:** With something you like or enjoy about the work (*Compliments*)

- **Notice:** Simply notice something about the work (*Observation*)

- **Wonder:** Inquire about anything in the work that caught your attention; this is the time to give constructive feedback to the composer

- **End:** With something you like or enjoy about the work (***More Compliments***)

After all of this discussion and investigation and after the composer of the piece absorbs the feedback, invite them to speak about what they were trying to accomplish and if the comments were helpful.

Reminder: Don't forget to add this to your portfolio!

TABLE A12.1   Grading Rubric for Music Maze

Criteria	Best Score	Better Score	Good Score	Points
Music as Information	**40 to >35.0 pts** The music perfectly matches the goal of the assignment and enhances the gameplay experience.	**35 to >30.0 pts** The music somewhat matches the goal of the assignment and sort of works with the gameplay experience.	**30 to >0 pts** The does not match the goal of the assignment and does not match gameplay.	40 pts
Technical Mastery Music transitions, Intensity levels, Clean looping	**20 to >17.0 pts** Transitions are clean and smooth from start to loop to end. Music intensity levels are clear and effective, and looping is musically accurate.	**17 to >13.0 pts** Transitions are mostly clean and smooth from start to loop to end. Music intensity levels are generally clear and effective. Looping is musically accurate.	**13 to >0 pts** Transitions are not clean and/or smooth from start to loop to end. Music intensity levels may be unclear or not present. looping may not be accurate.	20 pts
Audio Balance Mix Balance, Quality of Audio, No Distortion	**20 to >17.0 pts** Mix Balance – Instruments all clearly heard. Quality Excellent, with No Distortion.	**17 to >13.0 pts** Mix Balance – Instruments mostly heard well though some may not be. Quality Excellent, with Occasional Distortion.	**13 to >0 pts** Mix Balance – Instruments frequently unheard. Quality Acceptable but may have More Distortion.	20 pts
Artistic Approach Orchestration is clear, Coherent music approach.	**20 to >17.0 pts** Very clear orchestration, very coherent musical approach.	**17 to >13.0 pts** Orchestration is mostly clear. Musical approach is largely coherent.	**13 to >0 pts** Orchestration is less clear. Music approach lacks coherence overall.	20 pts

Permissions: GAI.

Assignment 13

Mood Board

RECOMMENDATION: CHAPTER 8

Grab the Mood Board Game Lesson from the Game Audio Institute at this link: https://www.gameaudioinstitute.com/crc

Context: Middleware can be strange and difficult to understand. After all, it's a completely separate audio engine that sits between the designer, composer, and the game engine itself. This means you have to understand what's going on for all parts of that equation, as well as learning new tools and concepts. Context is key here; without knowing the questions to ask, students are often lost and unable to grasp how middleware relates to the overall process. We developed the Mood Board to give students that context. It provides the first step in the understanding of what it's like to integrate FMOD studio with Unity.

The game itself is really not a game at all, it's a very simple music system with three levels of intensity and transitions that bridge between them. All the creative composition can be done in the digital audio workstation and then imported into FMOD Studio. Inside the project, there are demonstration tracks which display the function, along with tutorial videos and written documentation that provide context to the gameplay mechanic. This is a simple and common mechanic based on increasing levels of intensity and used in many games.

Transitions between pieces or sections are often challenging, so making smooth transitions between in the intro to the intensity levels and from these to the outro is a vital part of this Game Lesson. Students get a chance to work in FMOD Studio and then get to experience downloading and installing the FMOD integration into Unity. This helps to build an understanding of how middleware works and integrates into a game engine on a fundamental level. The student gets a chance to express their creativity writing music within a set structure, and implement that music into the game. This is an experience that should bring up more questions as lightbulbs go off!

Assignment: In this assignment, you will compose an interactive score that builds in intensity. Below are some general procedures. For the complete picture and much more detailed instructions we strongly urge you to read the Step-by-Step Guide and watch the video tutorial (*link provided in the same .ZIP file as your Mood Board Game Lesson*).

DOI: 10.1201/9781003414728-26

LEARNING OUTCOMES

- Compose an interactive score that contains all musical elements

- Prepare and edit your music for the game via your DAW of choice

- Implement music into the MOOD BOARD Lesson via Step-by-Step direction and Video tutorial

- Play the game, and if changes are needed, iterate by going back and re-export your music to adjust

- Create and submit a playable Mac/PC Build

Asset List

- Create intro and outro segments (Two bar intro; Two or four bar outro)

- Create three loops, made up of layered instruments or instrument combinations (Four bar loop)

- Each loop in the set of three must be the same length and tempo, No more than 30 seconds maximum length

- Import all assets into the FMOD Project under the Event named MusicBoard-FMOD

MOOD BOARD – Composition Pipeline and Builds

For this assignment you're going to finish working on your music loops in FMOD, test this out in the Unity Editor, and then make a Standalone Mac/PC build of the MoodBoard project, based on the directions in the Step-by-Step PDF, and submit the build to this topic via a public Google Drive or Box link.

- For Mac users a build will be an .app file. Compress/Zip this file

- For Windows users the build will be in a small folder with a few files in it. Note that this is NOT the Unity project folder. For best results make the build on the Desktop, that way it will be easier to find.

Discussion Questions: Was your music successful in transitioning from level to level? Was your music successful in building intensity or changing intensity from level to level? How smooth were the transitions from the intro to the loops, and the transitions from those to the outro? How does FMOD communicate with the Unity game engine? What were your biggest problems? What were your biggest successes? Did working with middleware change your compositional process? Do you enjoy working with audio middleware?

Some Gentle Rules for in Class Critique and Respecting the Creative Process

As we enter into group discussions, the goal is to have everyone express their point of view so that it might help to illuminate to the composer/artist the effect of their work on others.

- **Begin:** With something you like or enjoy about the work (*Compliments*)

- **Notice:** Simply notice something about the work (*Observation*)

- **Wonder:** Inquire about anything in the work that caught your attention; this is the time to give constructive feedback to the composer

- **End:** With something you like or enjoy about the work (***More Compliments***)

After all of this discussion and investigation and after the composer of the piece absorbs the feedback, invite them to speak about what they were trying to accomplish and if the comments were helpful.

Reminder: Don't forget to add this to your portfolio!

TABLE A13.1   Grading Rubric for Mood Board

Criteria	Best Score	Better Score	Good Score	Points
Technical Mastery Music transitions, Intensity levels, Clean looping	**40 to >35.0 pts** Transitions are clean and smooth from start to loop to end. Music intensity levels are clear and effective, and looping is musically accurate.	**35 to >30.0 pts** Transitions are mostly clean and smooth from start to loop to end. Music intensity levels are generally clear and effective. Looping is musically accurate.	**30 to >0 pts** Transitions are not clean and/or smooth from start to loop to end. Music intensity levels may be unclear or not present. looping may not be accurate.	40 pts
Audio Balance Mix Balance, Quality of Audio, No Distortion	**40 to >35.0 pts** Mix Balance Instruments all clearly heard. Quality Excellent, with No Distortion.	**35 to >30.0 pts** Mix Balance Instruments mostly heard well though some may not be. Quality Excellent, with Occasional Distortion.	**30 to >0 pts** Mix Balance Instruments frequently unheard. Quality Acceptable but may have More Distortion.	40 pts
Artistic Approach Orchestration is clear, Coherent music approach.	**20 to >17.0 pts** Very clear orchestration. Very coherent musical approach.	**17 to >13.0 pts** Orchestration is mostly clear. Musical approach is largely coherent.	**13 to >0 pts** Orchestration is less clear. Music approach lacks coherence overall.	20 pts

Permissions: GAI.

Assignment 14

Day and Night

RECOMMENDATION: CHAPTERS 8 AND 9

Grab the Day and Night Game Lesson from the Game Audio Institute at this link: https://www.gameaudioinstitute.com/crc

Context: This is perhaps one of our favorite game lessons. It works off a single in-game parameter of time. A simple rotating 24-hour cycle from the rising of the Sun to the setting of the moon, it also takes place on what we like to call Scott's Island, a nice place to visit. This lesson is a first dive into adaptive music, how to work with parameters, and a first taste of simple adaptive scoring. Unlike the Mood Board, there's no FMOD studio session provided, however; students will create their own from scratch.

This lesson takes the next step in understanding how middleware works and continues to develop ideas of how music can transition and develop over a time period, tied not to a timeline, but to a parameter. The context and function of the music are documented in both written step-by-step guides and video tutorials. This Game Lesson also contains sound design elements for a further challenge. The more adventurous student may want to not only write the music, but also develop ambient backgrounds that change with the passage of time. Overall this is a simple and very effective game lesson that allows students to be as creative as possible within a fixed parameter range.

Assignment: In this assignment, you will compose an adaptive score based on a single parameter. Read the Step-by-Step Guide and watch the video tutorial (*links to these provided in the same .ZIP file as your Day and Night Game Lesson*).

LEARNING OUTCOMES

- Compose an adaptive score tied to a single parameter

- Prepare and edit our music for the game via your DAW of choice

- Implement your music into the Game Lesson via Step-by-Step direction and Video tutorial

DOI: 10.1201/9781003414728-27

- Play the game and if changes are needed, iterate by going back and re-export your music to adjust

- Create and submit a playable Mac/PC Build.

Asset List

- Unlike the previous game lesson, there isn't really a set list of assets required for Day and Night. The step-by-step directions will give more information on this, but the total number of music and/or sound effects files will vary depending on your approach, though it should be no less than 15. All assets should be 16 bit 44.1kHz stereo WAV files, since the FMOD Studio events will be 2D.

Day and Night – Composition Pipeline and Builds

- This project will involve more work in Unity, but it's a pretty minimal amount. This Game Lesson is a simple example of a completely adaptive music experience where the music (*and optionally ambience as well*) mix is determined by a time parameter while you walk around on an island over the course of 24 virtual "hours" from midnight to midnight. As you walk around, the moon sets, the sun comes up and travels through the sky and sets, and the moon rises in the sky until the entire cycle is started again.

- This game lesson does not come with an existing FMOD Studio project already created. So the PDF guide and video tutorial will take you through the process of setting your own FMOD Studio project up, creating Events, assigning these to banks, building them, installing the FMOD Unity integration package, and then finally using the FMOD banks inside the Unity project.

- Once successfully tested, you can then export the results as a Standalone Mac/PC build.

- **NOTE:** Similar to the other FMOD Studio game lessons, you will need to install the FMOD Studio Unity integration in this project. If video tutorials are more to your liking, you can access this playlist of unlisted videos covering the complete implementation of the music and sound effects for Day And Night here: https://www.youtube.com/playlist?list=PLVKIvIgin2rF1OxIfvdFERmei2QCOZjS

Study Questions: Was your music successful in transitioning smoothly from day to night? What were your biggest problems? What were your biggest successes? Did working with middleware change your compositional process? How do parameters change the way posers think about time?

Some Gentle Rules for in Class Critique and Respecting the Creative Process
As we enter into group discussions, the goal is to have everyone express their point of vie so that it might help to illuminate to the composer/artist the effect of their work on others

- **Begin:** With something you like or enjoy about the work (*Compliments*)

- **Notice:** Simply notice something about the work (*Observation*)

- **Wonder:** Inquire about anything in the work that caught your attention; this is the time to give constructive feedback to the composer

- **End:** With something you like or enjoy about the work (***More Compliments***)

After all of this discussion and investigation and after the composer of the piece absorbs the feedback, invite them to speak about what they were trying to accomplish and if the comments were helpful.

Reminder: Don't forget to add this to your portfolio!

TABLE A14.1 Grading Rubric for Day and Night

Criteria	Best Score	Better Score	Good Score	Points
Technical Mastery Music transitions, Intensity levels, Clean looping	**40 to >35.0 pts** Transitions are clean and smooth from start to loop to end. Music intensity levels are clear and effective, and looping is musically accurate.	**35 to >30.0 pts** Transitions are mostly clean and smooth from start to loop to end. Music intensity levels are generally clear and effective. Looping is musically accurate.	**30 to >0 pts** Transitions are not clean and/or smooth from start to loop to end. Music intensity levels may be unclear or not present. looping may not be accurate.	40 pts
Audio Balance Mix Balance, Quality of Audio, No Distortion	**40 to >35.0 pts** Mix Balance Instruments all clearly heard. Quality Excellent, with No Distortion	**35 to >30.0 pts** Mix Balance Instruments mostly heard well though some may not be. Quality Excellent, with Occasional Distortion	**30 to >0 pts** Mix Balance Instruments frequently unheard. Quality Acceptable but may have More Distortion	40 pts
Artistic Approach Orchestration is clear, Coherent music approach.	**20 to >17.0 pts** Very clear orchestration, Very coherent musical approach.	**17 to >13.0 pts** Orchestration is mostly clear. Musical approach is largely coherent.	**13 to >0 pts** Orchestration is less clear. Music approach lacks coherence overall.	20 pts

Permissions: GAI.

Assignment 15

Create a Technical Design Document (TDD)

RECOMMENDATION: CHAPTER 9

Context: This thought experiment will help you to understand many of the elements that go into composing music and designing a music system for a game. It is important that we are able to clearly communicate to programmers and designers our goals with the music system. The questions below are just some of the things that we might expect developers to be comfortable with when programming music and sound. The answers to these questions will help to prepare the programming team so they can plan the work time needed to make these events happen in the game.

This requires us to be familiar with some technical terminology and will give you practical experience, so you will already be familiar when tasked to do so in the real world.

Assignment: In this assignment, you will be tasked with creating an imaginary game and then coming up with a coherent description of all the technical aspects of the music and music system. Include answers to all the questions and sections below.

GENERAL INFORMATION

Team/Game: (*List the name of the game team and project here*)

Style and form of the game: (*A short description of the look and feel of the game, include scenarios, narrative, and characters*)

Gameplay mechanic: (*A short description of how the game works, including game loop, screenflow, and transitions*)

Schedule: (*List the music development timeline including delivery dates*)

Game Engine Information: (*List what game engine will be used*)

Audio Delivery Quality and Format: (*List bit rate, sample rate, and file type here*)

Target file size for all the music in the game: (*List how much space will be allotted for music in the game*)

Technical Design: TAD (*Technical Audio Documentation*)

DOI: 10.1201/9781003414728-28

- **Music Triggers:** How does the music trigger in the game? how many triggers are there and furthermore please explain the proper starting and stopping as well as placement of all music events

- **Mixing:** Who will make sure the music is playing at the correct volume? Please explain the mix system and proper blending, volume balancing, and EQ'ing of all music elements

- **Looping:** Where will loops be used? Please explain the form and function of the triggers assigned for seamlessly looping music and ambient background tracks

- **Transitions:** Please explain the proper triggering of transitions between menu screens and levels. Cross Fades, Stingers and other technical means of blending seamlessly between screens and gameplay levels

- **Randomization:** Please explain how many pools of music and sound classes for randomized playback will be needed

- **Pitch shifting of music:** Please explain the use of and need for pitch changing algorithms to speed up and slow down music tracks and other sounds

- **3D Sound:** Please explain your vision for the use of distance attenuation as well as occlusion and obstruction algorithms for foreground and background music

- **Resource and performance management:** Please explain the proper timing and weighting of music as well as any optimization of music and sound during gameplay

- **Mixer snapshots:** Please explain if the game will require the use of separate mixer states for game play levels and Menus

- **Parameter based music triggering:** Please explain if the game will require the implementation of parameters, for creating adaptive scores

- **The use of third party audio middleware:** Please explain if the audio system needs to use any available 3rd party audio engines and code bases to more completely integrate sound into the development pipeline or to create composer controlled parameter driven adaptive soundtracks.

Reminder: Don't forget to add this to your portfolio!

Assignment 16

Create a Website and Artist Statement

RECOMMENDATION: CHAPTER 10

Context: It is a fact of life that in order to build a career we have to network and develop community. One way to do this is by writing a short artist's statement that explains clearly what you are all about. Think of it as a brief pitch you might give to your favorite game designer if you were stuck in an elevator with them. Additionally, you should also have a clear web and social media presence, so that you can apply for jobs and link to examples of your work. This is your chance to take all the work you have done in this course of study as well as any other work you have done and create a killer portfolio!

ASSIGNMENT: WRITE A SHORT ARTIST'S STATEMENT

An artist statement is a written description of your art that helps your audience understand your creative process, ideas, and inspiration. Here are some tips for creating a good artist statement:

1. **Identify your audience:** Before you start writing, think about who your audience is. Consider what they might want to know about you and your artwork.

2. **Keep it concise:** Your statement should be brief and to the point. Avoid using overly complicated language or jargon that others might not understand.

3. **Be authentic:** Write in your own voice and be honest about your motivations and intentions. Avoid using clichés or generic statements that don't reveal anything about your creative process.

4. **Describe your process:** Explain how you create your artwork, from the initial concept to the final product. Discuss any materials, techniques, or tools that you use.

5. **Discuss your inspiration:** Share what inspires you, whether it's a particular composer, a place, a historical event, or a personal experience. Explain how your inspiration influences your work.

DOI: 10.1201/9781003414728-29

6. **Provide context:** Discuss the themes or concepts that you explore in your music. Explain why these themes are important to you and how they relate to your audience.

7. **Edit and proofread:** Review your statement several times to ensure that it is clear and free of errors. Consider asking a friend or colleague to review it for you as well.

Remember, a good artist statement should give your audience insight into your creative process and inspire them to engage with your work.

List of References

INTRODUCTION TO BOOK

Steve Horowitz: Photo Credit: Charles Russo
Scott Looney: Photo Credit: Kimara Dixon

Chapter 1

Koji Kondo: "Interview from Legend of Zelda Super Best Collection", translated from Japanese by Glitterberi https://glitterberri.com/special-interview-koji-kondo/
Micheal Sweet: GAI Interview, transcription. Scott Looney, Game Audio Institute 2023.

Chapter 2

Will Wright: *Lessons in Game Design*, video lecture by Will Wright. Computer History Museum, Recorded November 20, 2003 YouTube. transcription: Steve Horowitz
Lessons in Game Design, lecture by Will Wright.
Chase Bethea: GAI Interview, transcription: Steve Horowitz, Game Audio Institute 2023

Chapter 3

Matt Levine: GAI Interview, transcription. Steve Horowitz, Game Audio Institute 2023

Chapter 4

Austin Wintory: "*Abzû* soundtrack complete OST" - Video, composers YouTube Channel, Music by Austin Wintory, with text commentary, transcription: Steve Horowitz, Game Audio Institute 2023.
https://www.youtube.com/watch?v=mCL0jRV_xb4
Lena Raine: "Mastering Video Game Music: Celeste, Battlewake, and More".
Interview by Jett Galindo, iZotope Contributor January 8, 2020.
https://www.izotope.com/en/learn/mastering-video-game-music.html

Chapter 5

Steven Spielberg: "Lucas and Spielberg on storytelling in games: 'it's not going to be Shakespeare'".
Article by Bryan Bishop, published on *the Verge*, June 13, 2013.
https://www.theverge.com/2013/6/13/4427444/lucas-spielberg-storytelling-in-games-its-not-going-to-be-shakespeare-usc
Danny Bilson: "THQ's Bilson: Cutscenes Are a Cop-Out," by Fred Dutton, Contributor.
Article, published on Euro Gamer, Updated on Mar 9, 2011.
Winifred Phillips: "Information in Trailers, Cutscenes and Cinematics" (for the game music composer) Article, Posted by Winifred Phillips on the composer's own website. October 11, 2022.

Chapter 7

Guy Whitmore: GAI Interview, transcription. Steve Horowitz, Game Audio Institute 2014.

Chapter 8

Guy Whitmore: *Peggle 2*: "Storytelling Through Adaptive Music".
Article, Game Audio Network Guild User Blog published: 02/25/2014.
https://www.audiogang.org/peggle-2-storytelling-through-adaptive-music/

Chapter 9

Rich Vreeland: "Serialism & Sonification in Mini Metro," GDC talk 2018 published Apr 26, 2019,
Video from Composers Site transcription. Steve Horowitz, Game Audio Institute 2023.
https://www.youtube.com/watch?v=FgV4hSfsl00
Daniel Brown: GAI Interview, transcription. Steve Horowitz, Game Audio Institute 2023.

Assignment 09

Martin Stig Anderson: *"Limbo* – Exclusive Interview with Martin Stig Andersen," Article, Designing
Sound, Published August 1, 2011 by Damien Kastbauer.
https://designingsound.org/2011/08/01/limbo-exclusive-interview-with-martin-stig-andersen/

Index

Note: **Bold** page numbers refer to tables and *italic* page numbers refer to figures.

9 781032 540085